Urban Conservation

NAHOUM COHEN
ARCHITECT & TOWN PLANNER

Urban Conservation

The MIT Press
Cambridge, Massachusetts

Library of Congress Cataloging-in-Publication Data

Cohen, Nahoum.
  Urban conservation / Nahoum Cohen.
    p. cm.
  ISBN 0-262-03268-6 (hc: alk. paper).—ISBN 0-262-53161-5
  (pb: alk. paper).
  1. Urban renewal. 2. City planning. 3.Architecture—Conservation and restoration. I. Title.
HT170.C64 1999
307.3'416—dc21   98-43963
                                          CIP

For Yael, Ira, Tami and Yori.

Design: Elisha Benovich
Computer Graphics:
Shai Schwartz

© Photographers:
Motil Mark (Azur)
RCHM England (Cover)
N. Aviv, Zuki (Paris)
Benovich & Cohen
Mandelberg; S. Wolf.

Printed in Israel, 1998

TABLE OF CONTENTS

Introduction

Planning Conservation
Modern Plans
Urban Pattern
The Inner Order of the Urban Fabric

Conservation is a cultural necessity.

Due to the increasing tendency of city dwellers to move back into historic city centers, urban conservation is becoming an ever more urgent issue. Its urgency stems in part from the general disappointment in modern urban planning, which moved residential areas outside of cities, without successfully planning new urban areas that offer everything expected of a modern city, including nearby and easily accessible workplaces, as well as rich and diversified cultural activity. Lacking the appropriate infrastructure, life in these areas demands that every move be scheduled in advance to avoid being caught in a traffic jam.

So while the trend of moving back into city centers cannot yet be considered significant, it would seem highly likely that it will continue on an upswing, placing the issue of urban conservation at the fore. The surge of interest in residing in historic city centers cannot be attributed to socioeconomic factors alone. It

The formation of the urban weave is the result of both geometry and systematic building. This conception in building and designing palaces and mosques in Bukhara, is filled with patterns reminiscent of local carpet weaving, thus reinforcing the commonly used term, "urban fabric", especially as used with respect to planning. The experienced eye will no doubt sense a principal weave in the orthogonal grid, as well as a secondary weave which is octagonal and more elaborate. Geometrical sophistication leads into repetition of basic modules, to resemble jewel- like facets.*

*The historical conceptions of ancient cities, such as **Babylon** in this 19th century illustration, is romantic, symmetrical and very regular, nearly utopic. While this concept is, of course, pure myth, it helped form conventional European landscape and design attitudes. Study of the past must be more factual, if it is to contribute to the new understanding of the urban structure.*

Maps such as the one below (changes in the planning of the city of Cologne, Germany, last century), show attempts to keep current and existing urban structures. When necessary, changes were considered. The changes show proposed measures for connecting several existing squares and focal points, with the actual town pattern dictated by old grids. Local land division, based on agricultural plots and dimensions, unsuitable for urban use, was to be cut and altered. This is the way new quarters come to life, bringing about some urban renewal.

Western towns have their own typical patterns and webs, because of local repetitive design rules. The similar attitude to what constitutes a "building", as well as a repetitive division of land, similar height regulations, unified local form and a long lasting scale, all create the urban fabric. The points of focal interest, all formed by prominent squares, wide avenues and waterways, with public buildings to "embellish" the pattern, imply a visual culture, a network of solid and permanent life. This network seems more persuasive today than much of the "neighborhood" planning done over the past 50 years.

Rising interest in urban renewal often results in international competitions. The aim of such efforts is to discover the existing urban structure and suggest ways to ensure its continued existence. The profession was influenced by these attempts of studies, into post modernistic trends. The above illustration is from a competition for the renewal of Belgrade (winning entry by a mixed team). The somewhat conservative approach is the result of declining modernist attitudes. It is an outcome of renewed study and respect for the past.

must also be examined within the context of some basic facts:

Historic city centers are made up of a web of buildings and streets from different periods that create various cultural and urban strata. Over the centuries, they have finely honed their urban character and now offer quality urban culture. New cities and suburbs, however, lack any feeling of history and are devoid of any sense of cultural continuity.

Forsaking the esthetic patterns common to cities of the past, the modern approach to urban design, with its broken urban spaces, has ignored esthetic elements such as the street and square.

Proper urban conservation transforms historic cities into hubs of cultural activity, making them much more than merely residential.

To a large degree, historic cities manifest characteristics of self-preservation, and it would not seem necessary to enact special legislation to preserve the original urban plan.

The reality, however, is that the many failures in existing approaches to conservation have brought that initial assumption under question.

This is especially true when conservation extends beyond nostalgic or esthetic preservation to city life as a whole. Successful urban conservation is significantly more than merely preserving a few buildings. Unless a comprehensive approach to conservation is taken, more and more cities will lose their battle against urban blight.

Modern pressures are numerous: commerce, changing land use and zoning, transportation and growing population density. These all place new and substantial burdens on the existing city structure. Traditional cities have been hit by urban sprawl, and consequently, their service radius has expanded relentlessly. Measures must be taken to preserve or protect the very elements that attract people to move back into the city, and this means doing more than preserving buildings alone. If historical elements are not correctly integrated

*Photographs such as these of bombed cities, (**Dresden**) are quite familiar. Repairs in these instances, were done very quickly and did not produce a model for renewal. Further, studies undertaken at the time had no such aspirations.*

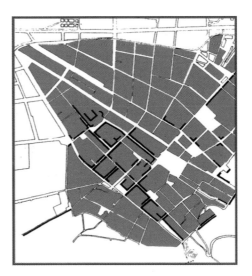

Urban lartifacts (Cuzco, capital of the Incas), are present in the form of old walls. These marks of days past are influential in marking and forming the present scale of the town, bearing some notions of the past into the future. Thus, buildings disappear, with abstract notions of urban scale, width of streets, geometry of road patterns remaining for centuries. We are immediately faced with the question of what constitutes large scale conservation, buildings or geometric patterns. Such questions will be carried into the planning of new extensions in towns.

The internal division into parcels of differing proportions, is testimony to the way preservation has taken shape. Buildings are the result of the way land is divided. The final character of a place is therefore dictated by the local division of the block.

In further examples in east London, architects provide superb buildings, with new symbolic, clean overtones. They also look forbiddingly strange, while providing work places close to rail terminals. Design is perfectionist and execution immaculate. This slightly oppressive modernity, clean and respectable, huge and total, cannot be accepted locally. It has no life of its own, existing only because of its daily infusion of employees. Converging trains make those working places possible, nobody can guess for how long. Contribution to urban life on such a scale is minimal. It only perpetuates alienation between home and work, and the inherent dualism is persistent.

Different patterns yield much information when examined and studied. An urban web, which emerges over an extended period of time, can be organized in many ways. The example provided is of **Mainz**, Germany, and it includes two periods separated by about 150 years. During those years much has changed, except some basic structuring of blocks arranged along streets, to prove the resilience of the town, despite its normal growth.

As can be observed, preservation depends on carrying out clear instructions , given by planning authorities. To be effective, these are supplemented by detailed design plans. It is no less important that the builders be experienced in this sort of work and materials, and are careful in execution. This has been done in the above example in Chelsea, London. It is very clear that the result can be fully enjoyed by the pedestrian, as it fits into the urban and local scale.

in daily life, the entire process will fail and urban centers will continue to empty: the past will simply become both a cultural stumbling block and burdensome to the public.

The type of planning needed is an entirely new field and is, therefore, somewhat experimental. It will call for a variety of quantitative analyses and in the end, conclusions regarding laws and at times for an experimental approach.

This is not a matter of designating city areas where a number of buildings or individual objects of historical significance are to be preserved. Conservation, on an urban scale, is concerned with the urban fabric as a whole and not with architecture alone. The successful conservation project will make use of quantitative analyses and will be aided by comparative and economic studies. The detailed conclusions drawn from such studies will be integrated into normal planning procedures, and, when necessary, bylaws and regulations will be enacted. To do this, planners must identify the basic urban structures and underlying qualities calling for acts of conservation.

The next stage is to formulate it into a method that allows modern planning to benefit by preserving focal elements of the past, while integrating new and modern qualities. A city must be able to survive normal wear and tear without remaining too rigid for change. Planners should therefore be able to identify lasting urban qualities.

Urban culture is the result of human development and one of the peaks of its achievements. When this common goal is agreed upon and understood, conservation of the urban fabric can become a permanent part of architecture, design and planning. On the other hand, we often see that conservation not

Conservation becomes a massive endeavor. Large public and private buildings spend big sums on preservation. The impact is important, as big contracting firms join such schemes, generating technical research and restoration grants. (Paris Opera.)

The center of Frankfurt (Opera House), is a densely built modern environment. It is well connected to what was left of the old fabric destroyed in the War. In some isolated cases respect was given to the old scale, now absent. The town center operates well during daytime, and as can be expected, is totally deserted at night. It is only half useful and held together by financial institutes, important commerce and retail outlets. No residential use remains, thus there is no reason for an urban meeting place. These commercial centers are designed to have an internal, commercial purpose, and no vestiges of communal, street level meeting place. People are only exposed to publicity. Urbanism used to be a background to free activity, but is being replaced by commerce, a much stronger presence.

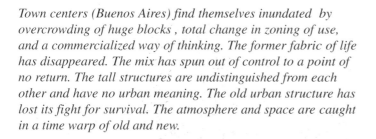

19th century architecture is preserved in Paris as a matter of course, partly because urban planning and reinforcement of the urban web have dealt with it successfully. This conservation is virtually self-driven.

Town centers (Buenos Aires) find themselves inundated by overcrowding of huge blocks , total change in zoning of use, and a commercialized way of thinking. The former fabric of life has disappeared. The mix has spun out of control to a point of no return. The tall structures are undistinguished from each other and have no urban meaning. The old urban structure has lost its fight for survival. The atmosphere and space are caught in a time warp of old and new.

A tremendous number of huge buildings have burst on the existing townscape of Rio de Janeiro. While efforts are being made to save some tourist attractions, the results are likely predictable.

understood to be conservation of cultural content creates many avoidable pitfalls and planning mistakes. This mainly occurs because of the prevailing tendency to consider separate buildings as cultural 'objects' and not as parts of the whole.

Planning Conservation

The lack of clear regulations regarding conservation in urban plans often causes great difficulties in day-to-day work, as departments do not know how to clearly formulate their intent of what to preserve. A vague formulation of intent, coupled with an improper definition of requirements has the potential to lead to irreparable damage. This can often occur during attempts at urban renewal as well, when poorly formulated plans destroy the existing urban fabric, without conceiving a new one, thus leading to yet another round of new urban blight. This is one of the reasons why urban renewal has not been altogether successful. By having a clear clause of preservation in every plan, a great deal of trial and error, sometimes only error, will be eliminated. One has to be very clear in what one is preserving, while maintaining a clear grid capable of incorporating new buildings.

Aerial photos from space allow us to view the extent of urban sprawl and provide us with the opportunity to judge and formulate the way we look. The old civic activity of living in towns can now be appraised qualitatively and quantitatively. Photographs take the place of maps and show truthfully the way we behave in our organization of urban life.

Urban planning and conservation should, therefore, be viewed as symbiotic, neither quite complete without the other. When this outlook is adopted, new buildings not only infuse the area with new life, but also maintain existing urban structure. Plans that do not integrate a solid legal foundation for reinforcing urban patterns with a clear vision of the future simply postpone problems of urban continuity. This is the reason for shifting the focus from individual buildings to a more general, contextual, collective and cultural outlook.

Proper interpretation of the urban context will guide planners as to how to incorporate the new into the old.

Central Frankfurt underwent major building programs, with very little restoration undertaken. The square in front of the old town hall was included in the restoration. Massive buildings of office blocks in this important financial center bear no relation to the historic fabric. Tall buildings are placed where they are for reasons such as presence of convenient transportation systems. No harm in that, apparently, other than that it does not encourage residential development. Thus the popularity of certain districts will fall, the reason for selection of the areas as lively business centers will disappear, and we will be left with an estranged urban environment, used only at peak times. The city gains in taxes, citizens lose the freedom of urbanity.

Conservation in England and specifically in **London** is the result of a long respect for buildings, building tradition and the law. This results in a natural predisposition for preserving regulations regarding heights, proportions etc. and is probably due to the love of architecture. The concentration of the effort to conserve the common heritage is on a continuous scale, and not sporadically spread out in single examples. The value of fitting in the existing fabric, as an infill element, is very much practiced and embraced. The rules which allow the infill are necessarily formulated by the relevant planning authorities and is well responded to by the designers. The common usage of keeping to the urban scale of historical buildings is to be admired. The result is that one can enjoy well-kept examples of historical buildings, not divorced from their neighbors.

Modern Plans

One of the recurring problems inherent in modern architecture is the inability to foster urban patterns with life of their own, with abilities to sustain forms of communal life.

New basic urban forms need more than implants of public functions, which are not organic to them.

Urban design, in the modern movement, has clearly capitulated on those issues, especially in the residential neighborhoods, with blocks of apartment buildings in high densities and tall structures. The unfortunate given name of these areas, 'solutions', only points out the anomaly of living in them. Urban planning has played a pitiful role in facilitating authorities and developers to play the game of providing 'dutifully' for the need of the people.

On the other hand, there are many examples of poor and neglected neighborhoods that are highly vibrant. Though these neighborhoods are products of natural evolution and simple architecture, they are teeming with positive urban values, which thus far have not been successfully imitated. The goal of conservation, however, should be correct identification of those elements and utilizing them in creating the future..

Urban Pattern

The successful urban pattern is better equipped to be the basis for sustainable life. There are a few general conditions to make this happen.

1. The relevant context, size, and character as well as the perceived or adopted concept of the whole. Every change will then occur with a goal in sight, in terms of building the actual detailed plan. Thus, every new planning move will not be a half-baked trial to correct a few manageable but nonessential mistakes. As long as the whole is identified, and its structure is clear, decisions will be carried out more quickly and clearly. The new can accommodate itself in a well-identified and structured past. Some infill patterns are justifiable in these terms, and have, therefore, become successful.

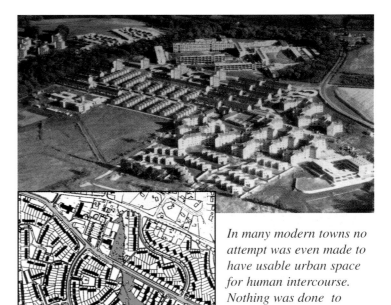

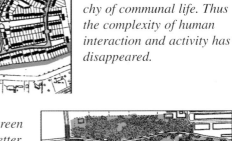

In many modern towns no attempt was even made to have usable urban space for human intercourse. Nothing was done to implant a cultural hierarchy of communal life. Thus the complexity of human interaction and activity has disappeared.

The concept of public green space has somewhat better connotations, but has remained unusable because of size constraints and lack of communal feeling. Inner green spaces are better, but wrong proportions and repetitions make the spaces look both unfit and void.

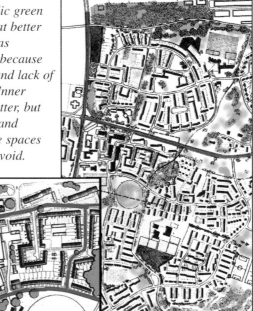

The result of urban renewal loses much historical charm by inherent carelessness. It tends to produce a measure of estrangement , often caused by not quoting or respecting the past. The use of local methods and patterns was absent, and it is hardly surprising that we find ourselves with places void of past connotations, even though some local grids were adopted. We are in the presence of bureaucratic dryness , and into the heights of planning absurdities.

Sofia, *Bulgaria, 1996. Central location, hit by local urban blight (certainly like a disease or cancer), utter deterioration on a massive scale (above). Development plans unapplied for some 15 years, have led to a self-perpetuating situation. The local plan was initiated with the hope of promoting a new underground train system and was soon abandoned, for political reasons.*

The world is filling with absurd designs, creating more and more visual conflicts. The issue of who created them is immaterial. The new and the old cannot be reconciled.

Residential solutions such as these (near the old Berlin wall), were supposed to bring urban renewal as a possible solution. Lack of study and a clear decisions as to what has to be renewed, cause solutions to become foregn to their locality.

2. Identification of the unique and special elements in local forms and general patterns, not only as building types but in terms of space. Zoning will have a role here, as it determines the nature and scope of human activity in a given area.

3. Components in the surrounding city fabric should have an influence on local elements, allowing for better ties and preventing urban isolation that is often detrimental.

The above will become the means of encouraging the present towards self-preservation without ignoring the new.

We are now acting on the city level, identifying and creating self-perpetuating systems. Modern planning is lacking in terms of its urban lexicon. Very few, if any, urban components have been created or invented in this century. Instead of developing new planning tools and blocks to create clear spaces and urban forms which can compete with elements such as boulevards and squares, quite the opposite has occurred. We have managed to destroy and clear the lot, leaving emptiness (some of it green), unusable in urban culture. One of the aims of this book is to classify the well known but neglected urban types and to preserve their use and meaning.

Even places famous for their cultural elitism, such as Boston, have failed to stop the prevailing disruption of urban cohesion. The production of such modern creations, is beyond belief, throwing the center off balance, obliterating it as a possible place of human meeting. This state of affairs looks more and more like a backdrop to some film production. There is no way that the human mind can face and bridge the gaps of such visual occurrences. Two opposing messages are offered, and each is at a loss to explain the other.

Another new and faceless reality, on a similar scale, in Eastern Europe. For 50 years schemes of public housing have quickly turned into banality. The complete lack of urban structure is

What are the elements worth preserving on the urban scale? What constitutes and creates the given element? How does it relate to the geometry of the planned environment? The values determined are not always consistent with those of individual buildings. This is the reason for quantitative and comprehensive identification and cataloguing of those elements. The results of such

disastrous to human identity. The authors of these plans must have known the results of such thinking, one of endless quantities of the same dwelling solutions. The lack of character displayed shows the collapse of urbanistic thinking. Buildings are thrown on an empty background, no analysis of possible relations is even attempted. Modernistic theories behind these new environments are at fault. There can be no other way out except by the study of existing urban examples. That is one of the aims of urban conservation.

Planning of Hemel Hampstead, England. Plans of linear town centers conceived in the sixties were much in vogue then. This solution was limited from the start, as the success of such a forced, utopistic anomaly could not be expected to last. It was an isolated island of semi-intensive use, but without a background of high density to sustain it. Backed by an indifferent web, it was related to it only minimally. This sudden drop of intensity cannot sustain activity for long and will enhance no natural growth. It only looks nice on paper and furnishes some short-lived ideologies.

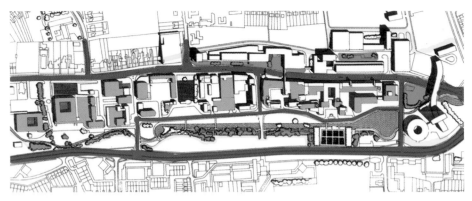

We get environments which though clean are artificial and foreign. The endless growth of tall buildings is normally void of much meaning either visually or conceptually. One feels that it would have been better if buildings were hidden away. The way things emerge, there is endless competition between a few tall giants, striving for visual attention. As far as using the center for the high densities created by office blocks, the adverse influence on city life is constantly felt, meaning that a necessary compromise has not been found.

Attempts at beautifying certain places in local historic quarters, most of them preordained to disappear, tend to stress the hopelessness of such efforts in a locality which looks doomed. There is no point in decorating in bold and hopeful colors, which at their best will fade and peel. The old looks even more neglected and the new with its decorated walls will soon follow.(Right.)

research are less than practical and are not easily implemented.

The urbanity advocated here took many years to evolve to its present state, but as we well know, much has happened that allows the present disregard of urbanity as a way of life. Furthermore, the estrangement from traditional urban features is happening in a period in which humanity is significantly concentrating in cities. Unfortunately, these cities do not show a great civic coherence, physically. That is the reason conservation comes into play.

Conservation attempts to introduce some urban context. It is still almost impossible to design a continuous street front or a good urban space containing continuous activity.

This is partially rooted in the unwillingness to respectfully study the past and create a system out of it. This is to happen first in planning terms, design coming later. The discovery of fabrics and typologies on the urban scene has been done before, but has never been woven into a workable planning methodology. This may enable planning theory and practice to have a stable historical system that includes present form and terms with comprehensible values. It is perhaps obvious, that every town will have its own unique characteristics. Every place has developed in different political and geographical circumstances and will have different attitudes towards planning. We will be looking into the common qualities (in our terms) that will accommodate the local pattern.

Center of Sofia, Bulgaria. Historically this town center contains some old patterns which cannot be introduced, unharmed into the newer patterns. Unfortunately , they have been neglected far too long. They are will most likely disappear, causing pain and a deep sense of loss. Occurrences such as these can be avoided by foresight and political intervention at the right time. (Above and below left.)

Historic Brussels is undergoing a major crisis. Upper floors are out of use. Population has deserted the center. Only the last vestiges of tourist use are present. Real authenticity has disappeared. Chances are that it will be all demolished sooner or later. First marks of the future high rise are present. Sticking to the past will prove difficult and expensive. If no good reason is found to preserve the fabric , it will be left to deteriorate further. Return of population to these centers may be made possible only by governmental interests, which unfortunately do not coincide with the local will.

*Restoration of parts of town center of **Plovdiv** (Bulgaria).Work was done to blend 19th century styles with more modern ones. This town is known as a preserved heritage city and enjoys some tourism in summer. Part of the success is the well-maintained public circulation between the historic center and the newer parts of the city.*

Conservation of small palaces and private mansions in Paris is becoming more and more common. At the same time effort is made to keep local preservation work on a very polished level, with the help of a systematic approach, which looks after legal , municipal and technical details. This attitude can be observed troughout, and is illustrated here, with a not particularly Parisian building. The methods adopted can deal with many types of buildings. The fact that they have accomplished just that, proves the need for a total urban approach. This is done once the consensus for environment protection exists.

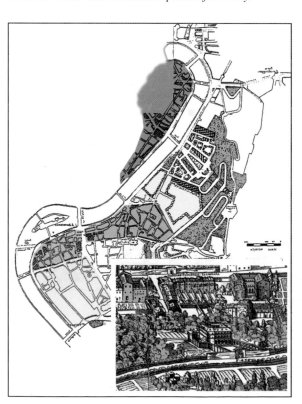

The existance and collection of historeical masterial, such as maps, make respect for the past possible and relevant. Fewer mistakes will occur; present mistakes happened when these studies were skipped.

The Inner Order of the Urban Fabric

In the different studies on the phases of urban development, we not only find marks of long term influences of taste, ideals and architectural ability mixed with evolving technical potential, but also geometrical divisions which form obvious patterns. This essential and underlying geometry is not entirely simple, as it is the result of some conflicting basic forces, along with a number of geographical constraints.
We will list some of these forces:
A. Public appropriation of land for common use, i.e., parks, roads, etc. This will strongly influence a broad

Streets with normal densities are always more inviting and do not disrupt possible conservation. The density achieved is not much lower than the one achieved by high rise blocks. These streets have greater chances of survival, permitting important preservation to take place on a city scale. The presence of good transportation , a clever taxation method, suppression of noise and pollution, will keep urban life present in the center. Relating to the existing web can create the framework for the survival of central districts.

*The result of urban neglect is more than just the loss of buildings. The harm done is long term and spreads easily into the neighboring web. It becomes increasingly difficult to stop and reverse the blight. This process has its own internal mechanism with a lot of inertia, which can persist for decades. In some cases the effect is well known in advance and is the result of a political decision or miscalculation. Neglect is the reflection of the problems of local population, often poor. Neglect sticks on to the existing framework of dwellings, hits the water and sewer services, roads are ruined, prices and ownerships are hit. (Town of **Jaffa**)*

When comparing between historic towns , one is struck by the richness of old divisions , closely interwoven into a pattern, producing perfect town squares and excellent urban ties. Those, of course, took centuries to develop, and hopelessly obliterated in the process of renewal. In the present restoration process, strange widening and changes are performed, clearly noticeable as not pertaining to the local scale. This tendency of overcorrecting the past, has done much harm to many localities and should be abandoned. The harmful effect was started by disregard of ancient land division and this has a bad effect to renovation. Historical patterns of the town of Leipzig to the right.

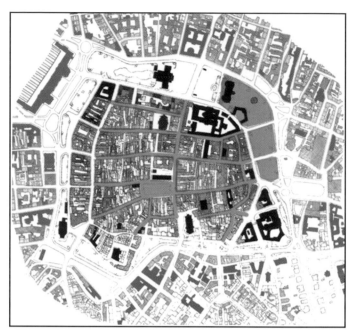

A partial study of the local historic web , done in the town of Leipzig. Some public buildings remained after bomb destruction, on the background of the town structure above. This attitude was taken with the main blocks and important parcels, especially those with public connotations. Old divisions into the smaller parcels were not protected, further destroying the historic scale of the center.

The overall result of these efforts reads at least as a well ordered endeavor , not total destruction the urban center. Of course , some public buildings now seem lacking any historic background, and this can have a strange effect on the understanding of the local pattern.

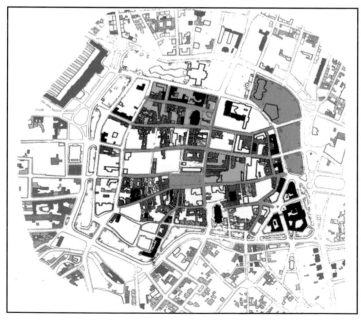

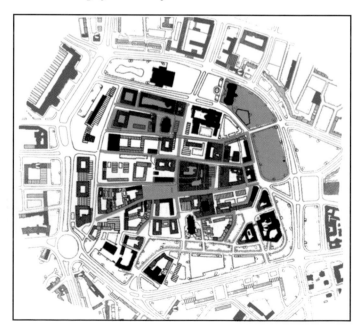

and general overall geometry that is not always entirely regular.

B. Division of private land – the subdivision which is constantly and subtly changing. This division is of a more precise, albeit secondary nature. Nevertheless, it will strongly and significantly influence the nature of the building pattern, creating the framework for future building. This refined secondary system is the result of economic factors, as reflected in the size and shape of individual plots.

C. The geometry of heights of buildings is created through a complex system of regulations, mostly of a planning nature. Its effects can be seen on urban space, influenced by the aforementioned forces.

The basis for conservation is formed by the meaning that is assigned to these space-forming and historical forces, some of which are two thousand years old and long range in their behavior and influence. Careful study of the historical forces will not only shed light on ways and means of town formation, but will enable us to maintain continuity while creating new elements. Not only does this mean creating infill architecture, but also advancing the concept into new planning on a larger scale. This may enrich us with something we have lost, namely the ability to create urban space in a convincing, unbroken way that is not haphazard.

The attention given to the old will pay for itself not only in terms of

*Efforts to prevent total disruption of local old neighborhoods (**Jaffa**, Israel). These attempts too little, too late to prevent the totality of urban blight. Present renovations of a few buildings, even when successful, will not have the strength to hold the local web together.*

The tradition of creating a pattern certainly exists in Paris. In this example of an early 19th century church, it is clear that the intention was to produce a continuity in urban appearance.It also tries to be articulate creating a universally understood presence in an important world capital, while fitting into a pattern.

The pattern of infilling into an existing local web has always been put into practice in London. The evident respect for the surroundings, does not restrain the imagination. On the

contrary, it sometimes helps draw out some creative forces . The unbroken continuity is contained in this example of originality. It is not difficult to implement, once some clear rules are observed.
*(**Vicinity** of King's Road in Chelsea).*

Amsterdam is built by neighboring principles and is, therefore very clear to understand. This is self- reservation at its best. There can be no better environment for town conservation, as conditions perpetuate continuity. All new design looks natural, and what can be learned is that one must 1) look for simple rules and 2) assume respect for patterns.

*Examples of filling gaps in **Paris** (1995). Some new local plans and bye-laws, contain clearer instructions as to how buildings can be brought back to life.*

These laws, while granting a great deal of liberty, also include rules of respect for neighbors. One of the innovations is the effort of these renovating plans , to include whole districts under a systematic conservation plan.

Plans also stipulate heights to be respected, related to volume of roof. Examples are very varied , so as to hint to the possibilities offered to the architect, sometimes too striking in effect.

The simple rule of adopting the volume of the block works here quite well. The human eye understands quickly the meaning of the volumes, and proceeds further to read the particular new detail.

conservation, but also by creating urban concepts long missing in existing vocabularies and lost in the vacuous 'so-called' experimentation. Planners must begin following the fabric and pattern of urban volumes and public spaces created by discoverable geometry in existing towns. Of course, this is not to advocate blindly copying the old. Concrete dimensions, sections, materials and details are all much too complex to copy. Planners must familiarize themselves with this lexicon of urban form and be able to converse with it, use it in conservation and understand its implications for future use. Local standards of culture and thought are not to be swept aside for the convenience of expediency and politics (or vague modernity). The result of this 'easy way out' is, as we can see in innumerable neighborhoods, failure. We have to accept and agree on a correct urban hierarchy of form, system and geometry. It is not to be the usual hierarchy of function, focal points of commercial or bureaucratic and municipal activity or roles. We shall be studying the conservation rules of space creation. On its own, this will not create life or renew urban culture. It will only foster a careful approach to form. Sometimes, as is well noted, conservation comes late in the day when the problem is past its critical stage and there is already the clear decomposition of building known as urban blight. The real contribution, thus, will not be through conservation alone, but with judicious planning and openness to its necessary culmination of urban culture as the focal point of human encounter. Conservation, therefore, is brought here as a planning concept and tool. It must be viewed as a way of analyzing the urban whole, contributing an attitude beneficial to planning in all aspects. This will mean that the new and the old have to be considered in very similar terms, and this is where continuity can be maintained.

Patterns, geometry and urban forms are to be discussed, while overall scale will be reevaluated and used. These attempts are resisted by authorities as an impediment to the tendency to look 'forward'. It is rare to find normal townships that will embrace this not altogether

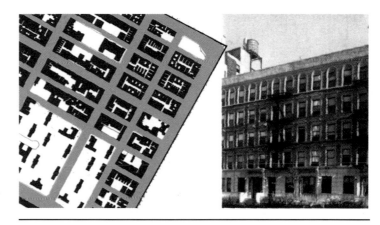

Conrad Levenson, Architect (1980). Example of filling existing building patterns in Manahattan. Existing town structure is clear in indicating designs that will not disrupt the locality. In this respect, there is nothing innovative, but the constant filling in the same pattern means that there is self- renewal. (above and below)

In the city of London, big chunks of the fabric are left and preserved, in spite of manifold pressures. There is still much left of what can be called London quality, when considering different urban elements. This is due to the basic consideration of the main blocks, including their composition, and the keeping of existing land division, both of which will tend to preserve the old quality. Much more could be achieved, as regards coherence and unbroken masses, by controlling heights. It seems that the apparent unification of small parcels has lead to breaking some of the rules, to create buildings visually incorrect as far as old patterns are concerned. However, as can be noted, this mixture of styles and heights still appears at street level as a valid contribution to the human scale.

The proportions of the urban space necessary for the conduct of normal activity are present. This, in turn, is possible because public ownership (of streets, etc.) is kept intact, with a continuous building front. Urban space is an entity that can be somewhat self- perpetuating, and its disruption will mean very brutal , forced and drastic moves. It is easier to try to respect the existing situation.

Central square in Prague. The consciousness given to general conservation in eastern Europe is widespread. One of the reasons for that may be that most of the restoration is done by governmental resources. Other reasons lie with the overall connection people have to their heritage.

clear outlook of integrating the old with the new in a controlled manner.

We shall continue to be attentive to the way towns are formed and try to have a critical and professional influence. If it is recognized that current planning and construction will become the focus of conservation in one hundred years, then the historical context of planning can be grasped. Are we creating a culture fit for conservation efforts? Is our creation fitted with self-preserving inner qualities? Can we begin the self-preservation process now, or do we condemn planning to oblivion, fit only for instant use – a disposable receptacle of changing importance, as politicians and new modernity would have it. This may be the most interesting and pertinent question. Changing concepts of reality will remain cultural (and self-perpetuating) only if we need them to be. Urban context is the perpetual place where this can happen. Its disappearance is convenient only to manipulators of politics.

A very productive approach of infilling the existing old patterns. (Center of Frankfurt). Full respect was paid to old ownership, the old parcel was adopted, as well as building heights in the neighborhood. Local conditions went unharmed, at the same time permitting the utmost liberty imaginable. Freedom was very wisely used , apparently by talented architects. This example will prove that the new can embrace the old pattern , while remaining striking and fresh.

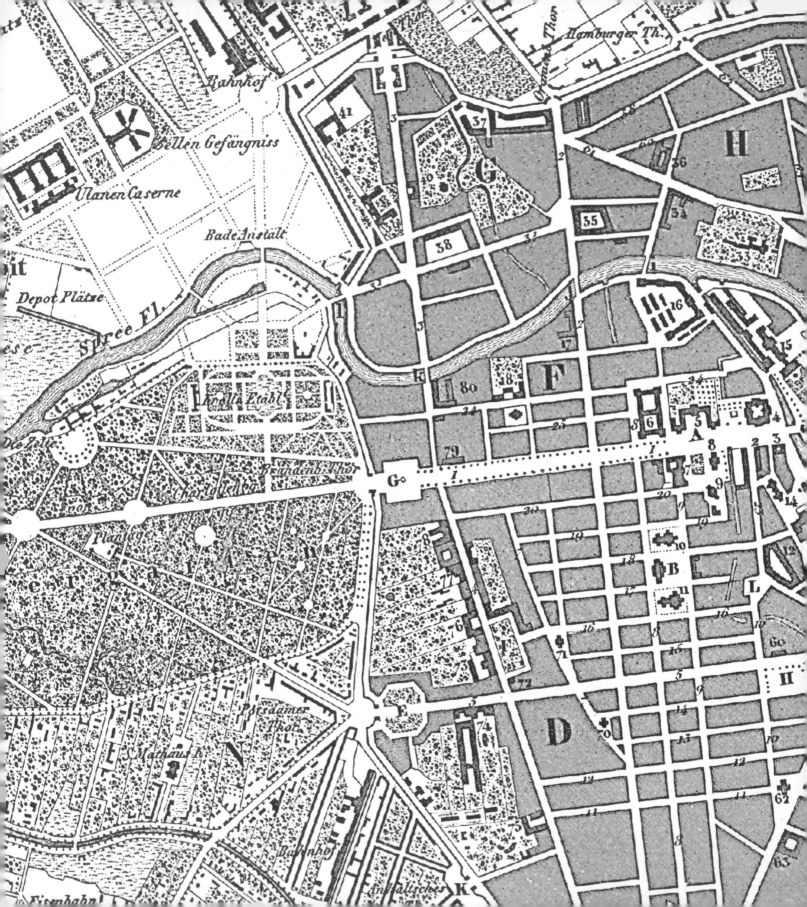

PART ONE

Principles of Conservation

B ring the preservation of the individual building into its urban context, in order to have more coherence as the end result.

Conservation in the urban context will be easier to manage than using pure esthetic grounds or historical justification for isolated examples of architecture.

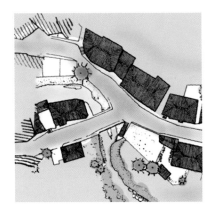

Chapter One
General Views

The Principle of Conservation
Historical Values
The Scope of Preservation
Coherent Urban Culture

Introducing Urban Conservation. Preservation of individual buildings is examined within the context of overall urban settings to ensure that preservation efforts yield products that are in harmony with their surroundings. When viewed as part of a given urban context, conservation is more easily understood than it is, when pure esthetics or history is used as justification.

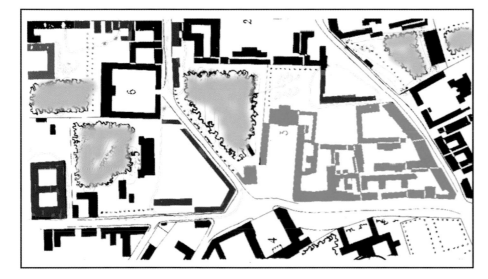

*Transformations in the urban structure and web can be minimal and very beneficial, if correctly and clearly applied.Here new urban space is created, while the main principal weave is retained. At the same time the clarity of major routes is enhanced. **Warsaw**, 19th century.*

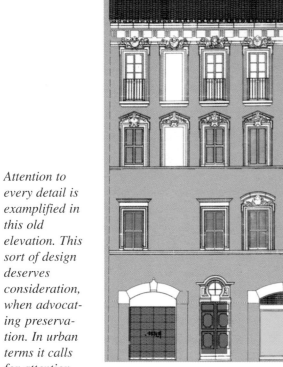

Attention to every detail is examplified in this old elevation. This sort of design deserves consideration, when advocating preservation. In urban terms it calls for attention not only to particular workmanship, but also to the cultural trend to which it corresponds.

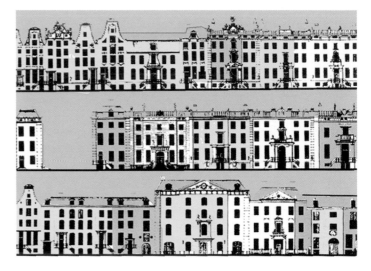

The great importance attached to the main elevation of a building, responds to a certain formula, which will allow for some private and personal expression in every attempt. This is clearly pointed out in old drawings. Design restrictions will always permit diverging from particular formulas, yet retaining local flavor. Conservation acts similarly.

The principle of historic conservation is illustrated by the Colliseum. The urban role of archeological conservation is almost self evident. There can be some planning problems, but there is no denying the importance of such historical presence to the life of city. At the same time, the city has adopted a building which cannot function too often or too well.

Urban conservation is not limited to the preservation of single buildings. It views architecture as but one element of the overall urban setting, making it a complex and multifaceted discipline. By definition, then, urban conservation is at the very heart of urban planning. Below are a number of principles necessary for full comprehension of urban preservation. **Urban planning and conservation are not contradictory, but rather complementary terms. Urban planning that does not take conservation into account is incomplete.** Unfortunately, most references to conservation in urban planning relate only to renovation or restoration.

While it is simple to appreciate renovated and restored buildings, it is far more difficult to comprehend that without taking a more comprehensive view of the urban environment, the renovation will remain specific and isolated, set against a backdrop of general decay. Without preserving the urban environment, no stop can be put to urban blight. Suitable guidelines must be established to ensure that restoration of one building does not lead to the loss of other buildings or parts of other buildings.

Piaza del Popolo *illustrates the principal contention , that of preserving towns' cultural continuity and not just individual buildings. The big square has important city axes, in several diverging directions, and a functional role. It also serves as a culminating and all embracing focal point, symbolic of local heritage.*

1. The Principle of Conservation

All aspects of a single building, structural or architectural, dealing with its use, age or fitness are beyond the scope of planning for urban conservation. **Urban issues begin where building and architectural considerations end**. Urban issues deal with questions of ownership, land division, private and public property, as well as arrangement of urban space as a result of changes over time, including change of use.

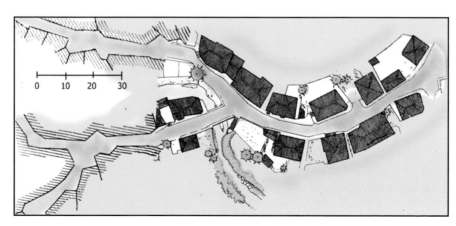

Conservation of a pattern (example of early European settlements) was a special challenge, considered as an "all or nothing" effort. It was also accepted and welcome by local citizens. Considerations had to be systematic, so as to apply to all property. The irregularity seems random, but it was always planned for privacy , good views etc. Original intentions were identified, recorded and respected, with minimal intervention.(Bulgarian village.)

2. The Ownership Principle

Public property and public considerations play a major role in urban aspects of conservation. Public property, the first sign of cultural wealth, cannot be left to decay, meaning that the public shoulders a substantial portion of the burden of conservation. This is true not only in financial terms. The burden may also include decisions regarding private upkeep, and building regulations. In light of the above, it is imperative to foresee conflicts by mapping the public domain. The renovation of historic properties necessitates funds beyond those that can be donated by private individuals. Only through public efforts can such funds be raised. The public will also be involved in passing the legislation necessary to facilitate long-term conservation, laws in the relevant planning bylaws and regulations. Private property, in other words the single building, is

The principle of historical continuity is clear when the presence of a church in the square becomes the main element which will justify urban considerations. This is the case in Piaza del Popolo, Rome, above.

Urban culture can be summed up as a unique human achievement, easily communicated to tourists or viewers. It enjoys a wide multinational consensus, as one of the indications of human heritage, and maybe a worthwhile reason for living in congested cities. This will constitute the antithesis of dispersion, of provinciality and suburbia, of life in nature. Urban life is concentrated because human nature often creates better under such conditions, and has developed not only because of economic necessity. This example of urban design can be observed in the example above (Trieste), and shows urban space at its best: the local view and its urban space are turned and sieved through the built environment, to become almost palpable.

problematic in another respect —enforcing preservation. Buildings may be privately owned by several individuals and institutions, not all of whom necessarily agree. The mapping of ownership must, therefore, be one of the first steps taken. Only when all urban authorities work together can the conditions for successful conservation be established. Ownership issues, however, do not begin and end with buildings; they also concern title to land. As we delve deeper, the importance of land division and title will become clear. It is also advisable to factor in land values when these considerations are made, providing a valid economic basis for the effort to conduct large-scale conservation projects in sections of the city.

3. The Principle of Historical Value

Conservation does not only consider modern factors, but also digs deep into the past, looking towards archeological and research findings for inspiration. The actual dimensions and geometry of the finds at archeological sites influence the course conservation takes, as does the urban dimensioning of old city components and their changes over time. Inherent to old archeological land divisions is a unique systematic development, which indicates to those involved in conservation efforts, the dimensions that must be kept because of their influence on local patterns.

4. The Principle of Enlarging the Scope of Preservation

Clearly, the single building and protected archeological site both have limited scope in terms of conservation. Only by relating buildings and archeology to their specific urban setting, can the role of the city be evaluated. It currently appears that urban conservation is becoming more widely practiced, making it influential enough to have broad implications.
Conservation efforts will not be limited to small areas

In the example of a preserved Bulgarian village, interior and external restoration enjoy a genuine conservationist attitude.(Started in 1964.)

or individual neighborhoods, and this will lead to a corresponding increase in the scope of conservation planning. Proper planning will take such factors as good urban relations into account.

The term, urban relations, as used in this context, relates to the overall sense of harmony between urban elements and the relation between those elements and the local populace. When a sense of equilibrium exists, human culture is conceived and enjoyed, and it is this very rich cultural life which is drawing people back into the city, thus providing the impetus for conservation. While such urban material obviously abounds in large, historical concentrations and not in remote, disconnected regions, it is also clear that the principles that can be applied to large areas are true for smaller areas as well.

The detailed results of the early endeavour of performing conservation on a new scale in an historic settlement, Bulgaria, 1964. Government was heavily involved , while village life did not stop. Conservation plans considered position of the particular house, as well as the unique pattern of local streets and roads. The coherent pattern that emmerged is valuable in its totality.

5. The Principle of Coherent Urban Culture

As stated above, the aim of conservation is to promote urban life characterized by a strong sense of continuity. Esthetic qualities, which will hopefully also be preserved, are not sufficient to achieve this goal. The value of day-to-day urban qualities must be rediscovered; the focus cannot remain on monuments alone. This means initiating a change of outlook, as sometimes preservation efforts will concentrate on urban space that is void of structures.

These unimproved urban spaces are of importance because they often constitute an important and essential backdrop for events and creations, providing a context which highlights the preservation and makes it simpler to understand. The background may be a particular topographical area or a natural park. Preservation efforts should be made in a climate of participation, proving to ourselves that we are not merely preserving stones, but concentrating on daily life. Once people understand the positive impact projects can have on their daily lives, they are normally happy to encourage and participate in conservation.

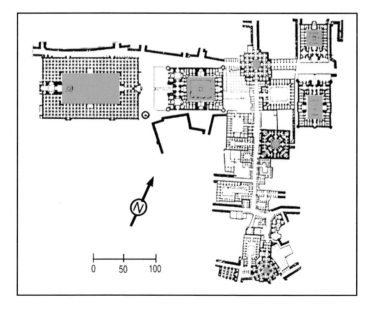

*The plans of a cultural complex in the city of **Bukhara** show the extent to which urban conservation can be applied (some 60,000 sq. m. of floor space). It is clear that only a public concern can deal with such projects.*

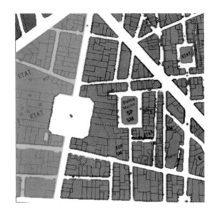

Chapter Two
City Structure

Webs, Districts and Blocks

City structure is not difficult to understand, once the principles governing it become familiar. It is assumed that a clear hierarchy is behind all structure and this also helps our study. We always start from a general plan, finding major and minor features as we close in.

An in-depth understanding of the city structure is a prerequisite for determining conservation potential and hierarchy. Thus, the city needs to be broken down into its most basic components. The illustrations provided serve as clarification.

1. Although every city is defined by a structure, often unique to its locality, it is still possible to state a number of general rules. In order to build a framework of general rules, the existence of some city hierarchy must first be assumed. To this end, it is helpful to try to compare similar towns. After a quantitative analysis of elements such as width of streets, heights of buildings and number of shops, the main dimensions of the area become clear.

This portion of north-central Paris will serve to point out, in principle, the major parts in the structure of the city.

Paris is known as a mixture of styles , lines and axes. To find the meaning and the structure of a town , one has to form a system of analysis. The system suggested here is general enough to be applicable to many towns.
In order to conduct and build a proper planning hierarchy, it is essential to have good, detailed maps (such as 1:25000). Well defined air photos are also available to help this process.

Parisian blocks are rather special, because they were cut in different directions in different periods. Their shapes tend to be disoriented, sometimes confusing. At the same time, manifold urban ties and short cuts are made possible and make the whole more negotiable, especially if compared to the orthogonal grid.

Discussed and analyzed districts and sections are seen from above, to help in clarifying the structure. The scale of the areas in discussion becomes evident, when heights and spaces, not apparent in the normal plan, are brought in, by aeral oblique photographs.

2. Every city is built on and contains different webs. These webs, either structurally similar or completely different, are complementary. The urban pattern is composed of the collection of such webs, as well as by the generation of natural lines (such as, direction of geographical features, wind, sun, coastline) and manmade lines (such as streets). Cities may be made up of any number of webs, each containing multiple sections. They can be comparable in terms of their major dimensions, age and methods of formation, as well as periods of

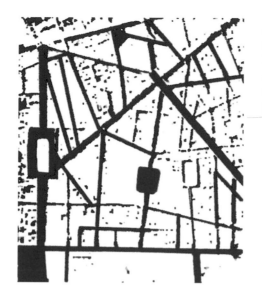

Marked in red , we see the somewhat arbitrary selection of districts, or quarters. The major city web is also clear. The city sections, consisting and built by blocks , is marked in blue. The different blocks are pointed out in purple and white.

historical importance or regression. Webs may also be the result of a basic grid that, over time, has changed and developed subdivisions. Such changes may be indicative of changes in local planning and of cultural changes as well.

3. This analysis will help prepare the next steps, such as definition of general aspects of local building. Local systems of building when looked at in terms of geometrical patterns help establish principles and sub-

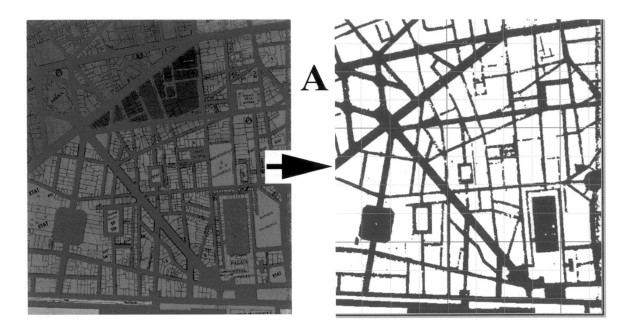

Paris 1990

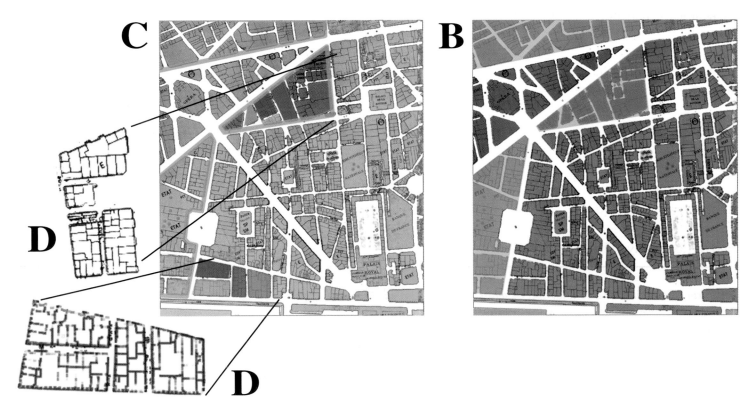

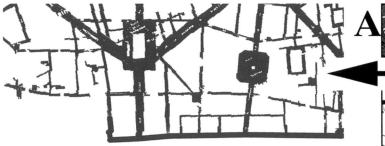

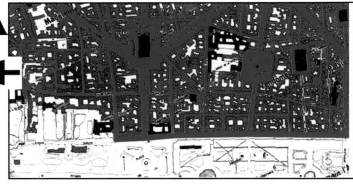

Paris 1750

jects relevant to conservation, such as uniformity, style and other qualities.

4. The urban web, once identified, is seen to be composed of several districts or sections. An urban section can be defined as differing from neighboring sections by a particular quality, such as height or geometry. It is, of course, part of the web and is influenced by it, but is defined as an entity in its own right. The district described above, while having a life of its own, will also be dependent on its relations with similar adjoining quarters. The changes that have taken place over time and that have influenced development in minor webs in districts or sections are generally more subtle than those in major webs.

5. Urban sections are made up of urban blocks, which define a section by their similarity, size and orientation. It is on this level that unique local mannerism, style or building characteristics become important and identifiable. Urban blocks can be defined as being surrounded on all sides by public land and rights of way. These are the borders sepa-

The structure of cities is also analyzed by maps , through the process of defining the following characteristics :

A. The urban web, that is the collection of all the primary and secondary roads, forming a pattern of the following entities, on which they are also based:

B. Major sections, precincts and districts, formed by common features or qualities.

C. The main blocks constituting the urban section.

D. The blocks have their own subdivision, that of the smaller plot or parcel.

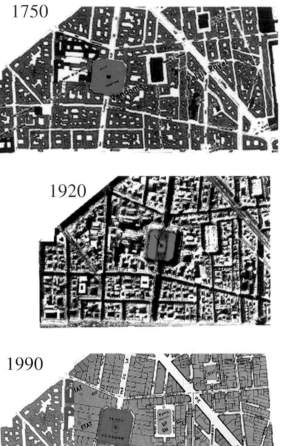

1750

1920

1990

Study of structural changes over time. This indicates what elements are important enough to have staying power throughout the centuries.

1700

rating and distinguishing blocks. Thus, the block is an independent entity, and the buildings on it can either be interconnected or separate. In addition, the block is an exceedingly well defined and measurable land unit, having a specific internal division. On this level different land uses (in terms of zoning) and intensity of the use, such as the number of stories in buildings per land unit, can be studied.

6. Blocks are further divided into land parcels, also referred to as plots, defined in terms of size, directions, relative proportions, repetition and quantity. The shape of the separate buildings closely mimics the shape of the parcel. This simple fact is too often overlooked in planning considerations. It can, therefore, be stated that the parcel is always the formative element in defining the evolution of a city. Parcels are the smallest building block of the urban environment.

7. In short, when looking at the components of urban structure, the following hierarchy can be established:

Parcel (also referred to as plot) - the smallest geometrically defined element of the urban environment.

Block- formed by parcels and surrounded by public land.

Section - a collection of similar blocks.

Web – a collection of sections, with similar attributes, form an urban web in a bigger precinct.

Urban network or city web – A group of connected webs.

City - the complex lattice formed out of a number of networks, developed over many centuries.

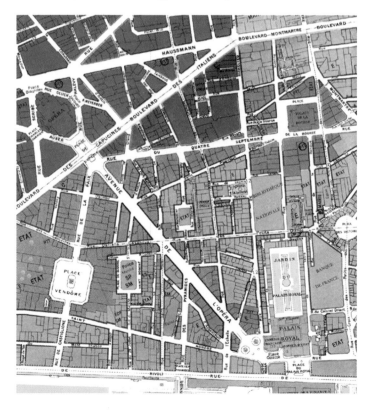

*Map of **Paris** , (contemporary ,circa 1990), is a very valuable contribution of the city plan, marking new developing potential and current by-laws. The web and the district quarter (in red), the city section (in blue), and the forming blocks (in purple) are noted.*

A good example of a congested, but clear urban space (**Napoli**).
Inevitably, spaces of this nature are not always the most desirable to live in. It only serves to clarify visually the meaning of a well-defined urban space.

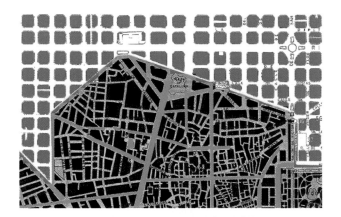

Two very different types of town structures meet in the city of Barcelona, creating a good example of the kind of structure one finds in urban conservation. The regularity and the detailed nature of the modern one (in blue), is very dissimilar to the green, seemingly haphazard one, containing the gothic city. When the two meet, one is faced by a striking cultural moment of comparison. As far as study is concerned, the two aspects of opposing geometry have to be defined.

Air photos are illuminating, especially vertical ones, and are widely used to identify structural components. In the present photo, height similarity is induced by shadows, as well as changes in details over time (if that is important in the conducted study). At the same time, relations, structural or other, are also possible. It is rewarding to compare a map with a photo, and thus be acquainted with both aspects. For example , it is difficult to judge precise road width, which can be an important element.

Details of city structure are made by a multitude of data. It is important to systematize all details in a way fit for use. The map contains the precise information about plots, roads, and buildings, all in their relative positions. Simple analysis will collect similar components. As an example, this has been done on plot sizes. With the help of an aerial photograph, one can decide on block repetition, or on a section of the city carrying some structural affinity with neighboring blocks.

Detecting the block formation, its similarities with adjoining blocks, is helped by size of plots, heights of buildings, period of construction and similar findings, some of them in maps, others with the help of photos. The basic structure (top) is simpler to identify, and once the rule is understood, physical size noted, it is possible to go into further detail systematically. (Central Tel Aviv)

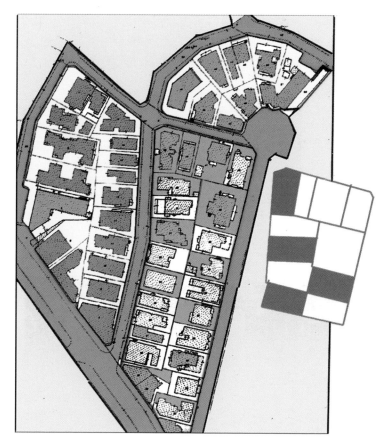

Chapter Three

Conservation as an Urban Tool

Quantitative Data
Physical Characteristics
Urban Economics

U rban conservation will be used after studies of the way urban qualities manifest themselves in different cities are completed. The qualities of urban culture, which have developed in certain cities' structures, sometimes as their result, will vary slightly from place to place, but their basic significance has to be discovered.

This conservation will mean better city planning. The examples cited in the present chapter are the basis of this realization - using conservation as a way of sustaining life in cities.

A general view of Budapest looks like a region worthy to be included in our discussions on urban conservation. Budapest has the size, density and special urban structure, as well as a general urban qualities that one would like to investigate and examine.

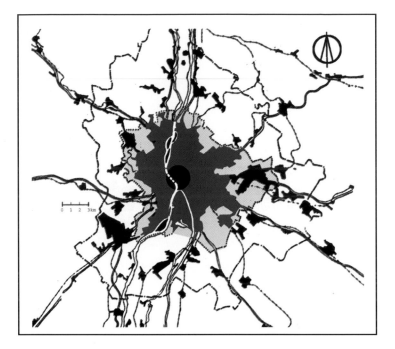

A network of patterns that are extremely illustrative in depicting the radial quality of the service roads of Budapest's surrounding region. The next quality to look for will be its size, intersections, and geometrical pattern. These patterns are influential in determining the nature of the internal roads and the way they are fed regionally. This in turn will show their necessary role in the city's function, and on its web.

Large-scale maps of the discussed region will help us understand the nature of urban quality as related to regional characteristics. The density in the built up area of a major city develops along well marked links such as roads, and is generally supported by a wide regional country- side.

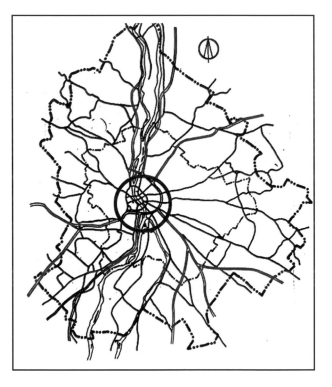

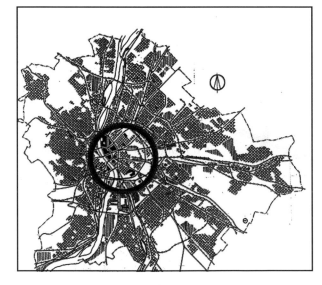

An urban map illustrating the main urban structure of a city, situated on a river and influenced by a large background region, tells us of the radius that is relevant to our considerations. As a result, we are able to formulate a wide outlook regarding the site that should be examined in terms of urban conservation. This overall view emphasizes the structure for which we are looking.

Which urban areas can be designated as potential conservation areas? A clear definition of the significant and quantitative components should be made before these areas can be sought.

1. Quantitative Data

In order to provide examples and study the issue, a numerical position that defines the size of a given region has been adopted:

1. Density – An urban area is defined as a region in which total **density** is 50 people or more per hectare.

2. Size – It cannot be assumed that serious problems would be reflected in much smaller areas.

Even here there will be a numerical demarcation, in order to conduct an urban analysis – 1,000 hectares which includes populations of at least 50,000 citizens.

This is the region that will be examined. Within this region, much smaller sections will be identified for further analysis.

3. City Background – An isolated city with a population of 50,000 is too small and the pressures of daily life there are insufficient for such an area to be suitable for this study. An urban area of 100 square kilometers (1,000 hectares), with a population of 500,000, including a preservation area of 10 square kilometers, is more suitable, and allows for a better perspective of the issues. With a better overall picture of the extent of

The main region of interest is central Budapest, the city's oldest section that is based on the river and is served by several radial roads . The regions' size, qualified by the map, is approximately as shown - 1/2 km wide by 2 km long, about 1000 hectares. It is surrounded by a semblance of a ring road and served by three major bridges, where the main bridge results from the radial cross-river roads.

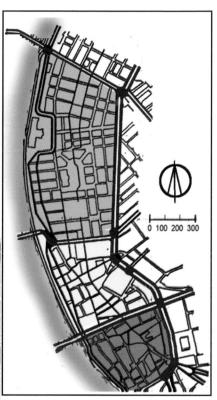

This basic structure can be seen to be influenced by the nearby region in a radial and concentric manner. Furthermore, it develops, for distribution purposes, other ring shaped connections and this determines how well fed the city is, by being well connected. Ill-connected localities will develop signs of deterioration.

This town fulfills our terms of reference, namely that we are looking into a region full of historical and esthetical values that are easily observed, and defined. The importance and centrality of this particular region, is apparent in terms of urban structure, major links like its bridges, in terms of the importance of public buildings of monumental value and the proportions of some clear urban volumes.

The above illustration shows what is meant by connections, urban shapes and proportions. We are clearly faced by a strong urban landmark, present in other European cities and developed along similar lines of structure.

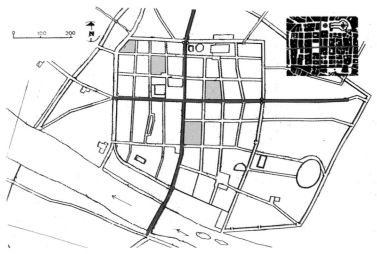

Florence is based on an old Roman network, containing an orthogonal system. This is why we can easily discover the basic features of the urban structure, namely: 1. Orthogonal roads 2. Roads perpendicular and parallel to the river. We start our investigation in this particular town with two grids that have an angle of 30 degrees to each other and contain: A. Ancient Roman walls and the orthogonal system pointing to the North and B. the urban wall that is parallel to the river, and results in a second system.

conservation in mind, it will be simpler to conduct an extensive analysis. A larger region, with a service radius of approximately 15 kilometers and a population of one million, will provide sufficient background.

4. Concentration – to classify a region in terms of land use (zoning), the concentration and intensity of business, cultural and recreational activities must be established. The remaining regional definitions will stem from an analysis of the components of the city web.

These numerical fields are a prime example of problems in preservation. To construct accurate models of urban structure, they must imitate regions where life-styles are typical of those in large cities.

The objective of this endeavor is to focus on the conceptual discussion, while preserving germane urban aspects and excluding all others. The complexity of urban preservation necessitates reference to an area of appropriate size, i.e., referral to a reasonable scale. In this context, the number of regions around the world that can currently be included in this definition can be roughly estimated at several thousand, the majority of which can serve as a testing ground for regulations as suggested by urban conservation (regardless of their location). Logically, the regions containing relevant information, mainly numerical, are located in Western countries (Europe and some sections of the United States) and are essential to the discussion. These are the areas that will be referred to, at least in the beginning phases.

In order not to err and use theories that cannot be implemented, there is a need for a realistic preliminary plan, which can be quantified and provide general statistics. Realistically, differences among places will exist, and there is a need to be flexible. However, the generalities we would like to draw will

The basic city structure is noted by a central core surrounded by a web at 30 degrees to each other. These two old regulative systems, play the central role in formulating the basis of this central area. The city has developed this asset as a generating formula to create a characteristic form.

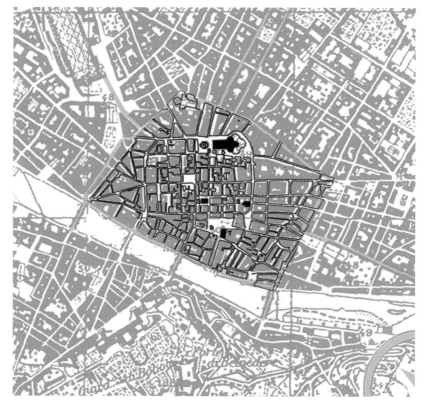

Modern day Florence, with its basic Roman grid, contains the old features mentioned. Orthogonality in the south-north direction joins the basic grid of blocks of identical structure. This is a square one, with several cuts into it, forming a well-defined quarter, humanly scaled and not larger than 25 hectares.

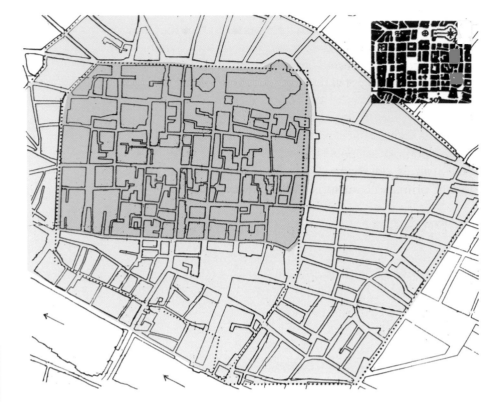

It is immediately apparent that the urban structure and qualities shown in this map are related to the secondary urban wall parallel to the river. It is also clear that the city blocks surrounding the older city are based on an urban grid that has its origin in the direction of the river. The establishing of these generating geometry forms our basic understanding of city form.

Delving into the structure of the city, one can look at it from two main points: 1. The black and white ones, stressing the size of the blocks and 2. The brown and black emphasizing the direction of the grid, that is the roads that form divisions to create the direction and size of the blocks.

be universal. Significantly large regions must also have particular characteristics which can identify the additional qualities to be preserved. A list of the local goals of the conservation project should be drawn up. Without this information, a comprehensive study of the problem of preservation, its size and components cannot be conducted. Identification will be made by maps specifically prepared for this purpose; maps which detail the urban components and their relevant characteristics. In the beginning, the following primary characteristics should be identified:

1. Physical Characteristics

Deployment – The area of the preservation region within the urban setting and background environment.
Land Usage – The general components characteristic of regional life (zoning)
Land Ownership – Identification of public and private property
Land Division – By grid lines such as streets, squares, etc.
Geometry – The general typology and measurements which make up the region, such as large blocks, distances, etc.
Three-dimensional – Building heights, primary spaces, and topography

2. Reference to the City

The relationship to the city web, its major transportation routes, as well as their hierarchy must be marked, and includes **the boundaries of the preservation area.** The relative size of the area to be preserved as compared to its environment (defined in percentages) and evaluation of its contribution and importance to the city, will dictate the scope of the undertaking.

All of the above issues will be reflected in the maps, tables and statistical/numerical analysis. In order to put the elements of the discussion in better proportion, similar types of elements from other cities should be noted. Problems should not be viewed as specific to a local area. On

This illustration presents some of the surrounding areas of central Florence, with the encompassing natural parks and gardens to the southeast, from which the center can be fully observed and judged, linking to the history of the place. This observation point makes the city consistently self-conscious of its formation and presence, and is helpful in presenting arguments for preservation.

The division of the city block is shown to be made up of the small parcels, the individual-owned blocks of land, which have a very long history. Here is where we can judge the size of the basic blocks that comprise the nature of the urban grain we are trying to discover.

the contrary, similar problems and solutions, or lack of solutions should be compared wherever they exist. For example, the study of existing squares is completely justified by the results of the comparative study of similar squares.

The criteria necessary for understanding the uniqueness of the site are established. Though this is not a discussion of issues such as style or traditions (but in a very limited manner) --the comparison proves to be useful. The focus on the dimensions and quantity varies from place to place, and as such will emphasize the relations between the different elements. It is not especially difficult to conduct these comparisons. The material continues to compile, with the help of cartographic and geographic processes. This material will be used by the researcher and will be made available to the planner.

3. The Urban Economic Dimension

One element that should be included is an appraisal table. In preservation, all financial issues and figures used are relative, varying according to the specific instance at hand. Without a financial benchmark (land and building values), the data is unmanageable and recommendations on a large scale cannot be made. This background material will be reworked, highlighting the potential components of preservation. This preliminary survey illustrates the size and the scope of the problem. Only after this step is complete, will the concept of conservation be clear. With a clear understanding of the issues, it will be possible to move on to the next phase.

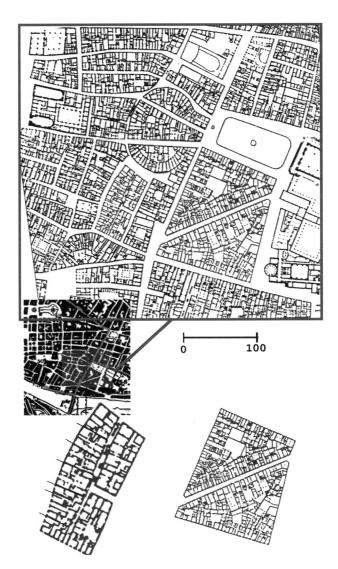

The main points of the basic elements of the city structure will be discussed later on. These include : A. The basic shape of the blocks in the town, B. The sizes of the city blocks and their subdivision into parcels, both dictated by the main grid or geometry.

Chapter Four

Identifying Urban Qualities

Major Characteristics
Essential Qualities for Conservation

The complex of mixture of qualities that call for conservation is not self-evident in all cases. In order to analyze and decide what is to be presented, we will try to understand the properties under discussion. When we deal with these properties in the methodology we adopt, we shall try to quantify each quality separately, so as to form a manageable basis of operation.

Too often, in the zeal of preservation, mistakes are made in preserving the many attributes (like tourist attractions), rather than essentials.

Instances of urban repetition like the one in Washington (middle) or in the town of Sopron, Hungary (left) the resort of Sorrento (right) show that some qualities are almost universal, revealing themselves in various parts of the world. This is the task that awaits us when we try to identify unique qualities fit for urban conservation.

1. Major Characteristics

Once the areas for conservation have been identified, questions arise as to what exactly should be preserved, how and by what means preservable characteristics are identified. The criteria selected for this task must be quantifiable, so that results can be judged.

Obviously, merely pinpointing the prototype for conservation is insufficient. Its uniqueness should be determined by comparing it with other prototypes. This comparison can then serve as the basis for deciding whether the prototype contains the unique properties. This is one of the reasons for comparisons with other regions currently undergoing conservation, or which will be doing so in the future. The properties we search for are varied. Often it is difficult to determine where one quality ends and the other begins. The precondition being that the characteristics should be unique and homogeneous- that is, they should

The old square in towns like Warsaw, which has been completely renovated and rebuilt, and other similar ones in Europe, historical places and streets, monasteries (the one in Assissi is shown), the Spanish steps (Rome), all evoke a feeling of history and place mixed with esthetics.

be both distinctive and prominent. Two major characteristics can be distinguished as follows:
Esthetic and historical qualities, both linked to durable cultural symbols.

Esthetic qualities exist for human pleasure. (These qualities must be able to withstand an examination of clarity.)

As was previously stressed, it goes without saying that the above refers to clear-cut examples of populated urban areas. As the **Historical qualities** and cultural symbolism advocated here are interwoven, the analysis to be conducted is used to clarify the extent and scope of the conservation project. Without this clarification, it is impossible to focus on methods of planning and make recommendations.

It should be noted that these qualities also relate to individual buildings. In urban analysis, it is more difficult to point them out, especially quantitatively. One should keep in mind, however, that urban conservation primarily preserves geometry and that architecture is based on that very geometry. Geometric qualities should, therefore, be preserved, so that they may serve as a background for esthetic qualities and not vice versa. Esthetics is very often based on geometric quantities. Therefore, geometry plays an important role in esthetic arrangements and must be discovered and defined.

The existing literature shows that while conservation projects in the United States tend to emphasize the emotional and historical, European projects stress esthetics. The reasons for this are obvious – the United States is searching for identity. In Europe, they have ostensibly already found this identity and have continued developing towards a complex esthetic megastructure. Following a survey of professional literature, we have compiled a number of properties that have been generally agreed upon by

Viewing this narrow street in Arrezo, Italy, we see the mixture of esthetic qualities, urban situations, spaces, historical values, workmanship, etc. The problem one is faced with, after discovering a region definable for research, is how to define, arrange and analyze the multitude of qualities one encounters.

In this old setting at Bruges, we are again faced with a mixture of a small square, bridge, river, style of building, certain volumes, certain urban densities and feelings of dignity and locality. How are we to define and mark these qualities? This complex theme of research has to include a system of hierarchy, to ensure coherency.

Venice has numerous examples of features of particular urban settings and an unmistakable feeling of place. In addition, it is known for the historical qualities that it preserves, linked by the canals and bridges. This particular instance of urban culture includes style, design and good workmanship, which have evolved during over four centuries. The combination of esthetics and history, workmanship and materials, all linked in the multiple web of canals and streets, is a unique and complex urban formula.

Public right of way through intimate urban configurations, give the feeling of surprise on the right, (Viterbo, Italy). The middle illustration is of a lively urban Spanish setting, and on the left of some unique style of building in the city of Boston. All these complex examples refer to conservation and indicate the need of systematic study.

most experts.

An area worthy of conservation (beyond considerations regarding individual buildings) is one where, to some extent, the identified qualities exist. (These are the qualities that those behind the conservation effort want to preserve at the various sites.)

The five qualities listed below are helpful in formulating the goals of conservation.

Obviously, in reality, qualities and criteria are not always clearly distinguishable from one another. Conservation qualities are based on the physical urban structure, and not purely theoretical. In other words, conservation is not an abstract issue, but can be legally defined and evaluated in economic terms. These general guidelines can be categorized and compared before work on the project begins.

2. Essential Qualities for Conservation

The following are qualities outlining the goals of conservation:

1. The Urban Setting

A clearly defined area with borders, situated within the overall environment. These borders can be easily identified. The nature of the area can be defined both physically and abstractly. The area has to be an obvious focal point in the environment, rather crowded and large in terms of its urban context.

2. Sense of Place

Sense of place can be defined as the emotional and historical associations, the view, presence of certain urban themes, provision of comfort and shade, relaxation, link to nature, topography and vegetation. Added to this are the simple urban understanding, spatial location, their selection and contribution to forging identities.

Another observable quality, in this case a very elaborate design and style with a proper, exquisite workmanship ability. This surviving mixture of volumes, style, preservation, workmanship needs to be properly defined if it is to serve as an example of conservation, from which we can derive methods of going about our attempt at systematic preservation and conservation. The formulas at which we are looking and trying to ascertain the qualities are the formulas that may assist us in places that are not as obvious as the one in this example. (Ghent, Belgium).

The materials used in different building methods and styles throughout history are somewhat surprising. The workmanship these materials necessitated, the diversity of local conditions in various urban settings conductive to unique usage are qualities to be looked into.

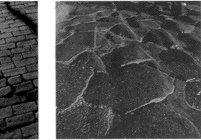

A walled-in city presents a very clear structure. We're looking at a pattern that has survived for centuries, has been naturally preserved in its setting defined by walls, is very dense and clear in its qualities, and thus helps to better define them because of this particular urban setting. On the other hand, seeing a feature set in an important urban position, such as an old bridge, positioned in a way observable from the human settlement above it, and forming a strong feeling of locality, one has to assess qualities difficult to measure.

3. Internal Links

Within the area, there is a singularity of places and links, concerning urban spaces and blocks. The spatial design (and not necessarily the particular building) that dominates the elements, positions, street measurement/length/height within the environment, is rare, and yet prominent.

4. Style & Design

This involves color, materials, textures, and silhouettes, as well as similarities and differences between buildings.

All of these elements are extremely important and unique, attracting attention. The three-dimensional and characteristic artistic style, such as a particular geometry, is what is dominant, and not merely local esthetics.

5. Workmanship

The materials used in the construction have undergone processing to make them appear original and authentic. These can include arches and domes, clay covered walls, and specially processed stone.

Construction methods refer to complete urban elements. They are not found in individual buildings, but are rather a continuous process.

These five central qualities assist in the formulation of guidelines to be used in selecting conservation areas. This will be **the reason** for conservation, after the area has been chosen. Now, we should continue to the background that will serve as the basis for the area's contribution to **objective and physical reasons for conservation**, as properties of urban structure which can be identified. This background, termed basic urban pattern, is physical and geometrical.

Clear urban structure is an important quality to look for. A main street in the town of Riga (Lithuania) is an illustration of the fact that clarity is closely related to structure.

Chapter Five

The Urban Web

The Archeological Background
Primary Urban Characteristics of the Web
Secondary Urban Characteristics
Nature and Topography

C ities are made of webs, lines and axes, caused by the formation of public rights of way (i.e. roads). Discovery of the city web, in the geometrical sense, gives a formal basis to our discussion. It will be seen that individual cities will have special and often unique characteristics, in similar geometry.

The urban web is essentially what defines the physical (not esthetic) properties of the specified area. This concept will be defined in further detail later on. The web is made up of several components, which determine conservation. These components will be the subjects of the forthcoming chapters:

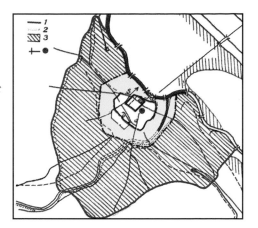

Growth of towns has a clear and somewhat symmetrical pattern of development and deployment. Early influences tend to leave their mark behind, and may serve as landmarks and indicators of structure and importance. The growth of early Vienna (marked in red) with late fortifications is shown. Inner city limits as existing today (in yellow), consist of old walls and fortifications dating from early 18th century. 18th century early town (hatched) and reinforcing walls of an early period (in black) are also pointed.

Modern Vienna, shown on its old structure. The logic of roads, blocks and directions stems from old Roman patterns, resulting in a radial town based on the canal and having the geometry and the orthogonality of its Roman foundation. This is surrounded by the circular form of the old walls, forcing outward radial connections, some of which later returned to basic orthogonal forms. Parts of the old town still survive, helped by the clear delineation of the old walls. Formation of present blocks can be derived logically from the major historical forces that the town has known.

The clarity of the pattern ,
pointed out in this manner helps
to analyze development and
shows the essential in the city
form, where its origins are and
what should be reinforced and/or
fully conserved, when dealing
with preservation patterns.
Understanding the basic urban
form is essential before we can
consider preservation. In fact,
when we see the changes in the
logic adopted in the formation of
different districts, patterns,
formative elements and
directions, and understand them,
we can choose our attitude and
assist the patterns that are vital
to the city form.

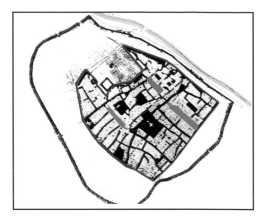

The old town of Vienna, which can serve
as a major example, is basically built on
Roman origins, inside city walls, on a
river bank, like in previous examples. It
has the orthogonal grid, present in
Roman cities, with the normal market
square and urban emphasis at the
crossings of the grid. Thus, the basic city
structure is clearly identified.

Aerial and oblique photography is essential to
analyze heights and geometric arrangements
when judging conservation potential.
This is where methodical planning
conditions are observed and realized.
The typical old land division is clearly
observed in the illustration, with some
new, more permanent planning. As we
can see, the main structure of the streets is
often related to notable patterns,
especially when they are based on
historical form. The city web creates
neighborhoods that stem from this
pattern, closing it and relating it to the
other city regions, which have their own
internal coherence. The districts are
subdivided into city blocks, marked in
color, which have roots in historical
ownership and land divisions. We have
thus observed the major components that
organize the city form.

The Archaeological-Historical Background

There are a number of explanations for why history spurs conservation. The ancient geometrical division is perhaps the most interesting as it provides a historical perspective of land ownership and development.

This has implications on conservation, emphasizing the major lines of division. The design of a place, beginning in the past, is a pattern formed by the division and which becomes the most fundamental characteristic of construction. For example, the contours of an ancient fortress which no longer exists, can contribute to modern urban accents, such as the emphasis of historical locations which have long since disappeared. They can also pinpoint changes in geometrical methods which may have also vanished.

Primary Urban Characteristics of the Web

The collection of streets and buildings establishes the atmosphere of a place as well as its spatial three-dimensional presence. The access roads preserve and indicate the size of the structure and emphasize their importance.

The basic web was created because of the various access roads. The importance of emphasizing the detailed study of this characteristic will be subsequently clarified.

These geometrical definitions are what conservation aims to preserve. For example, as long as major roads, characterized by size, create these urban structures, it will be easier to decide on their conservation in a precise and

This illustration will help to depict the approaches of urban design in traditional 18th and 19th century towns, in which clear blocks and links between town squares, boulevards and streets, with accents on different buildings at junctions can be clearly followed. This helps us recognize some major urban elements, and understand the result in terms of urban design. Town structure, urban grids and webs are also noted in this study of urban development.

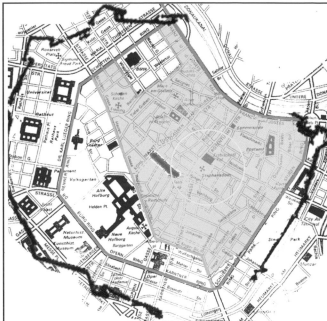

A closer look at Vienna will show the basis of the town's development, as it occurred from an early period through a Roman encampment, on to a basically fortified town which leans on the nearby canal. We can see the influence of the perpendicular lines directed to the canal, as well as systems continuing and clearly radiating towards the newer walls as they are being built through the centuries.

It becomes apparent that the old part of the town (seen on the right) has a clearly orthogonal style developed over the centuries in a radial manner, as towns based on one side of the river often have. Old borders and districts lines (in color) are kept. The major roads , districts and internal divisions are pointed out. All modern development stems from the old town progressing into the moderately orthogonal blocks, found to the right.

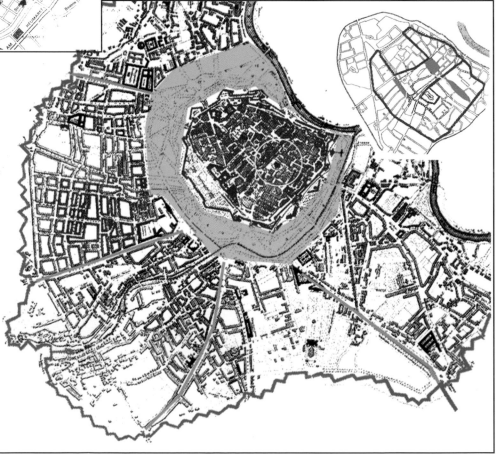

determined manner.

Identification of the urban structure largely depends on identification of the basic pattern, and it is, therefore, extremely important to understand it.

Pinpointing spaces within the urban web (such as various squares) and the links connecting them will also determine the nature and type of conservation.

The spaces can be pinpointed by careful study of the characteristic weave. This weave is the collection of the webs of streets and roads, which are primary in their role.

Secondary Urban Characteristics

Although monuments and castles tend to be more architectonic, their relationship to the environment and the web should be examined. This relationship is worthy of conservation, but only after its importance and place in the local hierarchy is established. In many cases, a link will also be established between the monument and land use (which has a tendency to vary over time).

When presented with evidence such as that on the left, where modern formations have totally neglected the historical development of city webs through many centuries, one cannot but feel helpless. The utter disregard met by the civilized approach based on historical development, results in the appearance, such as the one shown, in grave contrast with European traditions, of a completely inhuman state of affairs. Commercialized in an absurd and avoidable manner, we are inundated with these unnecessary blocks, created as a by-product of modern liberalism.

The organization in Vienna of the elements - streets, squares, views, spaces, urban parks - are integrated in the city system and constitute a logical outcome of city structure. We find ourselves with some organized urbanity containing the major elements as discussed. This approach is important to us since it is completely negated by the modern approach to the space qualities inherent in a traditional city structure, and organized urbanity is disregarded by many urban planners and designers.

One always looks for old architectural gems as they appear in crucial moments in an urban web and are considered, in our approach, to be a necessary outcome of a logically built city. They are to be regarded as good, but rare or random instances of successful design. This is not exactly logical, as good architecture cannot be "freakish", isolated as it often is. We may assume that the web and the so termed organized urbanity have prepared for it. In fact, architecture can be judged to be a contribution to a local sense of structure, and not vice versa. (Central Vienna.)

It should, however, be emphasized that the relationship to the environment is permanent, regardless of whether its use changes.

For example, public passageways within buildings (right of way) can take on a central role in considerations regarding antique conservation, even when their function or construction has changed.

Nature and Topography

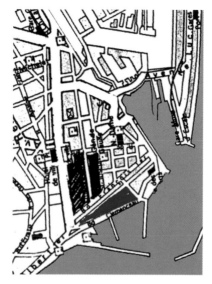

The old city of Le Havre underwent major renewal after its destruction in World War 2. Renewal has taken a modern approach which completely disregards districts, city structure, old patterns and block constructions with other major principal city formations as existed before the War. There is no regard for land divisions or parcels, and thus we are left with a barren piece of land, void of cultural connotations.

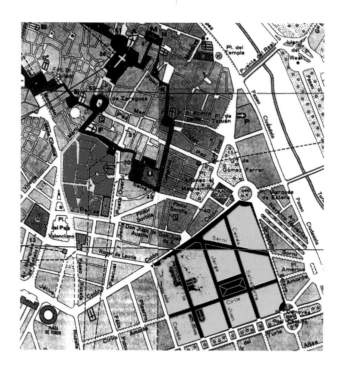

There is a clear progress in block shapes from the older type of central ones (blue) to more modern ones (orange), influenced by radial and orthogonal forms. The logic of the new forms is clearly seen as well as some esthetic and regulative proportions. In comparison the old town is more organic and not entirely repetitive in the shapes of blocks it has adopted. Physical sizes should be also noted and compared. (Zaragossa, Spain)

This aerial oblique photograph shows that forms built after the War took a completely foreign look and were mechanical in their design and formative attitude, having no regard for what was basically a clear city structure before these newer, modern building and design approaches. The historic approach that should have been apparent right away, was not difficult to adopt; modern thinking did not allow it. (Le Havre, France.)

Barcelona contains very illuminating examples of the urban grid with the contrasts inherent in historical towns containing different city structures. The new, 19th century modern grid, was duly tied and related to the older ones. We get examples of very modern and typical repetitive city blocks (in blue), as opposed to richer structures, mainly radial, subdivided into irregular city blocks which constitute a strong contrast, enriching city structure.

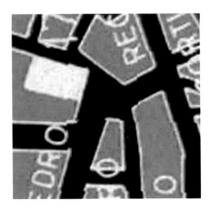

A closer look at the squares formed by the two different formations. Differences are very pronounced, stressing the fact that their creation, as major elements, is based on differing principles and attitudes to urban planning.

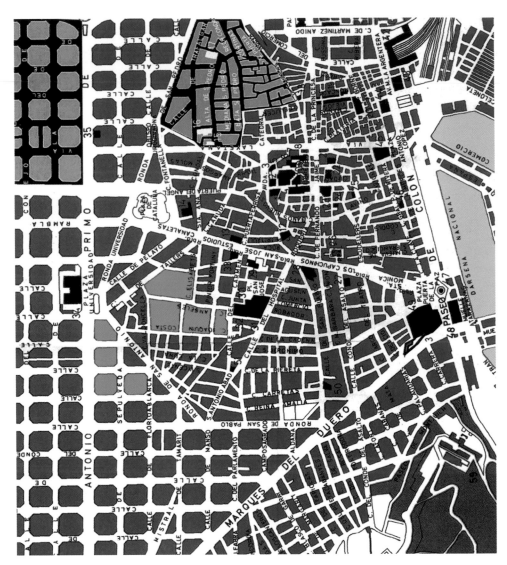

Examining Barcelona's city web, one can clearly see the opportunity offered by the meeting of the orthogonal and regular city division, with its regular streets, forming repetitive squares and providing an opportunity for a local meeting place in a very usable form. Nearby, we see the old divisions that form different squares which will also play their part in the town structure.

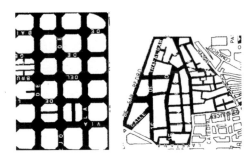

Values of the attributes of nature will determine the degree of relaxation – such as the relationship human beings have with their environment.

The characteristics of many regions depend on conservation of topography, while simultaneously taking full advantage of that topography (whenever there is public maintenance) by creating public gardens through which the entire area profits.

These elements, which create the uniqueness of urban webs and serve as a background, should be analyzed, and their contribution to conservation should be examined.

In conclusion, conservation areas should be characterized by the following principles:

1. General conservation principles, explanation of conservation activities – as related to the city or other selected area.

2. Definition of appropriate size – critical for clarity.

3. Identifiable properties – esthetics of conservation – as discussed in the previous chapter.

4. Unique urban properties – examination of the history of overall urban conservation

5. Defined Web – local examination of the web structure – through history, as revealed by its implementation and esthetic structure.

The city of Pamplona, Spain contains a mixture of old gothic and middle age patterns, meeting modern, regular and methodical arrangements. This occurs as a town planning approach in many towns in Spain.

Chapter Six

Main Issues of Conservation

Analysis of the Existing Situation
Urban Space
The Concept of Urban Conservation

The principal aim of urban characteristics is to define qualities that maintain the urban way of life. Thus, conservation will aid cultural values and not be limited to isolated examples.

In light of several failures in the 20th century, conservation has essentially been proven to be an understanding of the urban web and how it came into existence.
There is renewed interest in urban formation and a corresponding increase in the number of conservation projects. Beyond a discussion of methodology,

The basic consideration when conserving urban qualities is one of urban space, demonstrated in a typical mid-European street forming urban space, a street that shows the clarity and feeling of urbanity; mixed uses in dense situations with space as a clear concept which can be immediately identified. This is the public meeting place, and as such fit for urban considerations. Space is a quality that we will always look for because it has a strong presence and is a primary feature of city form. The street proportions, based on clear blocks with clear street facing elements, create space and are helpful when conservation attitudes are adopted. They become the physical entity that gives form to spatial qualities.

A town square (Veccia, Italy) is another example of urban space: a square which is a major element in the city structure. It helps the understanding of urban form and its conservation, being a clear example of the qualities for which we are looking. When discussing urban life, a square is a prime example. The block proportions and the open space are both qualities we can analyze and understand, so as to find a way for the preservation of their somewhat ellusive permanence.

background information is provided in the following sections.

Analysis of the Existing Situation

A. Urban conservation maintains that the urban situation must be thoroughly analyzed before there can be concise planning, effective preservation, retention of a sense of coherence between elements, and establishment of the nature of the relationship between the preserved and newly built elements. Such urban analysis begins with the large elements and determines the unique characteristics that define the urban area under examination. It can, therefore, be said that conservation efforts factor in the existing local life-style, in order to preserve those qualities which make up the unique local flavor.

B. When preserving a single building, it is unclear what authority will preserve the urban elements that are responsible for the formation of the building and which will continue to be influential in its future. Can it survive for a long period within a system that is

Gdansk (Poland) has undergone major urban conservation while regarding city buildings as architecture to be preserved. The space which is created by those buildings, is to be maintained with respect to its form. This will mean preserving not only the single building, but also an element that can be termed an urban overall quality.

unwilling and unprepared for active conservation efforts? In addition, how do we ensure a sense of cohesion between the elements? When observing the overall urban context, it is clear from the start that **the environment takes precedence over the individual.** The guidelines will relate to the overall context and, consequently, will relate to the individual building as well.

Urban Space

The most fundamental feature of urban planning is space, usually public space. Urbanism can be defined as the relationship between public spaces (stated in other words: what a visitor to the city sees and in what type of environment human culture exists). **Urban space creates the surrounding forms,** from which all types of successful urban life spring forth and flourish.

The modern conception of planning has turned its back on this approach, allowing public space to exist as an infinite expanse, without any defined structure – populated by scattered buildings that exist independently and do not produce urban space. In the modern conception of urban planning, space has been eliminated as a factor in urban creation.

One of the failures of modern architecture has certainly been its overemphasis of individual buildings as works of art at the expense of the building's background – the city, the web and the urban context, without which it is insignificant. A building without urban history is a theoretical undertaking in terms of style and artistry.

It is dissociated from culture, with no connection to its immediate environment and is, therefore, only partially understood. A building that is detached from its urban surroundings and that, in theory, could have been built anywhere, can easily be demolished, with no one noticing its loss. Urban quality is one in which space, and the buildings that shape the space, clearly comprise wholeness. Boundaries, centers or textures characterize this space. It has a complex nature – not linear, but visual, continual and generally without one significant order.

The recognition and identification of an existing situation, as exemplified in this illustration of conservation in old Jerusalem. One can see the success of a well-controlled development which unhesitatingly adopted some modern approaches, well introduced into an existing urban web, having a basically difficult form to analyze. Being a well known example of a dense city that has developed in existing city walls, and having somewhat anarchic structure, one can see that the heights, materials, logicality of urban form is preserved within existing squares with delineated and stressed forms.

Nevertheless, some preservation was necessary and some squares were adopted in order to preserve important landmarks, such as St. Paul's. Some of the landmarks were in the way. The development of completely new areas introduced qualities foreign to the existing neighborhood.

The comparison between this and the next illustration shows the outcome of large scale preservation scale in post-war London. It is the result of unplanned conservation with some minimal influence on urban planning, containing some unfortunate results. We can see that no rules were observed with respect to local differing districts, and their boundaries. This exercise in renovation was often accompanied by wide renewal, but the overall effect may be said to be of preservation. Part of the pre-war divisions remain. Only when ownership and parcel were not followed, and acquisitions not carefully carried out, were the problems of design and conservation evident. Increasing the building ratio, just because transportation was available, proved detrimental to visual quality, losing some local scale and proportion.

n instances such the one shown studies of proportion were undertaken, sadly only of architectural qualities. Disregard of proportions on the urban scale, combined with the development that took place, lack of consideration to structures that may have been related to important landmarks, show the pitfalls facing planners.

The borders can change or be rearranged. Its internal division into parcels constitutes a weave, interconnecting it to the neighborhood. (The weave or web being a form of arrangement of streets and spaces, typified by a progression, beginning with a predetermined order, then becoming an incidental one.) In addition, modern attitude tends to negate the existence of urbanism, viewing cultural life as advancing, undergoing dramatic transformation, with no room for historical perspective.

These unmanageable forces exist and create concepts that cannot be defined except through the universal prism of chaos.

Urban Regions

Variables in urban regions include the level of permanence and restoration, the proportion between public space, constructed volumes, building density and height.

There is an aspect of scale, of repetition, of streets and their shapes, of directions and orientation. Unlike old areas, modern space does not contain many variables – it is simplistic.

The designers of modern urban space seem not to be familiar with urban complexity, formed over many generations, but are satisfied with a shallow approach. Though post-modern space is moving in the direction of chaos by choice, it has unavoidably entered a self-destructive cycle. This tendency is still at its start.

The Concept of Urban Conservation

This is a discussion of the conservation of the web, not of individual details. It is impossible, as well as inefficient, to preserve single buildings. Moreover, there is no significance in terms of cultural or historical values in preserving individual constructions. Furthermore, as no urban standards have been formulated, there is no method of identifying the individual building. The same, however, can also be said of groups of build-

After clearing the debris caused by the war, new considerations were involved in London street design (except for large scale preservation like St. Paul's). The new considerations used as much building coverage as possible. This was carried out by adopting new angles of light, meaning that new city organization has been carried out in a proper lawful and planned manner. Some roads have been renewed and widened in order to facilitate communication. Some of the communication is still difficult locally, as blocks are not entirely self-evident and the web remains a bit anarchic. The public spaces are more pronounced. The local web was only partially considered when urban renewal took place, and some opportunity of a major study of city webs was lost.

Models such as these were used in order to carry out the new 3-dimensional designs of London, as clarity was lost, when the rules of city structure were abandoned. These models helped understand planning necessities, calculated not by urban qualities, but by daylighting angles, thus carrying no particular distinction or local contribution. It was decided, as seen in further illustrations, that local conditions will have to be disregarded.

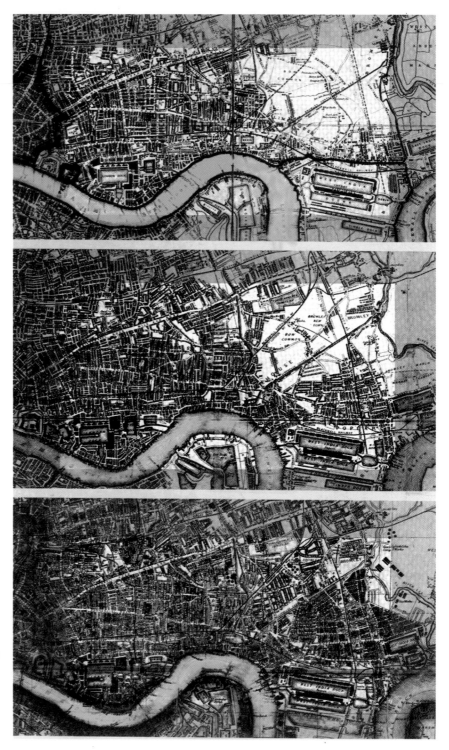

The development of cities over two
centuries is illustrated in these plans of
the development of London from a closely
knit, very dense city growing into the
surrounding country. It is clear that this
growth continued a principal structure -
existing streets and links into a cohesive
comprehensible pattern.

ings that lose all significance the moment they are removed from their environment – their context. That being the case, a "beautiful" building lacking its urban context will become completely meaningless. The so-called "beautiful" building will be turn into yet another 'pretty facade', until all the superficial layers fade away. It will also not be preserved without suitable standards to conserve the environment, and over time the environment will turn away from it.

Preservation of single buildings or a group of buildings is rarely successful and occurs only when no other alternative exists. It has become increasingly obvious that conservation of the urban context is the only viable alternative that is both flexible and has a chance of succeeding. Even historical buildings that have benefited from conservation efforts for centuries are located in urban settings that have held similar status.

The Level of Actual Conservation

Before approaching building renovations or physical reconstruction - also often the restoration system – it is essential that there be a clear conservation policy. The policy serves as the foundation on which other systems, such as restoration, rehabilitation or renovation (in this order) are based. Considerations in conservation result in yet an additional system of implementation – the juxtaposition of old construction alongside the new – the system of the future.

Future conservation models will operate on several levels:

1. Conservation on the urban level is done by identifying primary urban prototypes on a local level and establishing criteria to conserve these prototypes. This refers to urban elements, of which the individual building is a by-

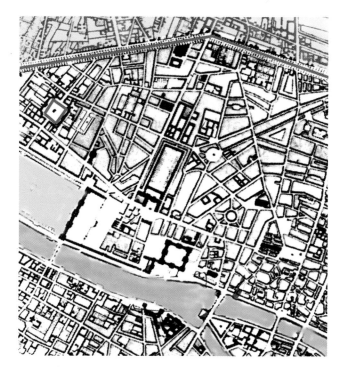

As can be seen from this old map, Paris has grown logically from the 17th century from what can be called agricultural plots, completely unmarked by structures and containing private land used for cultivation. The brown line denotes the city limits at that time. In the next illustration, one can clearly understand how the city forms, containing some of the existing divisions without totally disregarding them.

This aerial photo, shows the same district in Paris as the one in the map above, only in its present form. The existing divisions are the result of old (at least one hundred years) ownerships, which were extended to support the new construction. The brown line shows the limits of Paris in the 17th and 18th century, beyond it the part developed in a logical manner as an urban web. City structure is effective for many centuries, continuing its deployment in an understandable form.

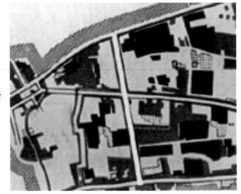

Old London blocks (demolished), shown in the illustration below, are based on an urban street pattern, (right), containing post war plans. The pattern includes (clearly marked) a road, linking three almost parallel major roads. Some of these localities were completely damaged during the war. Urban renewal was meant to reconstruct this East End district, without using pre-war patterns. The development completely disregards existing systems except for major roads. It does leave a lot of open space, on the one hand, but disregards urban qualities on the other hand.

product. On a detailed urban planning level, conservation models will identify the necessary hierarchy to determine which of the primary urban elements should be preserved. Primary urban elements consist of the following:

A. The web and regional division
B. The buildings within the region
C. The streets
D. The squares

The model will also examine all desired connections between these elements. Regulations will be the chief means for planning conservation on an urban scale at this stage.

2. Conservation on the architectural level – is done by identifying the architectural characteristics that prevent both stylistic distortions and disruption of the existing architectural language. This includes structural renovation or rehabilitation, or structural additions at times. In more extreme cases, **restoration,** generally more expensive (as a result of long-term neglect) is required. Continual, comprehensive, long-term maintenance may also be required for conservation. This holds true for natural elements as well.

1. The Need for Formulation of Planning and Conservation Guidelines

The outcome of urban growth (shown in the previous three phase London history) can clearly be seen in detail in this part of East London. The historic development follows block after block, in the same manner, continuing the same pattern, repeating it without divorcing itself from existing limitations. Unfortunately, these parts were destroyed in the war, and the local district was not kept. One can see that the pre-war situation had no character of its own, with a mixture of terrace houses, tenement blocks and various industries, not very helpful to each other, containing no open space. Nevertheless, it was urban. The new development uses a clean kind of plan, of a suburban nature, seen in the illustration above.

It is quite difficult to reach a definitive decision regarding the formulation of general criteria for conservation on an urban scale (beyond an individual building). The indecision begins at the regional level and continues down to the details. It is the intention of this study to simplify the decision process, even as it relates to the individual building.

Fundamental Concepts.

Essential differences exist between the concepts of conservation, renovation and rehabilitation. Each of these concepts alone is merely an element in the overall equation. When added together, however, their sum is conservation. Conservation along with additions to existing buildings or new buildings constitutes **urban renewal**. New construction is ongoing, both on an urban and individual building level. **Restoration and conservation are the more expensive endeavors aimed at preserving cultural assets important to the spiritual richness of the environment (historical or esthetic).** While these activities may not always be deemed economically worthwhile, frequently a change in zoning or function can make them economically beneficial.

Urban planners and planning divisions of various authorities involved in private planning, require a standard for judging the various options when faced with complex issues.

Planning norms must be agreed upon in advance if work is to be conducted efficiently. Without advance agreement, the processes of setting policy and defining norms will be awkward.

When the goal is to revitalize a region by new construction along with existing conservation efforts, this need is further intensified.

Run-down urban areas pose the central difficulty in conservation. While such areas have existing infrastructure, it is often neglected, throwing off the existing urban equilibrium.

Revitalizing areas infected by urban blight necessitates more than restoration alone. Often, isolated areas of valuable urban land are in close

The result of disregarding the existing structure can be bewildering, as can be seen in the photograph, with the surrounding traditional pattern marked in color. It is strongly divorced, utterly different and carries no resemblance to existing patterns. One can only wonder how this particular design can contribute to the existing, proximate, quarters of London.

It is very clear that the roads, (in red), permit urban qualities, not altogether lost when urban spaces are created, with some focal points (like the front of the British Museum) and with squares of different proportions. Green spaces, in the city web, can be very urban in character. They can be contained and not dispersed, like in suburban situations. Some quality can be achieved and kept, in concert with urban webs, streets and squares. (Bloomsbury, London.)

In contrast to the East End, this part of London was happier after the war. This is Bloomsbury in central London, near the British Museum, with its fine squares and urban pattern which is more orderly and well kept, with proper open spaces and good density, admittedly in a wealthier area.

proximity to run-down or demolished areas that could be candidates for filling-in policy.

The issue at hand, then, is a fusion of restoration, conservation and new construction, all of which are clearly planned and comprehensible.

To paraphrase Paul Goldberger: the principle that determines the criteria, guidelines and laws is not aimed at creating good architecture, which cannot be achieved in this manner. They exist to prevent bad architecture, and arc not even always successful.

2. The Policy Accompanying Conservation

A. Conservation Committees – These committees will take conservation guidelines from theory into practice. The authority delegated to the committee will be mainly in professional areas. Their goal is to ensure that existing structures are not harmed, and this is done by making various exceptions.

Conservation committees delay demolition of the region during the planning and operational stages. When the cost of preserving a building is lower than the cost of erecting a new structure and when preservation is justified from a conservation standpoint, then **buildings deemed dangerous must be preserved**.

B. Demolition Policy – No building in a conservation area will be torn down prior to the submission of plans for it to be rebuilt. In certain cases property owners may be obligated to renovate and rehabilitate designated buildings. Generally financial assistance, increased rights and other incentives accompany this obligation. The restoration of a building that has already been demolished is an extremely expensive, albeit rare, undertaking. This policy also covers thorough cleanup of the sites that require it, fencing them off in a manner suitable to the character of the area and keeping it clean.

Buildings that have been partially demolished (such as buildings sharing a wall with a demolished house) should have the damaged external walls repaired, including comprehensive technical repairs to the walls. Repairs should bring the walls to a fitting level of design. (They should, however, not have paintings on them, for that only serves to emphasize the problem).

This initial cleanup is vital and is conducted mainly at public expense, though there are occasions when owners are charged. The investment by the public, however, is not unjust as the region is undergoing improvements, which must be integrated into the law and development programs. Eventually the investment will be returned, as these improvements will yield betterment and accompanying taxes.

C. Infill Policy - Documentation of isolated, empty plots is collected so that construction on them can begin. This type of policy has the best chance of leading to construction organic to the site. It will serve as an example for the future and bring regional blight to a halt. This policy supports conservation efforts in order to fulfill and encourage economic growth, which will in turn prevent continued regional deterioration.

D. Clean Up and Initial Action – The initial steps in conservation, though not immediately profitable, are necessary to increase property values and spur a demand for residential areas within the regions. Apart from extensive

This is a case of rehabilitating and renovating an existing building, without changing its appearance and building a new foundation. The approach is one of maintaining appearances, considering existing architectural qualities.

Another instance of renovating and conservation of architecture, this time in Paris. The prevailing work is directed towards maintaining of building and style, and not urban qualities.

This photo of the illustrated urban block clearly shows the need to conduct a study and to implementation of complete urban renewal and not an instance of isolated architectural qualities (see elevation below).

work on the infrastructure (not necessarily municipally financed), demolished buildings must be considered. The manner of work on such buildings will be determined in the professional committees.

E. Background for Conservation Policy –

1. Population – public involvement in demanding conservation of cultural sites in their residential area. Questions regarding introduction of new planning for these regions interest all involved. A balance exists between the right of the public to protect these areas and the right of property owners to maintain property values. Contrary to previous belief, there need not be a conflict of interest. The very concept of conservation is aimed at increasing property values, and conservation efforts are generally successful in this regard.

2. Initiative – Who owns the initiative – the public or the property owners? If the owners plan well, interference in a private project is unnecessary, and they should be encouraged in any way possible.

Urban planning, on the other hand, must incorporate the background and history. It should be noted that current planning that does not include self-preservation systems, will be judged in just a few generations and will burden those involved with planning, just as the not-too-distant past has burdened us. For this reason, it would be wise to realize that urban planning, by its very defini-

As opposed to former examples of keeping single buildings isolated within the urban context, the preservation of blocks and city regions keeping existing urban structure and qualities, is becoming increasingly normal. A considerable in-depth study of an existing block in Rome, was carried out in order to preserve the qualities of such a unique historical block.

tion, integrates self-preservation mechanisms – some overt and others covert.

3. Conflicts of Interest – There is a tendency for each party to cast blame on the other. On the one hand are the users (or owners) perceived as stumbling blocks in the path of development (owners who do not look after esthetic qualities). On the other hand are urban authorities, which are viewed as unwilling or incapable of investment. Cooperation and fusion are the keys to ensuring high-quality, economically feasible projects that are esthetic. It is also helpful to avoid extreme situations, where everything is seen in terms of black and white.

4. Planning – Stagnancy leads to certain destruction. Take, for example, Venice's San Marco Piazza which over the past 500 years has undergone extensive changes. A greater effort should be made to enable new planning while preserving traditional values and keeping conservation in mind. This is the reason urban complexity is dynamic and continual.

5. Culture – An important contribution is the conservation of culture. The following question should be posed: how can high-quality planning be encouraged without excessive public involvement that may lead to the project being brought to a standstill.

6. Decisions – Decisions regarding planning, conservation and development should not be shrouded in mystery. Secrecy is only harmful. In any case, public openness limits extremism and only serves to help the situation.

7. Economic – Economic criteria will be adopted before the start of detailed planning.

F. Consensus on Specific Characteristics

1. Density of Future Construction
As one of the objectives of conservation is to boost the economic status of restoration and conservation,

Urban rehabilitation in a row of buildings, takes the view of preserving local color and street forms, in their present scale.

We see the need for urban conservation after the war, where demolition is indicated for certain parts, with a study of former qualities to be renewed. Major links, city squares or other prime urban qualities have to be indicated in cases like these, before any demolition can take place.

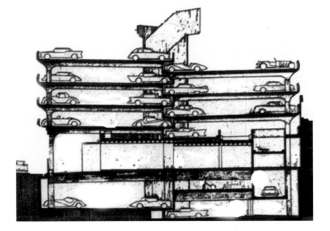

Urban conservation is increasingly becoming a consideration given to all city forms and not only to single buildings. It is becoming accepted by people as the apparent necessity of preserving urban life, not just esthetics.

To be successful, major urban conservation must always be accompanied by local car parks of various types, so as to be more user-oriented on an modern scale. Without this, many large projects have difficulties in drawing people in.

The result of preservation on a major scale can be as acceptable as the one bellow, (London docks), creating an interesting and nonviolent modern approach to design, one that embraces all design qualities and shapes them into a modern and acceptable way of creating urban spaces.

new projects are designed not to be overly dense. The demand will be for areas with a high quality-of-life. This holds true for residential density as well. The first step in revitalizing poorer neighborhoods is to provide larger apartments (reducing the number of units); otherwise, overcrowding becomes a problem, and may, in turn, facilitate a decline in the level of quality.

On public land, the number of units should be reduced, even by artificial means, in order to spur gentrification. This is extremely difficult to do on privately owned property, but even here, there is no call for unnecessary and problematic overcrowding. Regardless of ownership issues, overcrowding is quantifiable and controllable. There is a tendency to increase density due to the desire to reap immediate profits and the fear of the region's future. On the other hand, there is a fear of non-profitability and lack of reinvestment in the region. A shortage of public services, such as education and culture, cannot be ignored over the long run since they are major factors in urban decay.

2. Transportation and Zoning

A conservation region has a life of its own and should not be forced to 'go modern,' so to speak. Conservation regions are generally located near modern urban centers and can be sparsely served by transportation. Despite the shortcomings of such residential areas, demand for them exists, as many people do not want to live in row houses. In conservation areas, it is impossible for all residents to have parking spaces adjacent to their homes. Just as modern neighborhoods cannot provide a sense of historic identity, conservation neighborhoods cannot accommodate a large number of vehicles or serve as a thruway for heavy vehicles.

Neighborhood streets must remain, for the most part, for the use of the residents and should be closed to through traffic. Tourists or visitors to the area will not be allowed to park within the confines of the conservation area. That said, however, the urban existence of the region depends

Instances that have become well known, such as the renovation of the London docks, have created large-scale agreement on urban conservation and to the selection of preservable, useful urban qualities in old buildings. Such buildings find new uses in the urban web of the city proper, old warehouses and lofts are accepted, in large renovation and conservation projects, as a necessity.

Modern forms sometimes enter existing city webs, occasionally helping the formation of urban spaces and reinforcing urban qualities. We have become accustomed to modern forms and to approaches which have, in some respect, tended to accommodate themselves into existing structures, at times more successfully than others.

on its links to the city. In many instances, development bypasses these areas to such an extent that it is difficult to bring back the old vitality. Without transportation links, it is impossible to bring it back to reasonable levels.

The process of rezoning should be carefully managed, especially in terms of excess trade and irregular use, and is similar to the process described above, such as urban workmanship. This type of zoning receives priority in more appropriate areas.

The rationale of urban renovation after the war is demonstrated in Gdansk where it is clear that some respect was paid to the older city structure. Original blocks which were densely built, especially in the 19th century, have been renovated in a manner that will keep basic urban proportions and spaces as they facilitate our understanding of the old and keep some urban qualities.

Encouraging an influx or return to these areas by increasing land use leads to increased traffic and demand for parking. This also holds true when planning existing regions. Only with extreme care and a clearly defined plan, can these problems be overcome.

3. Encouraging Public Investment

It is important to note that **public means are never sufficient.** Therefore, public investment is essential. The public channel serves as a conduit through which private investment is regulated. According to this line of thought, it is not the sole conduit, but is still vital.

Private investment can be viewed as a desirable factor regarding continuance and encouragement of regional life. For this reason, public lands and buildings can be leased, rented or sold. Public owners are unsatisfactory in these regions as they lead to homogenous planning or stoppage due to a lack of means and faulty political interest, accompanied by a lack of desire. It is difficult to integrate institutional architecture in normal developments. The best opportunity occurs when several parties participate simultaneously.

Carlovi Vari (not far from Prague) - is an apt example of an urban effort of preservation. The vivacious clean colors render an athmosphere with a somewhat sweet effect.

PART TWO

Archaeology as a Basis

Archaeology shows the urban structure in a clear and unobstructed form, because it deals with the bare skeleton of human settlements.

The essential form is there to be evaluated, studied and formulated.

Using archaeology in urban studies will reinforce the belief that we are dealing with essential rules, not with whim and fashion.

Chapter Seven

Elements of Archaeology

Built Up Areas
Land Division

Insights offered by archaeology are, by their nature, clarifications of the patterns that create cities throughout history. Studies of historical cities are becoming more available and popular because of the insight they offer.

The ancient city of Ugarit can serve as an illustration for our search of direction and geometry in ancient cities, bringing us to some understanding of old city design. The orthogonal system was chosen quite early, even though not always apparent. It can be assumed that as building technology was based on a square stone, this fact was somewhat instrumental in the development of right-degree systems in building and in the formation of streets.

The contribution of archaeology to conservation-oriented urban planning is clear. Archaeology exposes historical qualities, including formation, esthetics and design, materials, construction methods, lifestyles and ancient culture as background material. Those dealing with archaeological research (in urban conservation areas) should also examine aspects of planning in ancient civilizations, as they have implications regarding conservation or, at the very least, reveal the origins of the urban condition.

The combination of researching the past and wise use of findings regarding the course of development of the urban condition will establish historical justification for continuity, as well as provide the means to separate the secondary issues from the main ones. Archaeological research supplies geographical data, the direction of historical construction, direction of apertures and roads as well as the causes and origins of a dominant geometry.

Archaeology and urban planning are, therefore, inherently interlocked.

Correct urban study, which exists due to continuity and is supported by archaeological research, is the source that can guide a quantitative statistical

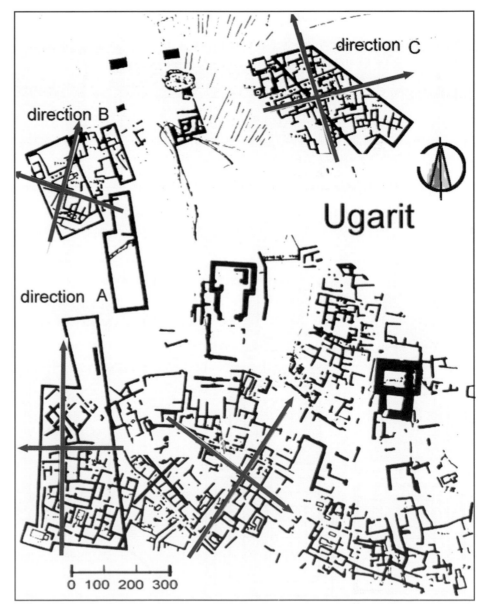

direction B

direction C

direction A

Ugarit

0 100 200 300

An ancient system of Chinese architectural design and approach shows systematic, very symmetrical land division, clear in its concept because of carefully thought out road delineation, internal courts. The whole was then molded into an orthogonal approach. This is a form of a Chinese model citadel. Spaces are immediately apparent, showing good control of geometry and design formation, with the strong ancient modular system.

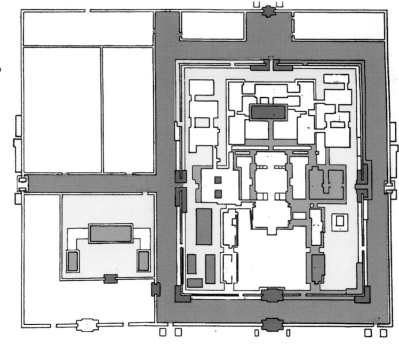

Ancient Chinese methods of building measurements indicate complete mastery of modular increments when designing courtyards and buildings. This has a major role in the cities, where a basic dimension of 125 X 125 meters is adopted(500 BC). This carefully planned geometrical approach shows that design can have regularity, enabling cities to grow in a controlled manner. The chosen system of orthogonal squares was important, when it was clear that it develops freely in length or width. A lot of standard land division was thus implemented.

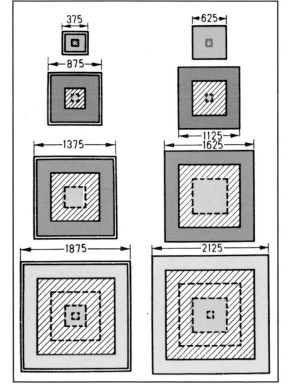

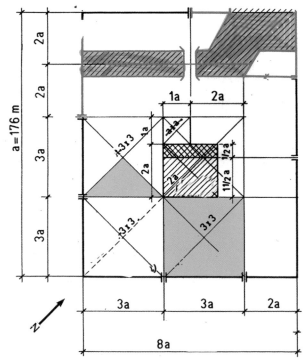

Regularity of dimensions in Ancient Babylon shows good control of land parcelation and town planning, as the land is rationally controlled and subdivided. This type of measurement ascertains continuity in land subdivisions, bringing a lot of possible use for a long time. This geometrical control also means that the planning will be very efficient, and means early acceptance of a central rule.

analysis. In order to advance conservation efforts, qualitative **and** quantitative definitions are necessary to formulate the correct plan.

This includes geometry, number of buildings, etc. whose origin in archaeological research and historical urbanistic methods is uncertain, and, therefore, requires further investigation. Such research is not always conducted by the archaeologist. For example, the former existence of a river might be determined due to the directions of construction in the surrounding area, even when those are extinct. The reasons for the direction of the original construction disappeared along with the river. Consequently, historical axes and directions have been and continue to be considered both irrelevant and impractical.

The ancient riverbank determined the direction of urban links as well as existing parcel divisions. Archaeology, then, is used as a tool to identify the determining order, taking researchers back in time until the river and the direction of the construction are identified.

The modern urban vocabulary of architectural means is a result of historical developments. Study of historical urban structures and their relation to modern urban organization can be very effective, assisting in the clarification of principles and developments and determining how they are to be incorporated into the new plan. Elements comprising the historical urban structure serve as an introduction of sorts to present-day conservation.

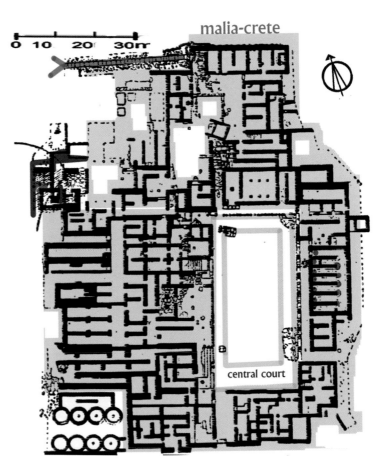

It is apparent that the urban organization is in a citadel form, around a central court and an easily defined and defended palace, which is well served by all necessary services such as food storage, water storage, sewage systems and allows for increments of buildings to be systematic and easily executed. The system used here is quite simple and had further developments, as simple arches, some vaulting, columns, etc.

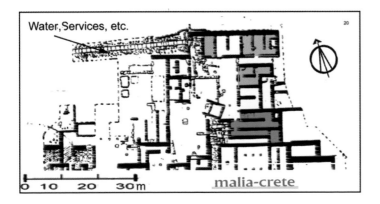

The ancient town of Malia in Crete about (1500 BC). Full control of the right angle is quite apparent, since all buildings are built in a precise manner. This is to show that we have here a complex, sophisticated and intelligent culture which keeps good control of different building necessities such as water services and food storage bins, while coping with several building types, some of them religious.

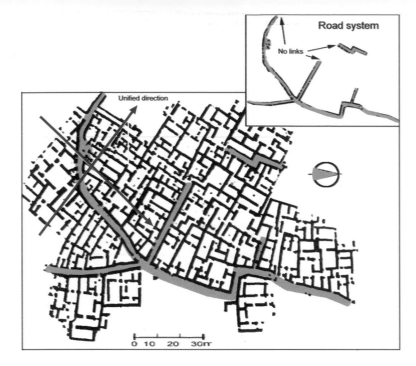

The land division in the ancient city of Ur of the Chaldees. It is apparent that only a small percentage of total land is taken up by roads. For this reason many internal passages are necessary, indicating lack of central control. There is a coherence in the direction of the buildings and less ability in dealing with topography, such as cutting roads across the hills. Internal division is quite systematic and efficient. There is a certain anarchy of roads, and their junctions create an early form of square. The early blocks are not entirely negotiable or coherent and, therefore, the web not very systematic, with a low degree of clarity. This type of early sites have some degree of ability to build in a regular manner. The irregularity of the web causes faulty interconnections, due to the early, undeveloped use of geometry.

Developing of the straight line and orthogonal systems of building, shows the rational ability of measurement and direction. It is clear that directions chosen were orthogonal so as to facilitate land division, with the primary aim of marking private property, as opposed to public property, mainly the roads.

Old Gurnia (around 1000-2000 BC) shows good understanding of road connections even though the city is built on a hill. The shape of the parcel or city block is orthogonal with a clear direction, despite the difficult topography, meaning that it has been properly planned. Roads are publicly maintained and clearly cut up to the buildings, facilitating communication, introducing steps and a degree of paving. Some of the communications are still difficult locally. The blocks are not entirely self-evident and, therefore, the web is still anarchic. The public spaces are the ones that help in orientation and control.

This introduction validates the survival of concepts over thousands of years. Study of the fundamental concepts guides the analysis aimed at determining the order of the components of city life. In this chapter the fundamental concepts in urban analysis are presented. As stated above, these concepts originate in the past.

1. Built Up Areas

The building area (the total amount of built up areas) which accompanies the general area of land of the populated area and, to the extent possible, the number of residents residing there at the given time, determines the initial quantitative scope. Even a rough estimate of the number of residents can explain population density over history, as well changes in population density over time.

The following information provides insight into the past and has implications on future research: reasons for density in urban formation; extent of density; maximum historical density, especially in cases of walled cities (obtained from the archaeological findings). Once those questions are answered, researchers can study how these factors limit town expansion, population density and ability to develop, including its maximum size – in quantitative terms. Current numerical data can then be viewed as part of a general historical context and, therefore, be better understood. The phases of a city's development are characterized by the rate of numerical growth within the walls or other boundaries. Fluctuations in density (the number of people per area unit) reflect the past urban potential of the area, teach us about economic boundaries in the past, and often the extent of the region in proximity (a type of service radius), as well as its size and volume.

2. Land Division

The proportion of private and public property (private parcel vs. public land) is of particular interest to the planner. Public property can be indicative of both the efficiency and the quality of the division. Land was originally

Land division in ancient Babylon,(from an excavation of the site). A high degree of public services, roads, public buildings, etc. are found. There is great coherence in building direction and division systems. A clear difference exists between the public area, which is wide, and private land. Blocks are formed and make for a very clear and regular web. A square and an important religious building are apparent. This type of organization is certain to sustain itself. A few improvements are clear. Roads have similar widths and repeat, clearly contained in a system. Building methods are similar, containing an inner court airing the different chambers. This is an implementation of a good system, being marked by some dominant buildings. The parcel sizes are similar, indicating good social organization that makes for a certain equality. We can see a regularity in the blocks, which appear to be more systematic than in earlier periods.

The Roman town of Timgad has rigid subdivisions, a square module of approx. 25 sq. meters, forming an overabundance of roads. Internal division is efficient. Because the system is homogenous, there is a necessity of constant upkeep and preservation. This coherence led to an addoption and establishment of this sort of town, somewhat reminiscent of Chinese organization. This particular city system contains a measure of irregularity, especially in public spaces; there is some freedom inbuilt in the hierarchy, probably important to civic functions.

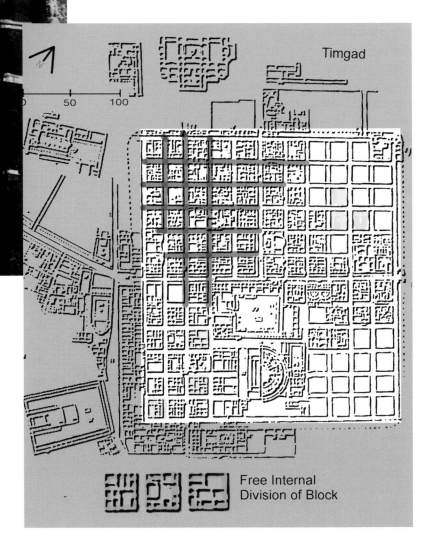

Timgad

50   100

Free Internal
Division of Block

The regularity of design and public works are apparent in this photograph of the ancient site of reconstructed Pompei. The care taken of the public right of way is apparent, as it must have been in constant repair. It is also apparent that the road is sufficiently wide to give proper and good access to the organized parcels which use it.

divided to indicate any type of ownership. Division of land to indicate ownership is the oldest type of land division in urban human organization. Private property was demarcated out of the natural human desire to clearly indicate the boundaries of family property (the land itself), thereby making a long-lasting statement of possession. While the division into parcels was initially physical, over time the division was granted legal standing, even prior to the existence of land registration and precise measuring. Demarcation of property is the human means of reserving a piece of land on which they wish to live, earn a living, organize and settle on a permanent basis (as opposed to being nomadic). This, then, is the foundation for establishment of an urban setting and the basis for conservation research.

In reality, there are a number of factors taken into consideration when land must be divided.

A. Size of the Parcels (or the manner in which land is divided) sheds light on the beginnings of urban formation. This is the smallest unit of measurement that can be exploited, a type of primordial "cell". The parcel dimensions will be extremely important further on. The form of the parcel determines the organization of daily life within it, as defined by accessibility, contact with neighbors and the general public, familial organization, etc. The basic parcel, in comparison to the modern parcel, attests to the rate of urban formation. A new division or link between parcels is a developmental process spurred by economic and social reasons.

It is interesting to track the development of a particular parcel. For example, subdivisions that face roads indicate that the front (often due to commerce) had be-

System of land division in ancient Rome shows that Roman rule applied not only to land division in cities, but also brought the system to bear on large tracts of land used for cultivation. The central government was conscious of maintaining a continuous system in governing different peoples in many lands. The method observed in the illustration is made difficult by streams and topography. There is simplicity in the division, with no real demarcation line between city or country. The size of the main square is about 180 meters and adapts easily to an urban grid. We can see this approach addopted much later in many parts of the world.

come economically important, justifying the division of the property into smaller units. Moreover, this denotes a change in the local economy, which was perhaps on its way to becoming a regional market or an important commercial center. Ancient unification of parcels can be an indication of centrality and wealth.

B. Direction of Land Division – The reasons behind land division (north-south or compass direction) are diverse. It is important to note direction, as ancient directions were established for essential reasons and which must be understood and at times, preserved. The physical, geographical location of a city is closely associ-

This aerial photograph shows the systematic approach to land division in ancient Roman cities. It is clear that the modular land division helps the formation of parcels, easily controlled and taken care of.

ated with this primary quality. The rate of urban development and its physical direction is a direct result of the selection of the initial divisions.

C. Private vs. Public Division – Along with land division, there is a need to differentiate between public and private property. This distinction reflects the consensus that the 'road' should belong to the public, since without it, private property is inaccessible. Furthermore, without roads, there would be no communication between parcels and homes, or between properties.

In each division, there are two major components: 1) **The creation of roads** 2) **The creation of private parcels.**

The boundaries of private and public property are determined immediately and dynamically. Agreement on these boundaries is a precursor to any type of organization. The percentage of land owned by the public (mainly roads) within an urban structure can provide the data for a

quantitative comparison with other cities. It can also serve as a measure of the financial burden on the public that maintains these lands.

This division also exists outside the city limits, in agricultural parcels. The difference in the division in urban and rural areas, however, is immediately apparent in their size, density and order. In addition, economic considerations lead to attempts to wedge as many parcels as possible on a city street. The factors taken into account and the size of the parcels outside the urban area are entirely different. Hence, the size of the parcel, as well as its direction and physical properties, teach us about the historical developments.

The aforementioned division is the reason a segment of land is marked as a **private parcel** (due to registration, physical demarcation, tradition or oral agreement). It is also the reason that the **through roads** (symbolizing the governing body or institutionalized organizational agreement) are marked as major arteries that nourish and sustain the urban formation. Together, these two elements form the principal urban structure.

D. The Public's Right of Way

Lines of communication were established that provided public access routes. These routes could be rivers, channels or aqueducts; access routes and passages to all granaries, bodies of water, areas designated for food storage, markets (which are the beginnings of the diversification of land use in the old world) as well as access to avenues, social or religious convention centers, etc.

As public property, roads have an extremely long independent life for the following reasons: they are necessary, maintained by the governing body and represent the consensus of the population on urban settlement. Roads are also clear indicators of both urban development and urbanization. The possible impact of that early chapter in history on the initial phases of urban development will be

This ancient town in Crete has also adopted the internal orthogonal system, in an early form, with unequal modules. It is mainly the direction that is kept to the right angle.

An ancient Japanese system of town planning, very
geometrical and controllable, with a certain module that
repeats itself. It contains a basic increment of one
square, leaving empty modules between the roads to
contain a sewer system. It is apparent that the hierarchy
contains the freedom to choose variations as one goes
far and away from the center, causing different land
divisions. The basic square can contain a variety of
modules.

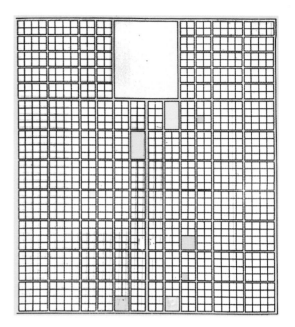

In an ancient town, Selukia in Turkey (7th century BC), we see the development
of public spaces and courts, as well as some building methods in different
archeological layers. The basic block has a rigid external wall, not quite
square. It was planned orthogonally, which meant that it was easier to
subdivide and make
for better public
ways and other
systems. It is clear
(layer 2) that some new
building methods
developed in time,
allowing for larger
spans and spaces.
This control over
geometrical means
allowed for the
appearance of the
module, which enables
regular increments to
be applied.

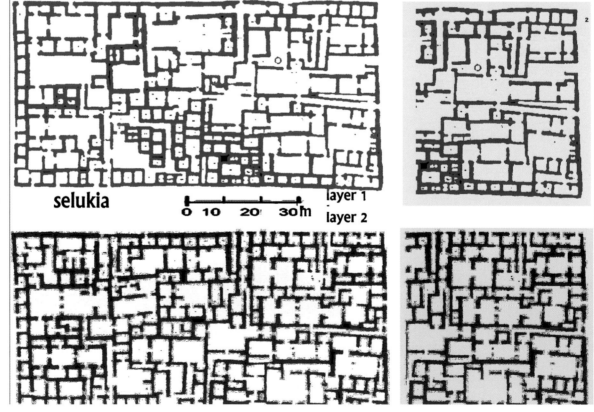

selukia   0 10 20 30 m   layer 1
layer 2

explored later. When analyzing the role of roads, it is important to note direction, length, size and area, as well as to examine whether the road was created before or after the division of land into parcels or perhaps during the division of property.

E. The Single Block Within the Urban District

The aforementioned classifications, that is, distinguishing between private parcels and public roads, lend significance to every piece of data. A by-product of this is the concept of the 'block' – parcels that are somehow adjacent and form an island of sorts that is surrounded by roads.

The block is an autonomous unit - a partnership between individual citizens who create boundaries between private parcels; from which we understand that the districts contain blocks which create them. Adjacent blocks similar in size create a district. This is the initial formation that granted the site significance and transformed it into more than a spontaneous urban formation. Within the block, certain partnerships are established between property owners, due to the shared boundaries of many of the parcels. Private agreements regarding borders differ from agreements to allocate roads. The former is an agreement between neighbors, between families, to foster the maintenance of shared borders, while the latter is an agreement between individuals and the general public (or with the governing body) regarding the limits of individual property and responsibility. These various districts created the old web and the beginnings of the city.

The Roman town of Arcolineum is very modularly organized, with a system of orthogonal roads and buildings. This geometry allows the right angle Roman tile to be used in a very early period. It is obvious that the adoption of a sophisticated system allows an advanced method to develop.

Chapter Eight

Historical Formation

Roads, Squares and Public Buildings
Block, District and Web
Layered Structure of Towns

Structured elements of the urban patterns crystallized long ago and have served human culture satisfactorily. Their recording, analysis and study all help the cause of urbanity as their primary concern.

This old Byzantine church has some prominence in the city web of Sophia , allowing the principle of conservation of antique buildings to uniquely add qualities to our urban culture. The presence of such objects serves as an element of advocacy to keep remains of archaeology alive. It is also an inducement to carry out historical studies, especially into the existing web.

The structural hierarchy mentioned above was constructed to contain city blocks and to suit various needs. This chapter will outline several of them to emphasize that the type of geometry which builds cities, must be complex and flexible.

1. Roads, Squares and Public Buildings

Places of worship, ancient cemeteries and open squares hold a place of importance in the annals of ancient planning. Their existence provides, at the very least, an indication of urbanization.

Spiritual centers have made a historical contribution to the development of town squares and other types of public areas, which in turn provide insight into the development of urban areas.

Public squares are established as a result of road expansion, designation of market places, ports and other meeting points.

The very nature of the square, however, testifies to the need for common symbols, a place of assembly, a symbol of general or tribal power, similar to a symbol of holy places. Often, these values – religious, governmental or social – co-exist and are, therefore, mentioned together.

Another example of the living remnants of an early Byzantine church, in Sophia (Bulgaria) shows an archaeological site in the midst of a town center. A question is implied: can heavy modern buildings, be compared to the old urban church, and the answer is rather sad. This early example of building, is better looking than its neighbors. One may note that the orthogonality of the old building is easily adopted into the modern orthogonality.

The Acropolis in Athens is another illustration of how modern development completely bypasses old sites, while maintaining them as old treasures. These old remains do not visually influence much of the urban development. Modern Athens does not resemble the old culture on which it is based, and we are fortunate that several examples remain. They are thought provoking, as far as our relation to past urban cultures goes.

The well known site in St. Geminiano (Italy) shows the importance of old cultures to newer buildings. A unique and extremely attractive human environment is created by this juxtaposition.

2. Ancient Ports and Gates

Ports and gates serve as markers of urban development, as do walls, watchtowers and other such structures. They are the first to create a need for roads. They either forge or sever the link to the outside world. Often, large traffic arteries spring up around them, both within and outside the urban settlement.

This, in essence, is urban clarity: the comprehension of the symbolic-geometric perception. It exists because the gate emphasizes the urban link to the outside world and therefore necessitates fundamental symbolism to stress this fact visually.

3. The Single Block and the District

The size and form of the single block, as a collection of parcels, is a result of the establishment of necessary roads.

This is an independent urban entity, which is important in the creation of webs. It is also important to note that a collection of neighborhood blocks, similar in nature, direction, size and form, creates districts – the result of the formation of the aforementioned components: private parcel, public roads and blocks.

4. The City Web

Walled cities symbolize the phase in which social formation is complete. It reaches the point of self-definition when subsequent generations receive well-defined and decisive urban structures, the achievements of previous generations.

The wall represents outermost limit of development of the specific city web.

Other cities testify to a time when the wall was broken down and the city underwent a complete restructuring, with different units belonging to different systems. This process created the current web. When the new web broke through old barriers, there were several types of breakthroughs in various periods, with each formula

The little town of Priana (Greece 350BC), shows the construction, in a low profile, of this high density settlement, using a precise geometric arrangement with some prominent public buildings. The density (estimated) is approximately 400 persons per net hectare, which is a considerably high density. The formulation of such a methodological design shows the high organizational ability of this urban settlement. This high degree of sophistication, in a remote culture, carries its abilities of organization up to the present. This example of a precise urban web, shows that urban conservation must have its roots in ancient urban planning.

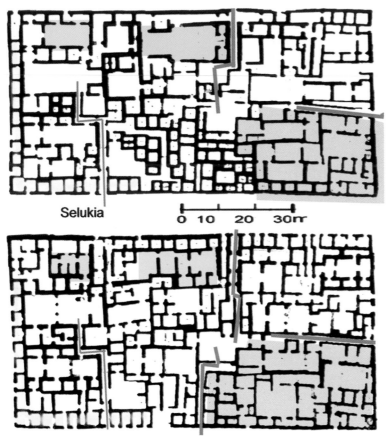

Selukia

0 10 20 30m

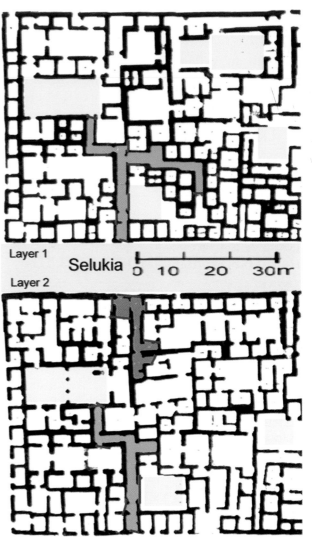

Layer 1
Layer 2

Selukia   0   10   20   30m

The early formulation of the urban block is shown to emerge slowly through time in these two layers of old excavations. In earlier times, there are some ill-managed buildings stuck to a better organized block. It later emerged as a densely built, but better-organized environment.

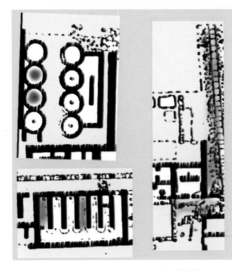

Organization of local streets is shown to happen, during the centuries, when some passages are completely blocked and others are made to provide better and wider communication to different parcels and plots of land.

Urban organization begins to take form, when we see that the urban services necessary to sustain life, begin to get attention. This becomes clear when we discover services such as rudimentary water piping and some degree of collective grain storage.

creating a different web with its own geometry.

Webs can be viewed as a collection of districts, each with distinct geometric properties and formed in different periods as a result of various factors.

At this stage, the human-historical hierarchy of the urban settlement can now be established. In descending order (the opposite of the chronological order of their creation) this comprises:

A. Formation of the urban **pattern**, made up of several webs and weaves.

B. Division into various **districts**.

C. The block created by **streets and roads**.

D. The elementary nature of the private parcel.

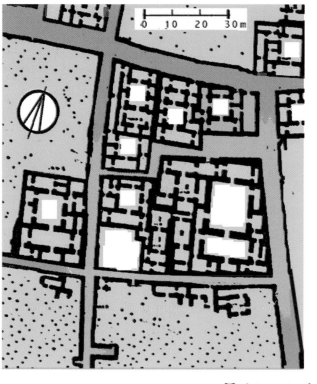

In the old town of Babylon, excavations helped to mark the emergence of town blocks as they remained for several centuries with the same type of building recurring, i.e. central courts surrounded by the different rooms and some systematic organization of buildings. The buildings are seen to have a high degree of approach from the system of the roads, which begins to be octagonal.

5. The Layered Structure of Ancient Towns

Towns built upon several archaeological layers are particularly significant to urbanization.

These different layers shed light on the given settlement in terms of both time and method of settlement. The changes that can be discerned when comparing the layers show how the residents in the parcel perfected their methods.

Periodic improvements in the outlay helped them gain advantage in areas such as regulation, measurements and passages.

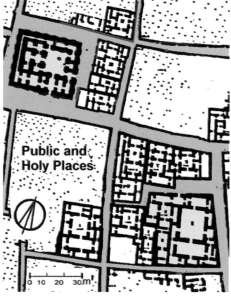

Public and Holy Places

The size of the different blocks begins to become repetitive. The sizes are marked as quite sizable blocks but repeating their dimensions.

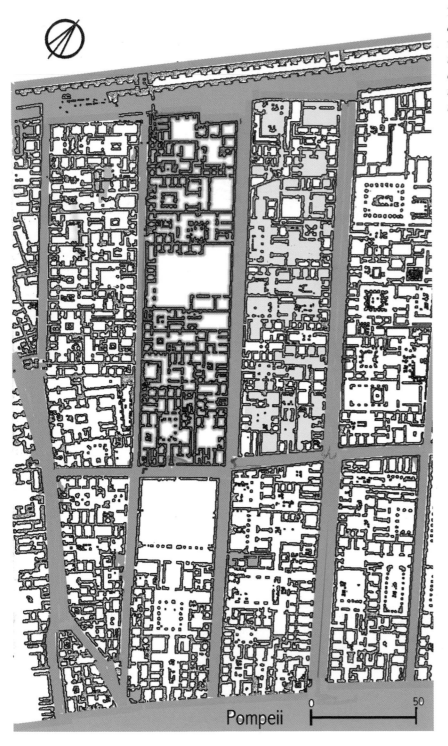

Pompeii

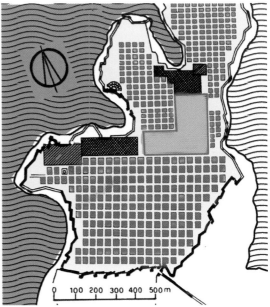

The old Roman town of Pompeii (left), is organized on similar lines as Greek towns, with the same high degree of sophistication in building orthogonal systems, roads, connections and communications along them. This system set out public buildings in the most matter of fact, democratic way.

*The old town of **Miletus**, Greece (500BC) above, where a few similar models dictate urban structure. The common plot width of 35-40 meters contains regular systems of public and private ownership. The realization of this system, without concern for topography, necessitated technical know-how. At the same time, it is unclear why this particular direction was chosen, perhaps as a measure of avoiding cliffs and being more parallel to the shore. On the other hand, a high degree of measuring site and organizing the system is indicated. This reliance on a module means ability of civic control and rule. This is indicated as well in the districts organized in a particular manner to keep the hierarchy clear.*

It is, therefore, accurate to say that the study of archaeological layers clarifies how geometry can be adapted to current needs, by showing the researcher how previous generations made adaptations to the urban framework.

In fact, this web is situated on another web, incorporating it to fit new needs.

To a certain degree, there is some conservation in ancient cities (e.g., preservation of holy sites) and flexibility, such as the repair of an old road, when a new one had been superimposed.

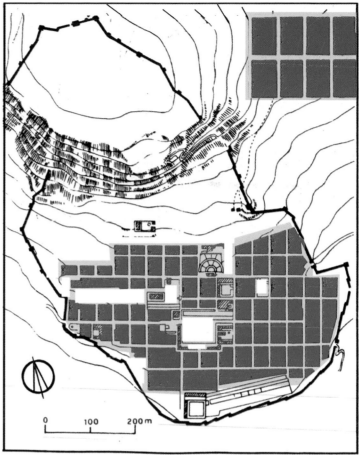

Priana's town plan shows the regular blocks, the regular module of the road system, parallel to the topography, the public buildings, squares and meeting places that have a necessary, high degree of organization.

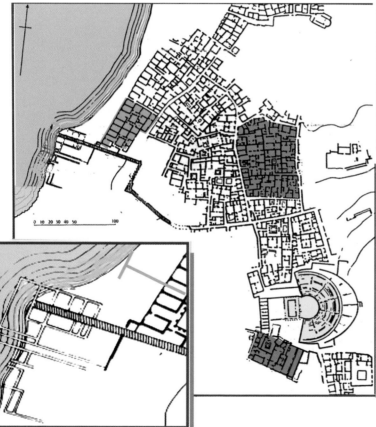

The town of Delos , Greece (on the left), shows the organization of a port in old Greek towns, which bears a degree of mastery in systematic building, and rational organization of services. One can see that at its initiation, the town (near the sea) takes the direction of the jetty, near the port. The organization of the living quarters and residential districts of the town, took shape differently. Public buildings take a prominent position in the town's separate squares.

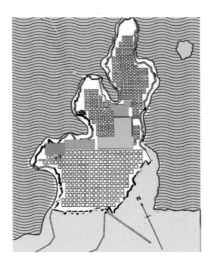

Chapter Nine

Analysis
of Findings

Type of Geometric Division
Block Size
Traffic Routes
City Web Data

Patterns of city life are self-recorded in archaeological sites. Some analysis of principal features, basic dimensions and principles are there to help our study of parallel elements in our cities.

Geometrical and quantitative characteristics can be measured and analyzed. The quantitative experiment is conducted to enable organized study in terms of quantity.

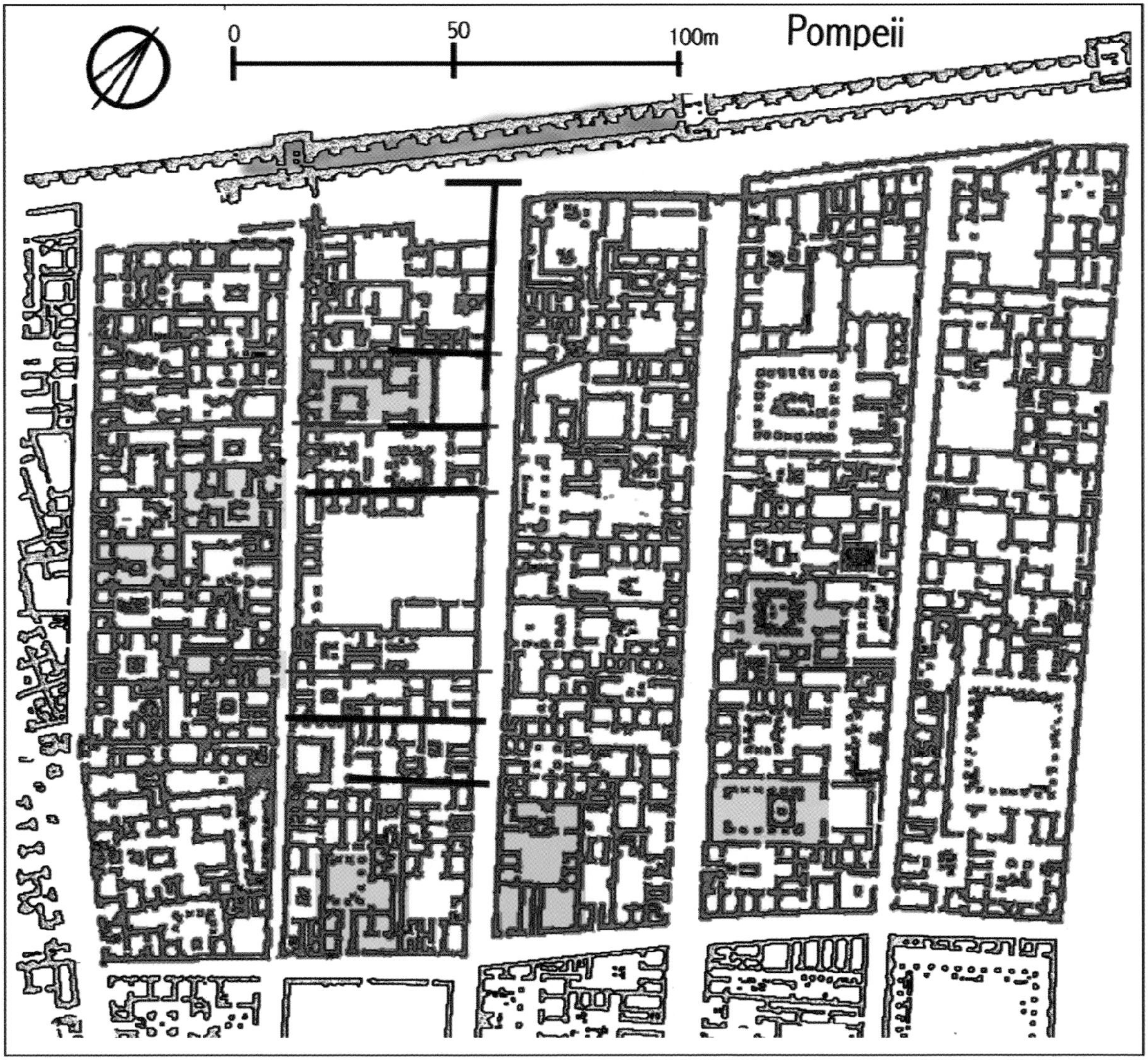

Pompei's hierarchy is less rigid than that of Roman camps. It is easier to live in and not just a blind copy of an old army camp. The long block is somewhat problematic for daily life, its length being an exaggeration, approaching 200 meters. On the other hand, it is a good example of planning ability in a coherent society that has led civilization coherently and successfully. A valid example for good planning, its influences are still felt today.

Pompeii

0   50   100m

The analysis of the hierarchy in planning, near Karachi, is pointed out by the prominence of the road system and the size of the districts to which they lead, the planning clarity exemplified. In this instance, it is only a start at ancient planning, where the difference in the road width first appears, marking main and secondary roads.

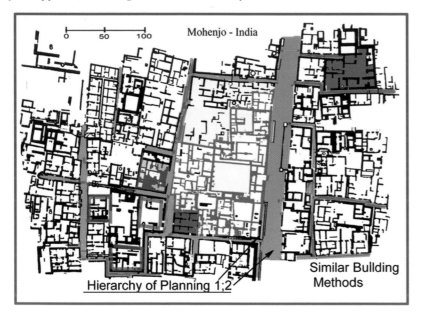

Mohenjo - India

Hierarchy of Planning 1;2

Similar Building Methods

We examine excavation plans (Ur of the Chaldees), for their major components. The main one here is the grid direction, which is kept coherent throughout time. What can be noted, are the limits of private ownership and the clear delineation of private blocks, an important part of planning, to be further shown in other examples. When analyzing, it is worthwhile to note the detailed approach to the building system, ventilation methods, etc., as well as the basic size of the block. This will partly explain the beginnings of the urban web and its direction, which is then adopted as a building grid.

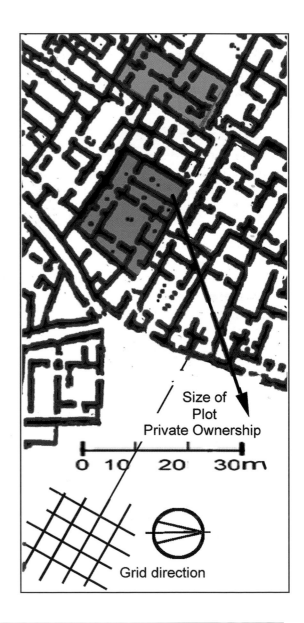

Size of Plot
Private Ownership

0 10 20 30m

Grid direction

To emphasize developments through history, the following examples have been divided into three categories: the ancient world, Greece and Rome, and other findings. An attempt will be made to take several quantitative considerations into account. This, however, requires the establishment of a number of principal standards:

The first comparative tool, or standard, indicates the possibilities for urban analysis and possible methodologies for development of research methods. Without a clear picture of quantitative proportions, there is no comparative tool for examining any form of urban conservation. Other measurements will refer to the following values and, when possible, will be numerical. These include:

1. Parcel Size

Average parcel size, as well as the length-width proportions, indicate the **standard of living**, purchasing power, and construction ability, relative to the surroundings, time frame and type of internal organization.

The type of use - which will distinguish it from its surroundings. When the use of the parcel differs from the use of parcels in its vicinity, it is often found in an area that is either a blend of commercial-residential or workshop-residential. These mixed uses are fundamental to understanding the nature of the city.

Future roads (changes over time) due to the existance of a new eminent use. Homogenous division indicates the stability of the previous system and its durability over time.

2. Percentage of Roads

As compared to the percentage of improved land (efficient division).

The proportion of roads is indicative of the amount of traffic. The percentage of roads in a crowded urban division sheds light on the actual extent of traffic congestion. A high percentage of roads, however, can also result from the manner of the division as well as the dominant geometry.

The old town of Shifta(Israel) excavation plan, shows the relation of buildings (3-dimensionally) to the urban web. The roads' system is pointed out, with ancient formation of squares.

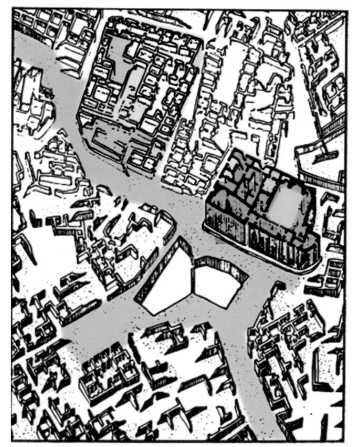

The city of Delos shows a high degree of orthogonal organization, especially at the port. It is noteworthy that some blocks built close to the city, probably served for storage. Multipurpose blocks are built logically into a coherent geometrical system. This systematic approach makes for easy understanding and use.

The plan of the city of Lambadis shows a big organized Roman camp, in which, by necessity, road organization is fully carried out. This is done with public buildings and protected sites as well. It is indicative that the small cells, serving the army as living quarters, vary in dimensions. The system is logical and coherent, at the same time not boring and clearly understood. The organization of such a complex settlement, which is fully equipped, starting from religious services and various urban necessities (such as food storage) is an example how such forms prove relevant even today, serving cities rationally. It is also evident that only central control can lead to such an able organization, which is based on hierarchy and clarity.

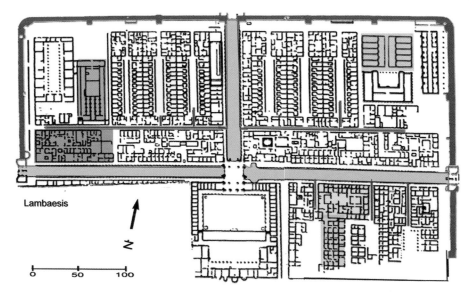

Lambaesis

0   50   100

3. Type of Geometric Division

The directions of the division indicate geographical and environmental constraints. A direction that follows certain laws (e.g., north-south), accepting topography as the starting point, or perpendicular (or parallel) divisions to the river, are all determined at the start of urbanization. The dominant geometry is not only a result of the selected direction, but also of construction methods and the measurement possibilities. Economic realities often determine size and create the urban web.

4. Block Size

Block size can be defined as the total number of parcels that create the block and the collection of private parcels surrounded by roads. The overall physical size includes measurements of length and width. Organization

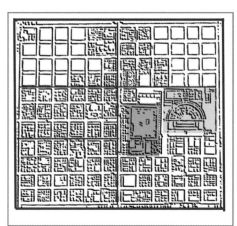

The city of Timgad, an ancient Roman camp, shows an entire simplified urban organization, with some main axes, perpendicular to each other and easily approachable by the use of the city square.

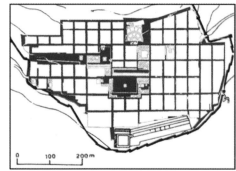

The city of Priana is an example of a coherent and perfected planning system, with clear orthogonal blocks, parcels, roads and public spaces. It can easily be cultivated, so as to become a basis of the understanding of the role of each component in the urban structure.

This reconstructed model of Priana shows the 3-dimensional structure from which we can understand the basic structure of the town, including urban and public functions in the hierarchy.

Old Cournub (in the Negev), shows some basic formations of primitive structures, starting to develop their system, which then culminate in more important, public buildings. Because of different building methods, the orthogonal system chosen to be regulative, becomes more important, leading to a more manageable urban form.

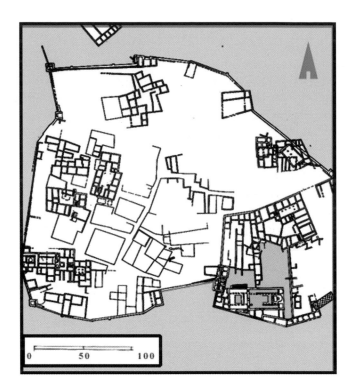

Ancient buildings, ruins and reconstructed Roman excavations, in towns in Yugoslavia (Split and Dubrovnik), show the role ancient edifices have in explaining the urban structure. A similar use of more recent reconstruction can be envisaged, say of structures we saw wiped out during the present century. This is a model of the possible use of old configurations in a civilized fashion.

of blocks within the neighborhoods and the position of the neighborhood in the urban area are the physical dimensions of city life with emphasis on traffic direction as well as internal and external developments.

5. Distances between Traffic Routes in the District

The block is created by the size and arrangements of parcels. It is also formed by the demands of traffic needs such as distances between sidewalks and roads (length/width proportion). These dimensions create the block arrangement in the neighborhood.

6. Conclusion - City Web Data

Numerical data regarding historical city webs has been established as follows:

Parcel Size – The form of the first cell.

Division – The length/width proportion – organization and efficiency.

Block Composition – Collection of neighborhoods, their numbers and character.

Type of Division – Direction and geometry, indicating the level of development.

Block Composition – the number of blocks and their character in creation of neighborhoods.

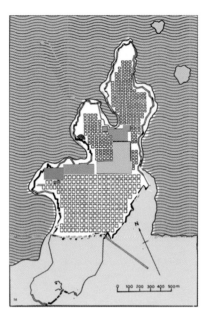

Another look at Miletus,(Greece) built while protected and surrounded by external walls. Geometrical and hierarchical urban organization in three separate quarters. Town center, with some public squares and buildings to stress its importance, acts as a link between the districts. Understanding this and other systems and being able to read the structure, will help in the study of their preservation.

An example of two of the important cities based on ancient Roman camps - Ratisbon (left) and Vienna (right), with their typical center point,where the junction is a crossing of the two main roads, and the orthogonal system of organization. Some of the ancient blocks exist in their basic form up to the present day. It is also interesting to note the similarity in the block size (around one half hectare).

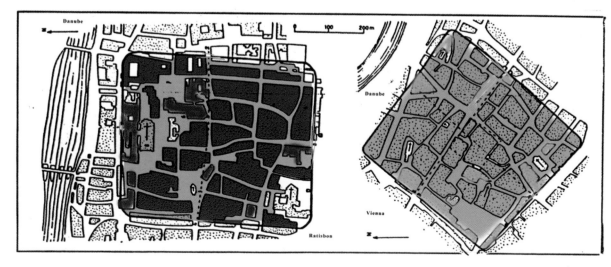

Block – Length/Width Dimensions - and repetition along streets. General urban organization and relation to roads.

Distances between Sidewalks – and the width of roads and public's right of way. It should be mentioned that it is not always possible to identify all these details precisely. Some will have to be estimated.

Quantify the following:

1. Percentage of roads

2. Parcel size

3. Type of division (geometry)

4. Size of blocks

5. Distances between passageways or roads

While the geometry of a given area dictates the possibilities there, it similarly dictates the limitations of the area. The possibilities of measurement themselves limit land use. For example, the orthogonal system of measurement, based

The analysis applied to ancient towns such as old Gurnia, in which we can point out, in yellow, the roads discovered and measured. The relation, in terms of area, to the total excavation is to be noted. The road area will measure the efficiency and importance of negotiations, transportation and communication levels and intensity, between the different parts of the human settlement, thus indicating different ways of reading the structure.

on the use of right angles (already known in ancient civilizations), was easily implemented.

Many human settlements were established with the right angle and geometrical arrangement as dominant features. This phenomenon has important implications when identifying human settlements as well as the structural and formative laws. Other systems of measurement exist and either create or enable different planning. Some may prefer a set, proportional and rigidly positioned model.

Moving on to modern analysis, it is clear that the findings of geometrical analyses are the principal tool for arranging the urban web, and, hence, are also a tool for conservation of the web.

Geometric strategy is naturally rooted in urban planning and is strengthened by continual movement on a linear plane (often in spite of topography). The direct simplicity created by this geometry facilitates conservation.

It is interesting to see in an oblique, aerial photograph how the organization is carried out and how the main roads are based on a system, throughout the town of Arcoloneus.

Public Ownership   Flexible Internal Division

Continuing our analysis of urban structure, it is possible to note in this ancient Indian town, the components of urban structure, namely a basic orthogonality, parcel depth, building system and a flexible internal division, demarcation between public and private ownership as well as size and hierarchy of the road.

Thiergarten

Botanic Garten

Pancras

Green Park

James Park

PART THREE

Principal Urban Elements

Urban structure is at the basis of planning; preservation is one facet of planning. Urban conservation depends on the basic form and structure of cities. The main components of urban form are those which constitute and determine the city web.

Cities' patterns will help establish the necessary background for urban conservation and preservation by pointing to the principal elements of its formation.

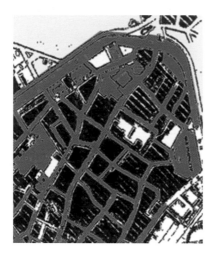

Chapter Ten

Formulating Urban Structure

Urban Web
The District
The Block
Division of the Block

The urban web is a discernible pattern with definable main features and a systematic development and deployment. It normally constitutes an agglomeration of a few secondary patterns, the result of historical influences, topography, regional remnants, economy and growth.

The following chapter discusses the urban system and its diverse range of functions. This system must be thoroughly understood before conservation can be carried out. In this chapter, we suggest a method of analysis that is suitable for study of medium and large cities. This method is also applicable when trying to gain insight into the past. It also enables present planning, restoration or conservation efforts.

The urban structure we have to identify here is characteristic of every large city and is, therefore, appropriate for use in this context.

This is an entirely new way of viewing the city, which is built on the same basic elements discussed earlier. Wherever this approach has been put to test, it has proven suitable for analyzing and clarifying various approaches to planning.

The process of constructing a model for defining the manner a city (urban settlement) was built as a human settlement is an important tool in the planning of urban conservation.

In the previous chapter, it was shown that certain elements repeat themselves. These elements are essential to urban structure and can be found around the world wherever socio-historical events have occurred, the result of which is centralization – or more aptly stated, urbanization. Let us now examine them from a conservation-oriented perspective.

We have discerned formative phases in the development of ancient cities, as a background to the formation of newer ones. It is, however, worth noting at the outset that the difference between these cities and new ones is not significant. The difference between

An illustration of very old agricultural land divisions of ownership, in the old town and its vicinity (Caesaria, Israel). The aerial photograph reveals facts which are not always mapped, and exists often as title descriptions, difficult to decipher or ascertain. The regularity in size and direction is consistent, and attributable both to value and geometrical ability.

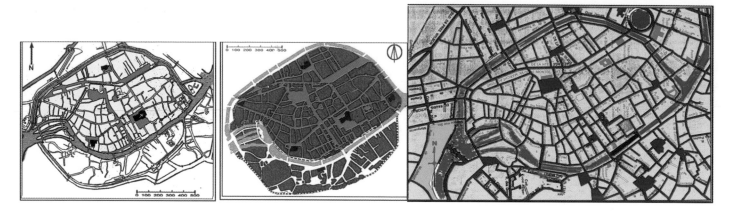

The consistence of city structure over time, in the city of Strasbourg. Present state (left), as structured by roads in the town center, can be compared to some historical maps (18 century and medieval on the right). From a walled and protected site, with the prominence of squares, churches, major market places, canals, etc. resulting in a clear unified formation of a viable mixture of components, the city has the continuous vitality of a growing healthy organism.

The structure of the initial land division will have a long lasting effect on the town's development (Manchester, beginning of the century). Major roads and the resulting secondary streets will result in land subdivision of a certain kind, in the same reciprocal manner that they were formed as a result of some historical process of ownership, topography, agriculture, etc. The first tracts of major division become apparent.

Comparison to the formative years of roads initial conception can be instructive (marked in red). This is the geometrical basis for the subsequent rise of the other systems, beginning with local streets (blue and yellow) , and followed by various public functions, such as schools (light green). Local roads (bottom ,center) often follow old field division, showing how far back our systems carry, and how far forward in the future the effects of our planning will persist. This can be one of the chief reasons for the care to be taken regarding conservation procedures, also for their extreme validity.

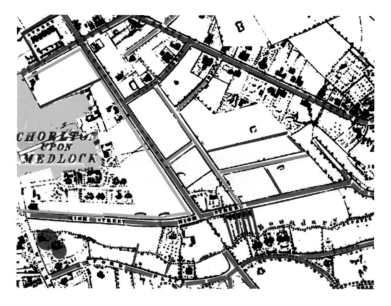

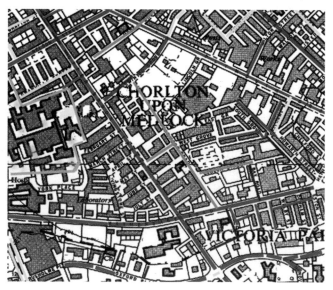

them is in the level of complexity of new cities as well as in their physical size, the large number of various webs within the new city and the diverse specialization in the level of land designation and use. It will be shown that public **presence** continually increases over time, as does public **ownership**. This was first reflected in roads and transportation networks, as well as in public gardens and public buildings in general.

Four successive phases of urban formation can be distinguished. They will be listed here in inverse chronological order, despite the fact that throughout time they generally built up from the small to the large. Definitions of the primary urban elements will also be provided, arranged from large sections to the division of private parcels. Those urban elements will then be compared to more advanced, not ancient, urbanization.

1. Urban Web

The urban web is a most general view of a settlement, but does not delve into the physical details. Through it one can see the general properties, characteristics of the urban axes and its diverse components, enabling the discovery of similarities between various cities. The series of public passages create a unique format or structure that is physically and geometrically defined. The most prominent and major passages (roads and streets) can be seen as arteries that nourish the district including the various buildings. By painting the public passages on the conservation plan a dark color, the web feature is emphasized and the result is a clearer picture of the urban area. Once the urban portrait is in plain view, the regularity of the emerging web comes into focus. This regularity can then be expressed in quantitative terms.

The formative elements in the city development can be read from a recent map of Brussels. A logical historical progress, from an old "walled in" form, containing a number of web patterns, irregular arrangement of small blocks progressing into a radial system. Outside the line of the walls, an ordered geometry takes over.

Formative development in the town of Frankfurt, Germany (from an old 18 cent. map).The walled in origins are clearly seen, with the internal partly regular system, parallel to the river, in contrast to the city walls. The circular road helps radiating development, in the process of which some existing irregular patches (in brown) are encompassed. This new system becomes regular in its geometry.

The city of **San'a** contains a few noteworthy structural elements. The old part of the town is regular, containing similar sized blocks. The later town developed (within city walls) in another structural way. It is to be noted the city contains a few undeveloped plots of land used for vegetation purposes. The differing parts of this town (such as the old city) can be called districts. We start by the division of the town into several parts, each defined by similar sized blocks. This will clarify the organization of its singular urban web containing separate districts.

The primary definition differentiates between a group of various geometrical webs (e.g., orthogonal) and webs that lack a prominent geometry, appearing to be random. Other definitions relate to issues such as building density, repetition and height.

2. The District

Whenever approaching urban structures, we begin to distinguish differences between close features that are differentiated from each other by internal qualities, despite the fact that they still merge with each other. These differences are the formative nuclei that established local features – variations in structure such as the size of the blocks, the distance between them, etc. We term these formally different structures as 'districts'.

A district, an uninterrupted accumulation of similarly featured groups (physical, restorable, symbolic, historical) is, in fact, a type of neighborhood – an urban subdivision or subregion for conservation that we examine with the physical-urban structure serving as a backdrop. An urban area with its particular web is made up of a number of districts. Each district incorporates various properties within its structure. It is important to recognize the limits of each district, the links to its surroundings and city, as well as the extent of change or possible change in the future. The district's internal continuity can also be defined according to its structural properties. These properties, both within the district and outside it, can be quantified and defined.

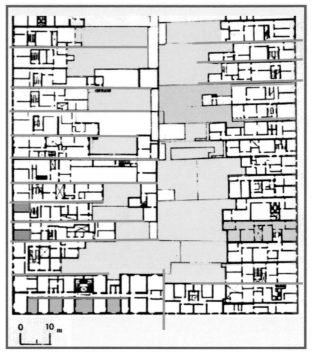

This close look at land division (Florence) illustrates how the block is built by divisions. Separate blocks and the similarity between them, the repetition, indicate how geometrical dimensions play a strong part in underlying and developing city structure. These similarities are also made by recuring building methods and same ways of overcoming the 4-5 meters spans. The argument that geometrical repetition is one of the norms building the block, is thus illustrated.

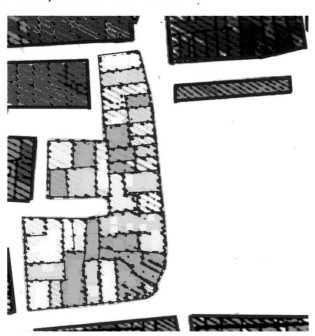

A much older city block in Florence shows undecided geometrical division. Even though it is perpendicular and orthogonal, its dimensions are not repetitive and not influenced by any module, allowing for a certain freedom or permutations in local district forms.

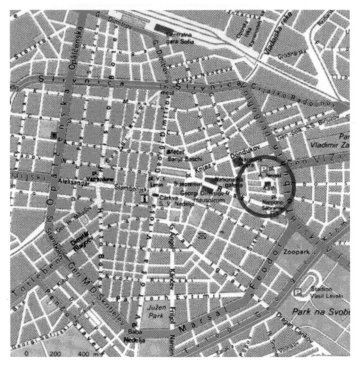

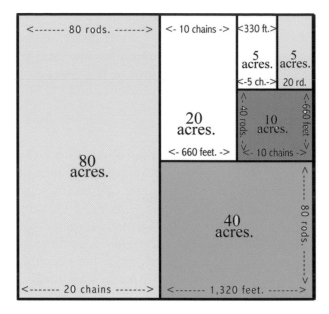

The system of land division used frequently in the U.S. shows the method of incrementalism based on strong regularity, actual measurements of area and not on geometrical divisions. Variations of the method are based on the quality of easily measuring and marking land, thus assisting in land marketing and quick development of settlements.

Sofia has a basic central web and circular roads, developing into a radial system. Internally, it has the normal orthogonal, perpendicular lines of roads and land division often seen in Europe. Parts of the town are strongly developed on an orthogonal basis; other parts rely on the radial system to swing about and form lines of development that allow for different geometrical values in the town's structure such as formation of irregular squares.

Calcutta is clearly divided into districts by regular deployment of an orthogonal system (marked in red). These districts are divided in a freely conceived manner and are, in fact, similarly structured, apart from a few additions of geometrical patterns, such as the one marked in green. The overall city web, however, has very clear delineations of an overall geometrical pattern.

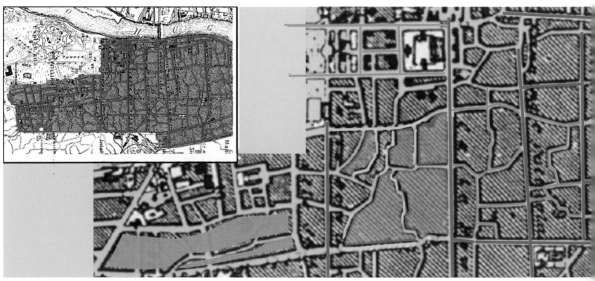

3. The Block

A coherent formation composed of smaller physical units. This is yet another formative phase, which is a predecessor to the others discussed. This is the unit that is responsible for the creation, construction and design of the block as a stable factor in urban life (often to the point of denoting human autonomy or authority within it). The block is rarely, if ever, dissected by public passages.

The physical continuity of parcels or lots, buildings and divisions is defined by public and city passages. This demarcation creates identifiable sections of land and which are, for the most part, privately owned (not by the city or public) – as a result of the formation. These are characteristics of the block. Shared borders and relationships between the divisions, as defined by the law and in planning codes, are created within the block.

The block is more cohesive than a neighborhood, because it contains joint ownership and a proximal legal relationship between the factors that mark them.

4. Division of the Block

According to certain laws, almost comparable to those of genetics, we now arrive at the smallest constructed cell: land division (parcel) causing some repetition of form. This arrangement or regularity is based on needs, neighborhood relationships, principles, laws

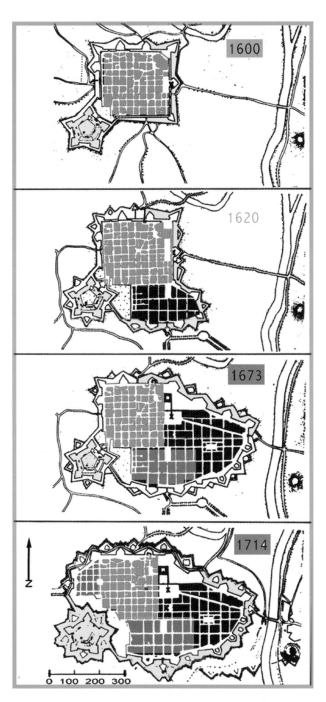

Development of plans in Torin (Italy) (beginning of the 17th century) close to city walls, system of city organization pushing the city wall. To a great extent, design of squares, streets and the ties between them are orthogonal through the ages. City walls change in appearance and geometry, through time as well, unlike the town of Nancy in France.

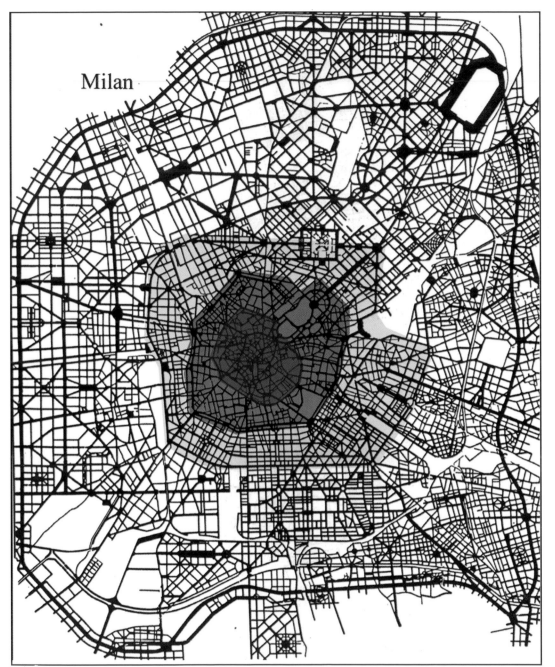

Milan

Milan's urban structure is instructive because it contains a variety of grids and webs. The differentiation of these grids follows a pattern of a centralized urban expansion, growing equally in all directions in a radial manner. Some of the grids are radial, most are not. This sort of example shows how individual urban structure can be, and the wide variety of possible patterns that are in actual use.

and mutual agreement. It is deemed successful if it withstands the test of time, otherwise, it disappears. In more modern times, filled with intense pressures – economic or other – the division relies on codes and laws incorporated in a more comprehensive law or code relating to outline plans as well as urban construction plans.

Improved and more sophisticated urban construction codes that do not ignore human and economic factors serve to guarantee the unit's existence. In the following discussion, the block is divided into the smallest possible unit – the land parcel. It is an independent entity and in terms of the authorities is owned and registered as a single unit.

The legal status of owner registration defines the long-term constancy of the most basic formative urban unit. On this parcel of land, within a geometrical framework, buildings that house people and activities are constructed. Even regarding this activity, a legal agreement has previously been reached. With the passage of time, the building, as a unit, becomes more vulnerable than the parcel of land on which it rests and undergoes various permutations. The underlying reason is that the continued existence of the building is dependent upon planning and construction codes, which differ from ordinances referring to the land on which the building sits. Real estate laws deal only with the land perspective. There is no link between these laws and construction codes. Both systems are driven by different economic principles.

The building, an additional framework necessary for human activity is the result of the system described above. The building serves as a station for services that nourish it. Consumers of the services, that is – the population – are attached to it.

The population is the principal owner and the factor with the largest turnover rate, within the **Human-Building-**

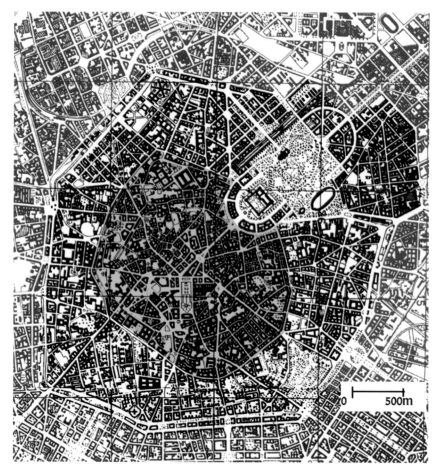

Milan's center, in which one sees in more detail the different districts surrounding the central area (in blue), clearly contains a more closely-knit and slightly ill-defined city structure. Definition and clarity progress, as the town expands radially. As we move further from the city center, the blocks become more rational and orthogonal, thereby sustaining a more defined web.

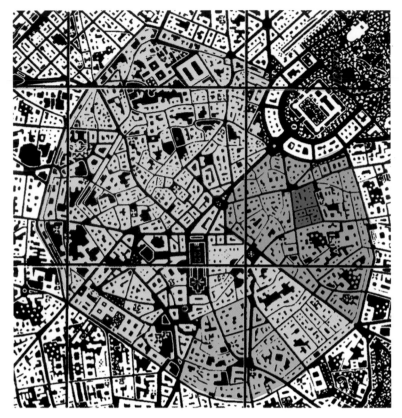

A close look at Milan's center shows the relation between the districts and the city blocks, as related to the geometrical web (defined by the radial roads). The nonsystematic old town, containing minimal roads and nonorthogonal directions seems haphazard. The block size shows a very densely built pattern in which a small amount of ventilating wells appear through the block shape.

The patterns created in Milan by the different webs develop unique qualities, allowing different connections to happen in a variety of ways. The connections between the central park and the different city squares and avenues, appear to be unique. This is one of the ways links are created between different parts of cities. When these links are analyzed in a variety of ways, trying to weigh their relative importance, we may realize how the city develops while different parts reach saturation.

Land triangle (the urban organization system).
The chronological phases of urban formation can be summarized as follows:

1. Humans settle within a land framework, creating a **building** within it. This framework has the first land unit attached to existing public service routes (roads, pipes, etc.) and nearby neighbors will act similarly.

2. Neighborhoods establish a section of neighboring units containing unique internal relationships as a result of shared borders. This is known as the **block.** The block can be

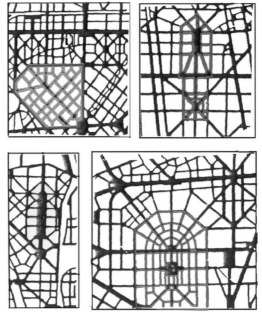

A closer look at the patterns in Milan shows the care and the method different designers used to build the city structure as well as the urban design employed in different districts or regions. This creates different shapes of districts and sizes of the blocks. Different patterns of town squares and street corners, as well as diagonal shortcuts between places of interest show a great variety. The analysis of these patterns and shapes calls for differing approaches in the conservation of the main elements.

Nothing illustrates a web pattern more than this manner of noting the development of a major city like Milan. The creation of the web is the result of the many approaches to urban design (clearly noted in different districts) in the arrangements of streets, avenues, squares and parks among them. This creates the immense variety of city design we meet here.

The town of Aden is also a 3-dimensional example of city structure not based on grids or Roman theories, but developed in a more irrational manner. The resulting structure is not conducive to town development and leads to a restrained development.

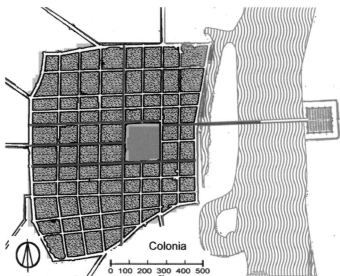

Colonia

0 100 200 300 400 500

The patterns in the old city of Cologne show a clear Roman arrangement with a clear-cut city square. Nothing could be more systematically arranged. This influenced a clear direction of the city on which much of modern 19th century planning has developed, especially in the United States.

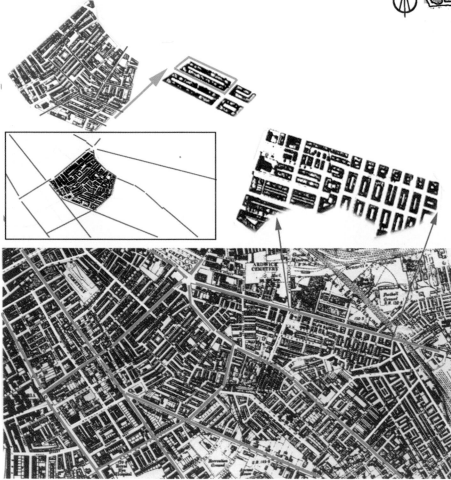

Few patterns in Manchester are as rich as Milan's and most do not offer such an abundance of shapes of features. They are easier to analyze, as we can see the pattern of the major and secondary roads creating districts with common structural elements. The influence of the webs on the internal block of the district can also be understood. Thus, the block is defined by rules of repetition, sizes and geometrical directions, externally, and plot dimensions internally.

duplicated, by similar, adjacent units, which are similarly nourished by even larger public roads. Concurrent growth of this type promotes urban formation.

3. Sections of adjacent, similar blocks create the next formation— a type of neighborhood with a structured nature, a large unit containing internal urban wholeness. This is known as the **district.** Within the district operate advanced community functions, justifying the close proximity of the blocks.

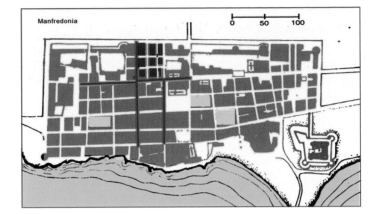

Another logical and rational approach to city design with similarity in the size of block and orthogonal, repetitive and clearly oriented system that is based on Roman concepts (Manfredonia).

The various blocks, each with its own reason for existing, move closer as they increase in size and create an urban language, though not of their own conscious doing. This urban language (a type of meta language) is capable of unifying all of the neighborhood 'languages' while creating a generality which appears as a site with strong internal cooperation.

Thus begins the formation of the **city web**. Often, a city is the result of several webs created by various forces over different eras. The picture currently in view, in which borders between webs are marked, is the result of a conflict between the web and the neighborhood. **Within these borders, we can distinguish several types of web structures that have engulfed one another.** As a result of these mutual links, there are a variety of domestic and foreign influences at all levels. Construction patterns, or prototypes, of buildings are created and will be the issues in conservation.

They are situated on urban links which contributed to their formation, including primary proportions, geometry of the section, distances and spaces, all of which represent a challenge in urban conservation. These abstract issues, whose origins lie in planning, and not necessarily in implementation, must be judged with the help of planning tools.

It is for this very reason that urban conservation begins in

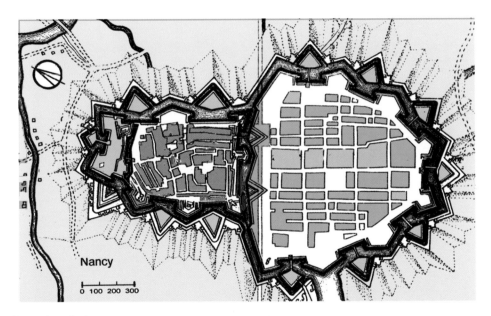

The influence of city walls is not necessarily very strong on the urban block or even on overall design, as can be seen in Nancy (France). Town development can be seen through the ages. Clearly, the orthogonal system of organizing blocks and roads is chosen for a system, while other considerations apply for the use of the wall system. These two systems do not emerge or influence each other, being both necessary.

Analysis of urban structure can stem from many examples. The example above shows Isfahan, Iran, in which a basic cell is repeated and fed by the minimal road connections with no hierarchy, showing stagnation of an urban structure that developed endlessly without the introduction of modern comforts or alleviation of poor living conditions. This town structure is typical, but not indicative of Western culture and seldom seen except in ancient villages.

Aerial photograph of Haifa at the turn of the 20th century shows an anarchic development of city form and structure, unable to conduct a very good progress into the 20th century. This exemplifies an anarchic cohesive urban development, of an haphazard structure.

planning and in outline plans and codes. It is impossible to separate planning and conservation. These are two sides of the same coin: **the establishment of a continual urban structure.** Only drastic measures can change structural continuity. Such measures can include its complete eradication, nationalization or distancing of the population. Once we understand that continuity is integrated within the formative laws, we will understand that it is unwise to destroy it. It is more worthwhile to adopt an attitude that encourages real growth and not extensive local destruction intended to replace buildings.

City structure is apparent in aerial photos when different city districts are accentuated. The structure of Paris takes some radial appearance according to the diagonal webs introduced by Hausman, as opposed to some orthogonality in the main direction of the avenues.

The superimposition of the 18th century city walls on modern Turin shows the influence of the old city on the new grids. The old blocks retain their shape within the new ones. Those out of old limits have a different countenance and density. Old orthogonal directions and grids have retained their strength and developed since the 18th century in the same manner and style without regard to the inclusion of the modern railway station.

Chapter Eleven
Main Components

Types of Urban Webs
Urban Content
Development over Time

T he major features of an urban web are the principal uses, the districts and regions developed and segregated. This will be discerned by similarities in the grain and sizes of the separate quarters.

Urban Totality

Historical sites always contain the same features: division into parcels, fields, roads, etc. of different uses. The totality of the division – either simple or com-

City web of a special form in St. Fueille-le Grand (founded in 1255). This particular city web is one of a district or region containing a repetitive formula, whereby all the roads are systematic and form blocks which probably contain similar building heights, technology and land division. Any measurements taken towards urban conservation in this particular place can probably be applicable to the entire district, as all of the problems encountered are similar. What should be pointed out is the uniqueness of this site.

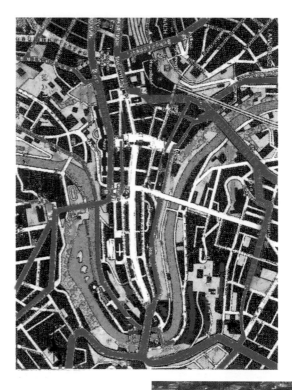

This shows the difference between the city blocks in their coherence, (old part of the city), and their related structure in other parts of the city. They all remain strongly connected to the principal city web, by stong ties. There is a unifying formula to this place, giving a breath of life to the old parts, which could have been cut off, and become lifeless.

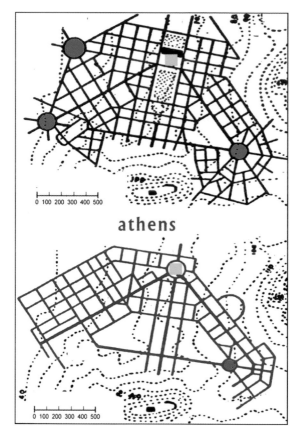

athens

An aerial photo of Basel illustrates the importance of the web in shaping the nature of a town. In our case the web comprises four long building blocks, of long history. All is based on the shape of this particular slice of the river, even more pronounced by the park on the bank, and strongly reinforced by the methodical block increment, due to a particular set of rules, whereby the height and similarity of division of land are carried out throughout the old district.

Two different approaches in alternative planning of Athens, show the importance of adopting a language and the influence of the set of rules when planning is applied to new quarters and extensions of towns. In the case above, it is noted that not much attention is paid to topography. On the other hand, some ties to the center are adopted by means of a diagonal. Both alternatives may develop into towns of similar attributes since they are similar in terms of symmetry, main access and main centers, as well as the sizes of subdivision in the two webs.

plex – represents the **city web**. Parcel division and road system, especially when it is simple to identify, is termed 'urban grid'. As previously stated, parcel size, direction and geometrical features are decisively important in urban analysis. This is the structural unit that comprises the whole.

Once a decision has been made as to which urban structures will be evaluated, the appropriate measures to identify historical parcels should be taken. The measures may include archaeological data, which assists in establishing the legality and environment in urban structures. The whole entity is made by several weaves. The city includes several various webs. We will detail a number of points emphasizing the main issue and its necessary analysis.

A web developed in Isfahan, has the different approach to planning in Islamic cities of the East, with completely local characteristics, as to private and public ownership. Public ownership of roads is tiny and neglected, whereas private property is fully developed with internal courtyards and different system of services. These towns are difficult to maintain in modern times. There is every reason to call this type of web "anarchic".

Types of Urban Webs

When discussing city webs, we can differentiate between a number of different types.

City Web – a web that is fundamentally an urban structure. The following forms of organization can be associated with this web: 1. Greco-Roman 2. Geometrical 3. Modular 4. Antique, possessing wide scope and 5. Other forms with especially large blocks. Frequently, when examining a walled city, the influence of the wall continues to be felt, even when the wall is no longer standing.

Some of the fundamentals in defining an urban area are density and concentration, along with a relatively high number of residents within the borders, and the regional background within a radius of several dozen kilometers of the country settlements found between cities. This background of country

The town of St. Paul in Germany will serve as an example of a coherent city structure, containing various elements that are at the root of our discussion. The first element is the road system, termed the city web, in public ownership, which determines the shape and size of different parts of the town; it further contains and creates the volume of the block in the districts, by a geometrical or other subdivision operating in the town in question.

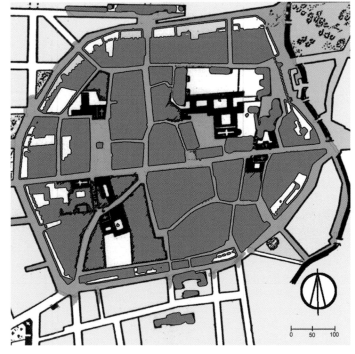

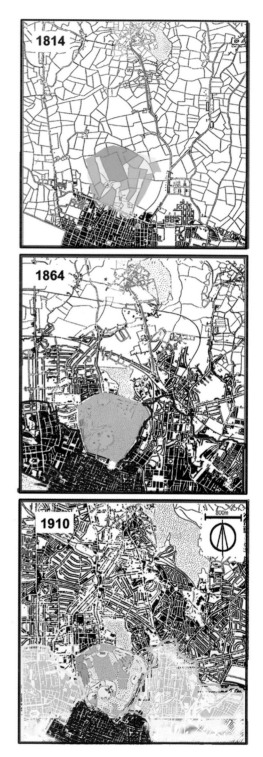

Bologna, where the web is colored, with lines comprising the road system marked in white; using differently sized blocks, it contains a very pronounced and unifying city web which has its own repetitions, not always similar but very coherent, containing elements of urban cohesion in their system. On the right, in black, we see different blocks with a character that shows prominent front towards street. These are recognizable city structure webs.

The development of city structure, has its origin in old land divisions and old approach roads. In this case, in London, in the vicinity of Regent Park (marked in green), the land divisions and main roads have influenced the growth of the city grain. In red, in 1864, we see the existing parts (built in 1814) reaching a significant portion of the surrounding land, by the green of Regent Park. At 1910, we can see the actual growth (marked in yellow) and the subsequent building in the next 50 years, all limited to the main radial access roads to the city, all carrying certain old land divisions throughout the building formations.

150

settlements contains and creates more cities of similar size, but with different urban nature. The process of city formation repeats itself in similar geographical rhythms, when the country backdrop is similar.

Country Web - development includes sectioning off agricultural parcels, with a basically disorganized central grid that borders on the agricultural grid. This web is interesting only when it serves to highlight urban development. It differs from its predecessors for it begins as an agricultural country settlement. At a certain stage, a need develops for the primary web to change and become more urban.

Free Web - A free and dense city web, it is reminiscent of the Casbah, fundamentally in anarchy and difficult to grasp. It is often termed 'organic' since its long-term growth remains apparently undisturbed by coerced geometry or other arrangements. The truth is that a even so-called 'organic' growth has its own set of rules that should be formulated.

We can identify large sections by general definitions. Here,

Petah Tiqwa, medium sized town in Israel, in an aerial photograph, is helpful in establishing the geometrical lines of the city web, enclosing different blocks or districts. This is one way of understanding city structure.

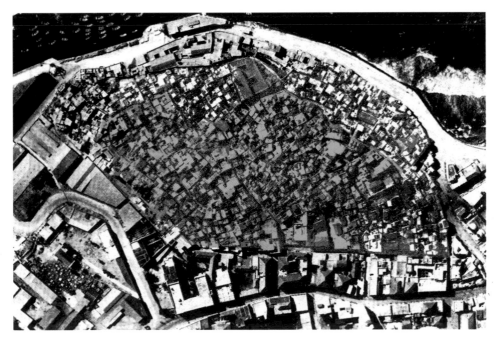

The web of the old city of Jaffa, mostly nonexistent today, is another example of an eastern city (Kasbah) that contains a very minimal road system (marked in yellow), making it a difficult web to maintain . However, it is a web that should be considered and sometimes appears in its irregularity as something of a country or village place, and can be called a free and anarchic web.

151

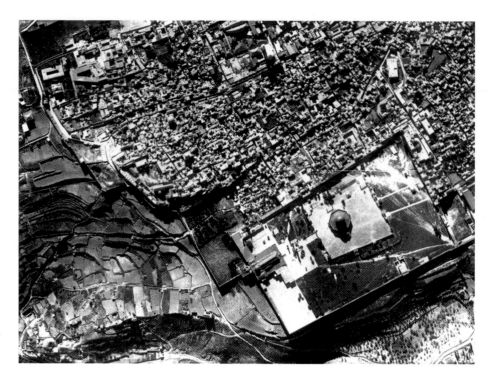

Another example of natural development of a free web is the old city of Jerusalem, which has a few basic orthogonal lines from Roman times, but these are almost lost, with free nonintervention by public measures in the city development.

Despite all that is said about old Jerusalem's free web, some orthogonal lines of old Roman roads can still be used to partially differentiate the city quarters and help somehow different developments, on slightly special local building lines.

there is no ordered and rigid planning. A regulatory system of registering borders and counterbalances barely exists, registration is scarce, the road system is defective and the internal division is unchecked. At times, sections of some form of structural framework can be identified.

The geometrical definition of the three aforementioned possibilities will be general and conform to the fundamental laws of web formation and primary measurements. There are, of course, various combinations of these types.

Generally dissimilar land division is an indication that division took place in different periods. Here, several types of webs can be isolated for the purpose of study.

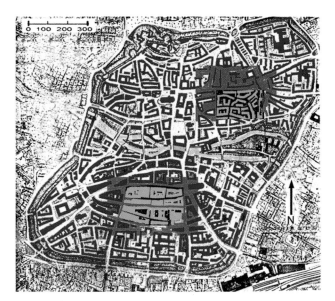

Old Nuremberg has undergone extensive rebuilding and refurbishing. As a result, the city was particularly cleaned, especially into its individual blocks, but has lost some of the old qualities when doing this. What has been especially taken care of are the public buildings. Replanning and reconstruction of the city web was only partially adopted. Some of the reconstruction looks unnatural, while the new regulations have opened most of the urban districts. Old city walls and their vicinities were turned into parks and some of the open land used for parking lots. In the lower part, some of the old city structure can be guessed at by the irregularity of the urban blocks. The newer, upper part, seems to be slightly more organized with a modern regulating system of building and design.

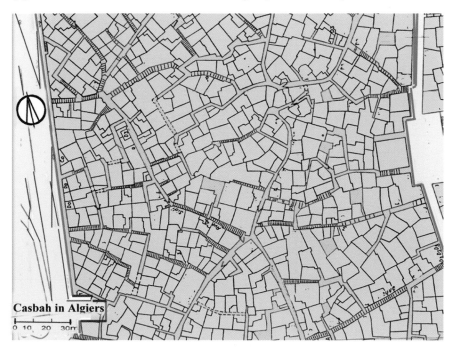

Casbah in Algiers

0 10 20 30m

Another example of a free web is the Kasbah in Algiers. It is interesting to note how every parcel has its own approach, a result of continuous subdivisions in their time. We can see that the Kasbah is a very difficult web to maintain but interesting from an urban conservation perspective, because many design qualities are inherent in this sort of town planning. This web, occasionally called an organic web, denotes a simple, natural evolvement, not frought with geometric concerns of pattern over time, a self-elaborating way with little public interference. It may serve as an example of very old origins of this type of division, which have somehow avoided geometrical and building methods concerns, as well as all public intervention or control, over the centuries. To be able to find one's way in such a place is nearly impossible, and our concepts of hierarchy are meaningless. After a certain size, this sort of conglomeration loses its own charm as well, to become unmanageable.

It can be agreed that in **London**, between Hyde Park and Regent Park, the grid providing the main direction is the west and east one, with the perpendicular secondary roads and the position of streets and squares, results in a clear marked subdivision, facilitating orientation, hierarchy and understanding of the development and structure of this particular section.

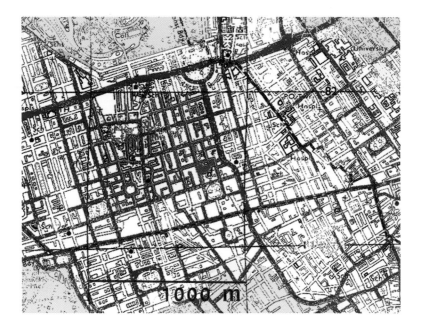

A different way of town development is noted in this example. An Italian town where the main street takes its direction from the ancient port, clearly shows how districts are developed separately, with their character evolving through the system, the size of the blocks and the urban design approach to the possibilities of geometrical arrangements.

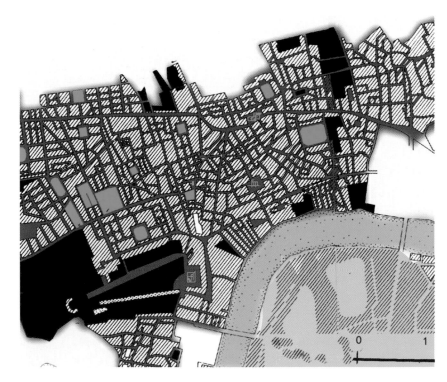

City webs can also be discussed in terms of opportunities they create for gardens, squares, parks and interconnecting facilities, as in this illustrated map of the central London, near the Thames; the importance enjoyed by the squares is stressed and made clear in this particular urban part of town.

Identifying the type and nature of the web, and how it is created, will make it easier to understand later on. We have a number of comments exemplifying the content .

Urban Content

As previously mentioned, the city and the web contain three components:

A. Land – the static and self-preserving element. Its division ensures its long-term survival.

B. Buildings – their survival is shorter-term, though property regulations preserve their existence.

C. Humans – in varying number and densities, variable characteristics, using and living on the land and in the buildings.

These three components, and their interrelationships, must be part of every urban discussion, in terms of numerical data, quantities and qualities, even when the discussion refers to conservation. Hence, the aforementioned geometrical and numerical analysis is incomplete if these components are not taken into account on a general level. This should be done without straying into sociological planning which, though important to urban planning, represents a chapter unto itself.

Development over Time

The result of urban development according to a formula, which we attempt to define, creates a structured urban life. Developing over time, the formula determines conservation laws to a certain extent. For example, although a revolution in style is detrimental to conservation, it is often necessary in order to incorporate new ideas within the web.

Conclusion

The principles of the urban structure analyzed here are the

Paris is noted by its very irregular web structure which forms an endless variety of shapes, block sizes, directions, squares and hierarchies of very different nature, which can only be studied by an analysis helped by aerial photographs.

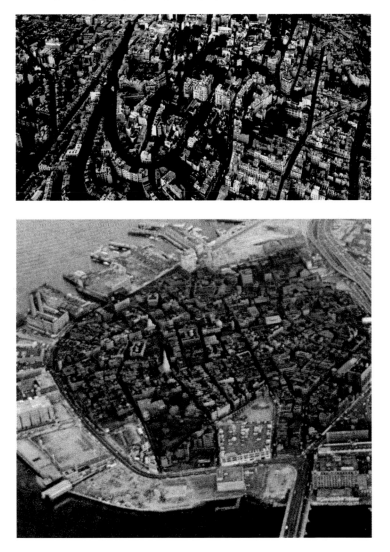

Boston, with the old part in color, is an example of an almost regular city web containing regular buildings in terms of heights and density, formulating a web that is clear to analyze and study.

Mexico city

The endless variety of different webs creating an overall pattern in their interrelation is exemplified here, with almost no relation between the different quarters in this town. Separate districts have their own internal structure, and are unconcerned with neighboring structures, which tend to become separate entities in the city web. This may create borderline problems and regions which are difficult maintaining by planning or by conservation.

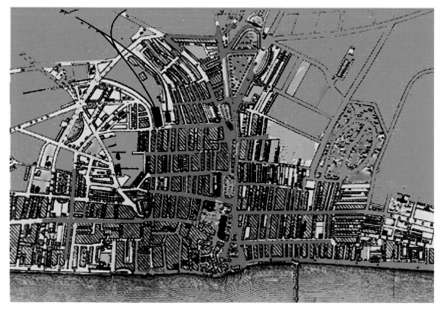

Brighton, with its very clear urban structure, from the central perpendicular lines to the shore road, from which, like tree branches ,stem secondary lines parallel to the sea, with major roads and connections, a clear hierarchical form, giving rise to blocks of similar lengths and other secondary roads parallel to the main street.

fundamental background in conservation considerations. These principles, combined with mapping, serve as a background for any formula of conservation principles. The components we have detailed thus far build the city. They must be considered when conservation plans are made. Thought must also be given to their development over time. It must be decided at what point conservation will end, as well as its nature and method.

At this point urban elements can be discussed in further detail. It is important to realize the importance of structural forms: each element is a reflection of the period in which it was created, was formed in a particular manner, displays a certain level of resiliency and flexibility to change. The urban structure, which was defined earlier as the creative force behind the city, determines to a large extent the continuation, understanding, quantification and definition in a conclusive manner. Overall urban considerations stemming from the above carry more weight and will influence conservation later on.

The following is a list of web attributes that construct the city:

Geometrical Aspects
1. Size
2. Relation to the environment and city
3. Nature

Functional Aspects
1. City function and role
2. Main land use and zoning
3. Transportation and traffic

The city of Hebron in an aerial photograph, shows development of a local mixed web, over a difficult topography, climbing on the hill with time.

Chapter Twelve
The District

Division into Blocks

The important city subdivision, called
district, region or neighborhood, is
formed in many instances by similarities in basic structures and pattern. It has its
defined borders and limits; it also contains a
life of its own.

Within a single city web are districts, distinguished
by their inclusion or noninclusion in the unifying web.
A collection of streets within the city web, each with

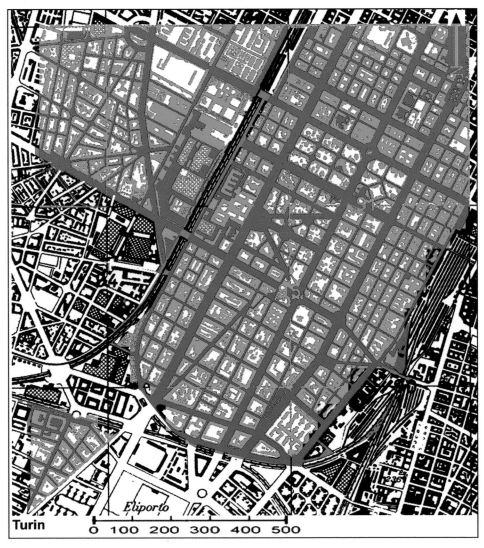

Turin

0 100 200 300 400 500

In modern Turin, it is interesting to note
that some places, persist in their old
division, apparent in some diagonals and
blocks, but include a higher density. The
new town is characterized by logical,
geometrical and orthogonal divisions, and
forms very clear districts, as we can see by
their shape, one in rectangular manner
and the other in smaller blocks,
constituting a different approach of web
inclusion. Diagonals in the web system are
interconnections between squares and
major routes, facilitating internal city links
and circulation.

It is amazing to see the modern inclusion of a complex road system in the old town, even though a lot of effort has been spent not to disrupt ancient qualities and land division, and to keep some of the elements intact. It is also striking that for 700 years, a certain structure has been maintained, helped by a strong character of roads and block sizes (Cologne, Germany).

When studying city patterns, we are looking for definitions of districts as formed by city structure; it is easy to ascertain the pattern characterizing the district. We can immediately notice that districts can be defined by a geometry or by the existing web, its direction, as well as from the building codes and bylaws, to which can be added technological features or styles, sometimes even historical details (Paris, France).

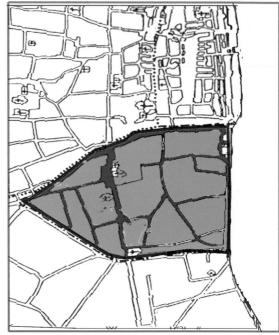

1250

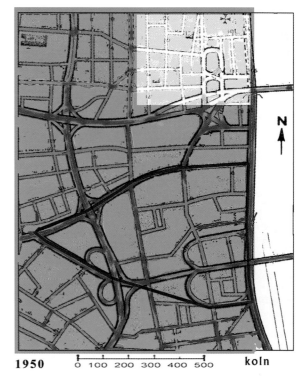

1950   0 100 200 300 400 500   **koln**

160

similar content, constitutes a **district**. Each district has a well-defined urban character. We term the entire entity of streets that create similar sections within city webs as **districts**, having a defined urban nature. The identified district includes a series of blocks. Blocks are groupings of buildings surrounded by streets. Their properties, including size, can be clearly identified. The city web is a collection of districts made of blocks with similar identifiable properties that can be laid out within the general web. The regularity of shapes that creates the district, along with the regularity achieved by the presence of similar blocks within the district form the basis for the urban conservation approach.

The District's Geometrical Aspects
1. District size, extent and demarcation of borders.
2. District adaptation to urban geometry and the web in which it is situated.
3. Width, formation and repetition of streets in the district.
4. District positional system, layout and height.
5. Internal division and measurements of the block.

The District's Functional Aspect
1. Use, zoning and their layout within the district.
2. Various mixed uses..
3. By-laws.
4. City and public services in the district.

The geometrical and functional perspectives are a summary of urban definitions. A city cannot exist without physical geometry and defined objectives. Conservation must follow these aspects closely, understand them and decide what should be preserved in order to ensure a continual flow of life.

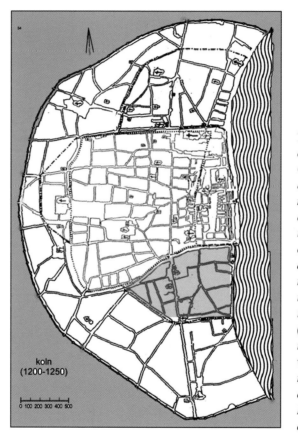

koln
(1200-1250)

0 100 200 300 400 500

The different districts that can be observed in a city like Cologne in its form in the early Middle Ages are marked out in color, being clearly different in their internal relations, constituting examples of different block organizations, therefore having a distinction in town. The one close to the river is older than the other (both in light blue). The inclusion of larger blocks as we go further inland, is typical. The older quarter contains an old settlement, a Roman road system and an open market square.

LUGO

AVILA

Warsaw's central square. It is simple to see how the different blocks are separated in the city structure and formulated by the roads and the differences in the adjoining blocks. Structural similarities in the district make the pattern recognizable but do not prevent us from seeing different principles in operation.

The formation of districts in the town means that certain similarities can be observed in the different blocks which constitute the districts. These similarities can be not only building technologies or heights, but block sizes, direction, internal organization and a special relation to the street. In ancient cities, blocks contained in a walled in district have the tendency to be similar, and are much easier to define, whether fit or unfit for urban conservation considerations.

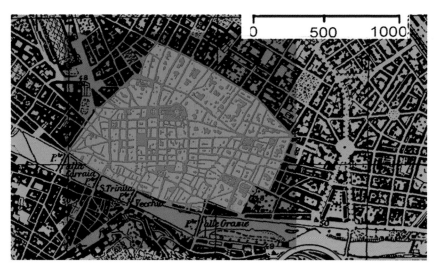

In the city of Florence, the oval shape of an amphitheater of Roman times has had influence on the webs and patterns, and has shaped blocks. This serves to illustrate the fact that traditions of land division have been influenced by ancient geometries and shapes.

Formation of quarters or districts is sometimes clear and easily grasped, as in the case of Florence. But the district marked in color has a mixture of several grids or webs, patterns which affect each other, while it is still apparent, in its overall structure, that there is a strong affinity between the geometrical patterns used.

Different geometries mixed, meeting each other to create districts and blocks, interrelated by a similarity in the land division, such as sizes of frontage or plots, acquire a strong homogeneity, while preserving the character of major parts in the old town.

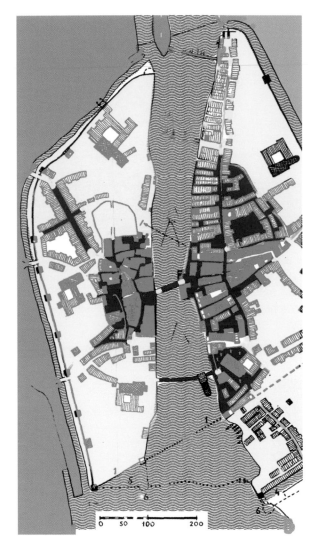

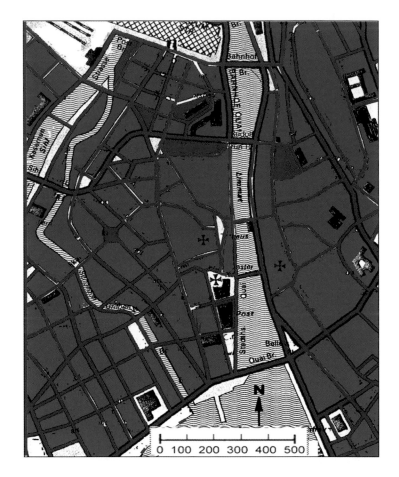

Zurich, shown in an old map, with its different grains in the periods which have built this city historically. Shown in stronger colors, starting at the 10th century, the progress is seen (in four different periods) up to the 19th century. One can see through the centuries the rules dictating this development, starting from simple blocks and evolving into sophisticated ones with a bigger internal space. It is also clear that the city has been strongly influenced by the adjoining river, and that is indicated by the parallel geometry.

The modern plan of Zurich shows that different blocks have undergone radical changes. Only a few ancient blocks have been maintained. The city web has clearly undergone changes over the centuries, becoming more clear-cut in comparison to the Middle Ages one. Such transformations, when studied, can reinforce the governing principle of the pattern formation, and to mark the different roads as they progress in time, making the patterns even more evident.

Division into Blocks

Public property (mainly streets and squares) create and direct the urban system. We can distinguish primary and secondary channels of communication within them. Fundamentally, the blocks were determined by public roads and communication channels. The size, division, repetition and regularity that shapes them, characterizes the district through the following issues:

1. Size of the Basic Block – Blocks created during the same period are generally of a similar size, dimensions and nature.

2. Position of the Block – relative to wind direction. The purpose of these two characteristics is to identify how blocks create districts.

3. Formation of the City Web – how the district builds and establishes the city web and how it links to it. This serves as a tool for further analysis of urban relationships.

Palace square (St. Petersburg).
Built in the beginning of the 19th century, it includes the famous winter palace, and is itself a preserved district. In the present case , this district is helped in its definition by the formation of the square, and not so much by the web.

The coherence of the old web in the city of Jerusalem is clearly grasped and easily considered as a district fit for conservation considerations. The studies in webs such as these have to further discover the smaller intimate blocks, in order to define a meaningful pattern that can be referred to when trying to formulate a structural principle.

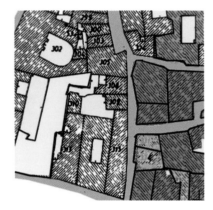

Chapter Thirteen
The Urban Block

Internal Divisions
Building Heights
Documentation

I n our presentation, the city block will be a forming element in urban design; a self-contained, walled-in unit of use and neighboring consensus. Its identity as a building block is an important element in conserving urban internal life because its success through time is illuminating in creating the success of urban relations.

The web of streets creates an 'island' known as a 'block' (or a group of blocks), that is, parcels surrounded by roads. The blocks have distinct sizes, mea-

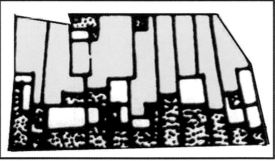

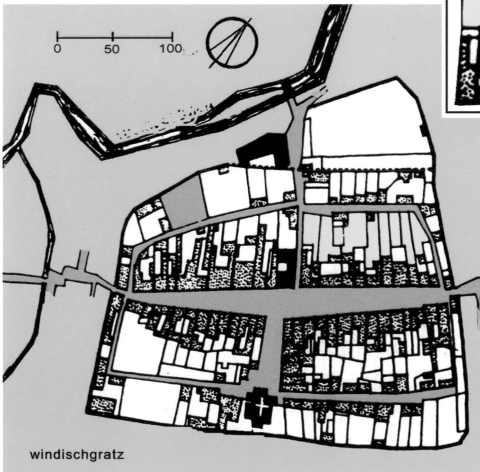

windischgratz

The old German town of Windischgratz. The old block divisions are apparent in this illustration and show that while they have been subdivided over time, they have remained true to the original nature of what the block looked like, reinforcing our recurring theme that the block and its internal division have cohesion and interrelation, that maintain each other for a long time. Secondary back roads also show that the town's original structure included many blocks that were more difficult to reach and those waited for a long time, before being subdivided into different parcels. That only happened when the back roads were formed.

Illustrative example of the basic peculiarity in the formation of a block, by land division and subdivision, existing barriers or enclosures (for cattle) organizing daily life, as well as including a pertinent system of building, to be fit for use, in such a system of land division. The grain of the buildings should be noted, as they are included in the block itself, surrounded by the necessary access ways from entrances and gates (not necessarily from the same direction). It is indicative that even in such primitive cultures, the main directions have some geometrical features.

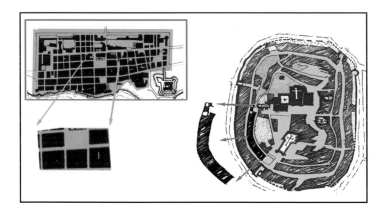

All the Roman towns in Germany show repeatedly the original formation of the ancient blocks, some being geometrical and important in the city's hierarchy, and others more accommodating to the town's structure; all have a definite character of their own and some unique qualities in the urban shape.

surements, directions, repetitions and similarities.

The form and shape of the block can be defined beginning with its internal structure – division into parcels, the nature of these divisions and the style of the building within the parcels.

The external structure is determined by size, creation of squares, intersections, typical geometry, etc.

Different shaped blocks in Paris have their source in old land division as well as the various changes that Paris underwent between the 18th and the 20th centuries, containing shapes surprising to the eye, but making at the same time an easy interconnection between major routes.

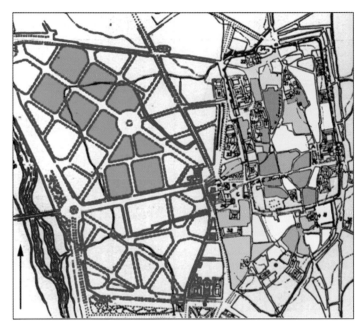

The old city of Leon, Spain, which has had few developments over the ages. Medieval walls enclosed the town, making for peculiar shapes, blocks of many directions and irregularities, some of which related to topographical difficulties, and some based on old land divisions. In a break with tradition in the mid-19th century, the town adopted a (then) modern attitude to urban design, with orthogonal and diagonal approaches to planning. The similarity of blocks can be seen in other Spanish towns, but it is important to note that they are not related to the existing in a normal way. In fact, they create a dissonant pattern when meeting each other. Only in a major square, some alleviating features may be found, in the nature of the space created, especially where the old divisions meet the new axes in a controlled way.

Paris's plan, in the illustrated district, shows clearly the similarities and differences of the shapes of the various blocks, making for the strong dynamic qualities present in this city pattern.

Old divisions in the city of Florence show
similarities in the formation of the blocks, but also
subdivisions and changes of character in each one
of them. The blocks are based on the Roman
orthogonal and regular division. The subdivisions
have helped characterize each block separately,
giving it an individuality and flavor, thus creating
an urban pattern full of internal life.

Block character lends itself to various approaches of its
analysis, one of which may be the importance of access to
parcels from both sides, back and front, all serving to define the
unusual urban character. This feature can be noted in some
places, where the service road in the back helps the front of the
block, served in a normal fashion. It can, however, be
considered as a rarity.

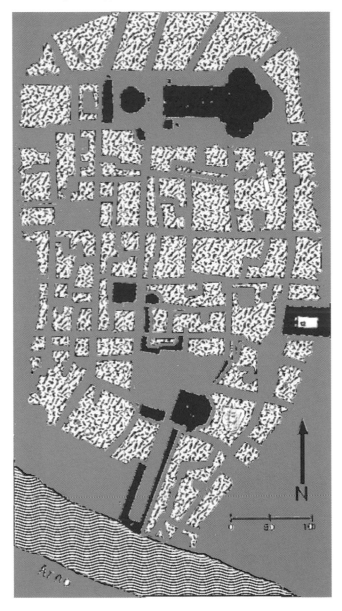

170

The Nature of the Internal Division

The block is divided into adjoining parcels that are often of similar dimensions. The parcel front, frequently reduced, has undergone divisions over the years. An increase in parcel fronts immediately lengthens the streets. A 10% increase in every parcel results in corresponding 10% increase in street length. Logic dictates that parcel width be reduced due to the high cost of streets (which is a public burden). In contrast, parcel depth is simpler to plan and serves to provide lighting and ventilation in the back. Public roads provide frontal lighting and ventilation. Each block can be identified by its unique fronts, parcels of varying lengths (varying front widths), which are characteristic of the differing typologies and periods. The reasons for their creation are economic, and they naturally undergo changes over time.

The different blocks, in the case of Venice, are formed by old canals which have served as roads and helped people, by different bridges and junctions. This constitutes a double communication system, each different from the other, one served by boat and one by foot. The shapes are quite viable, although the building methods are repetitive in their inclusion of identical plots of land, geometrical methods and spanning the similar internal divisions (see adjoining plan and diagrams). The Venetian blocks, surrounded by the canals, indicate that the right of way has a formative, basic influence on the any block's shape.

The original parcels that have been preserved are easily distinguished from parcels created later as a result of an economic need to subdivide the front for more space. The new division was created due to varying depth and width proportions, various parcel sizes, alignment and relation to public property (mainly the width of roads), limitations of walled cities, limitations by rivers and topography, ports and elements that mark the border as well as the webs. The type of division identified in this type of analysis determines the nature of the block and makes for strong interactive links.

Building Heights

The height of a given building was determined in the past and was limited for reasons beyond economics. These reasons include ventilation and lighting (blocking the sun, light and air) and selecting angles that dictate

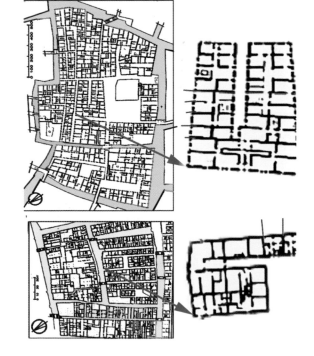

Divisions of the basic block in Manhattan, show the free-for-all system adopted in many places in the US. The regularity is not achieved by the internal divisions, but only by the repetition of a basic city block. Internal division can be fluid over time, and subdivide into very small plots or permanently remain a large parcel. Character will be kept, in such an instance, by building heights and regularity of the street front, not necessarily by repetition or similarity of ownership. In fact, it is probable that such a method will tend to be somewhat disruptive over time, as a multitude of functions can be included, in various sizes of urban divisions, as well as different owners and participants, making the mix hard to control, and not easy to grasp visually.

This modern system of land division has considerably changed the attitude towards land division and performed a unique transformation of city design, by a less rigid historical division. The claim of utter freedom is not always sustainable. Some disruptive tendencies and incoherent tendencies can be disruptive to urban qualities.

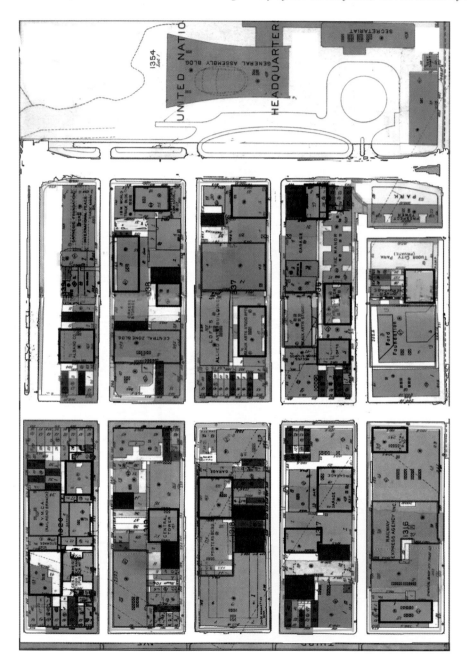

172

heights that can be regulated according to the mentioned requirements.

In other settings and circumstances, other factors determined heights. For example, the height ladders used by firefighters (London) or the ability of brick walls to bear the burden at its base without being too wide.

Factors that determined the height and volume of buildings in previous eras, along with the area of the parcel that can be used for construction, established primary con-

Olynthus, Greece, shows that a block can be subdivided into a logical, repetitive modular way, even for Western cultures. This sort of division is seen in the Far East as well. We see that secondary roads form the blocks, and those are of a similar and repetitive nature, thus forcing a strongly regulative code in city organization.

Modern Barcelona is a geometrical system of regulated block and road sizes, with small squares where roads meet at 90 degree angles. Internal block division has a free attitude to its size, sustained by a basic strong and interesting character in controlled proportions. This does not spoil the regularity and the ease of orientation basically predominant, even though the repetition can be monotonous and prevent some hierarchy to be developed and included in such systems, in the long run.

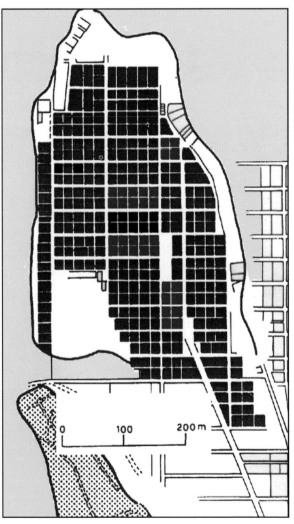

As a result of central London's regularity, helped by the internal secondary service roads, new roads have served land divisions in a very efficient way in daily life. The elongated plot of land is sometimes further subdivided, because of the inclusion of the secondary road mentioned. The regularity of the front roads, which have been kept for several hundred years, has formed the unique character of these streets and their very human and friendly scale.

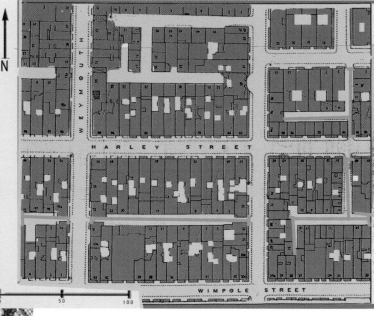

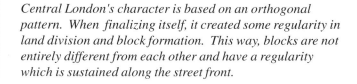

Central London's character is based on an orthogonal pattern. When finalizing itself, it created some regularity in land division and block formation. This way, blocks are not entirely different from each other and have a regularity which is sustained along the street front.

cepts such as building silhouettes, building coverage, building volume, internal height of floors and, in this manner, the general capacity of the city. The capacity and the volume, as well as the size, as stated above, are the principle components of the city's quantitative nature and economic potential.

The above describes how the city becomes three-dimensional (topography along with building dimensions) and it is essential that this important and typically urban element be emphasized in conservation. Without it, there can be no significance in urban design.

Repetition of the division, preservation of uniformity and rhythm, as well as height, create a constructed environment characterized by an internal regularity. The block creates urban volume and spaces familiar to us. Height is a partial result of street width and parcel division, which are what allow accessibility, light and ventilation, as well as privacy. Rhythm is part and parcel of the division; emphasizing our impressions of the clarity of the development and the flow of history of construction.

Internal organization in block limitations

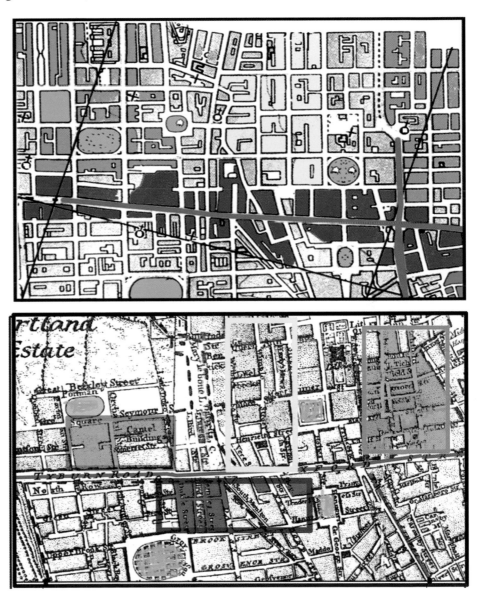

Historical division in central London, indicated by similar colors, shows that historically, the squares have sustained their life in very well, whereas the divisions had some tendencies to change themselves. We are looking at a span of several centuries. Oxford Street is marked in red, and so is the direction of Regent Street, where they intersect.

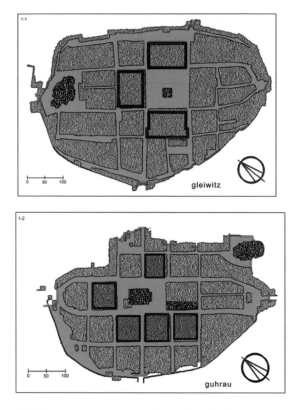

Old German town maps show that the block, in its formation, has many roles in the city. Those may be the serving and forming the front of squares, forming back roads or creating further divisions. The assumed patterns have a formative nature, which we may try to ascertain, as the geometry of a particular place, define its rules and the structural role it has.

Blocks in Piazza Navona (Rome) show the freedom of block development in this particular town, based on very old land divisions and having a peculiar set of rules, governing plot size and its position in the city web. Some of the blocks have fronts on both streets. Most have internal courts (ventilation). Some are very small or more regular. The character is maintained throughout, even though hard to define.

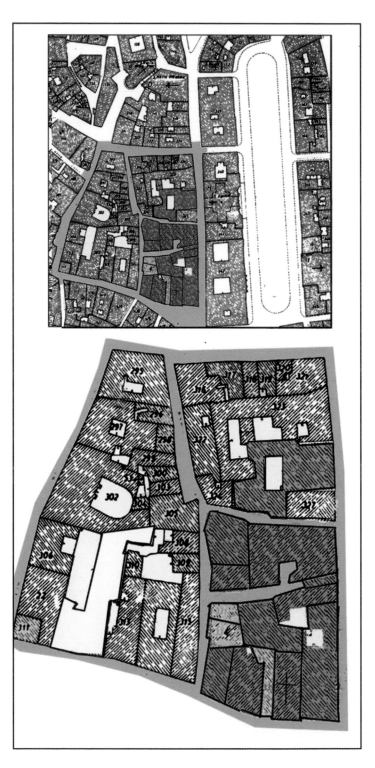

176

must be consciously characterized in order to be assessed in terms of its conservation potential. As previously mentioned, the measured elements – be they geometric or functional – can also be conserved.

Documentation of the Block

The Geometric Aspect:
· Count of various blocks.
· Distances between blocks.
· Primary measurements of the block, including height.
· Internal division – primary measurements.

· Typical cross-section of the block.

The Functional Aspect:
· Ranking the importance and link of the block to the district.
· Objectives, use, existing codes within the block.
· Internal function, borders, connections to public land.

Collection of blocks in Tel-Aviv (Israel), illustrating formation, collection and the conglomeration in an urban pattern.

Chapter Fourteen
Streets and Axes

Streets Create Blocks
Covered Bridges
The Street Front
Essential Documentation

One of the reasons of having a city life is the clarity of the streets, patterns, dimensions and relations. By the dictates of a clear structure, district blocks are being brought together to create and formulate a street, thus answering an important human need - a clear protected space for human congress.

Central alleyway and superbly designed London shortcut (Sicilian Ave. near Southhampton Row). Densely built, planned for mixed use (shops, offices and dwellings), ideally situated, on a pleasant human scale, economically viable, architecturally expressive, it can be considered as the precursor of the "protected" streets of today. It does not need protection, its planning and design provide that. An example of Italian style Edwardian design, using Sicilian marble. A superb example of on what planning and conservation can collaborate.

1. The street creates and differentiates the blocks.

In doing so, it emphasizes the design of the interior of the city, thereby enabling the blocks to exist in an exposed public manner . Practically, as well as symbolically, the street is the result of a mutual agreement of cooperation and land allocation to create a joint traffic artery for the benefit of the community. The existence of such a roadway is easily identifiable testimony to the social character of the community.

A well-defined road clearly shows that there was a public consensus to create a point of contact for locals and passers-by without undue regulation. An ill-defined street with unclear spatial dimensions cannot become such a meeting place. From a social value perspective, it actually determines that the meeting is unnecessary because a forum was not created or indicated.

Streets and roads within the city are defined as public property. The property was either designated public in advance or taken from previous private owners, due to laws of eminent domain, to benefit the public. The public maintains these roads as well. The acquisition itself is historical and the street represents a segment of urban history, and thus the length of the street is a representation of the urban weave. To a great extent, the street (the front, nature, form) is a reflection of the city. The acquisition and the division reveal the urban nature and content (as revealed through aerial photographs). Homes and walls conceal the heart of the block from observation. The creation of inner space in the back, which is not integrated as part of the street and which is controlled and selective, creates an artificial fa-

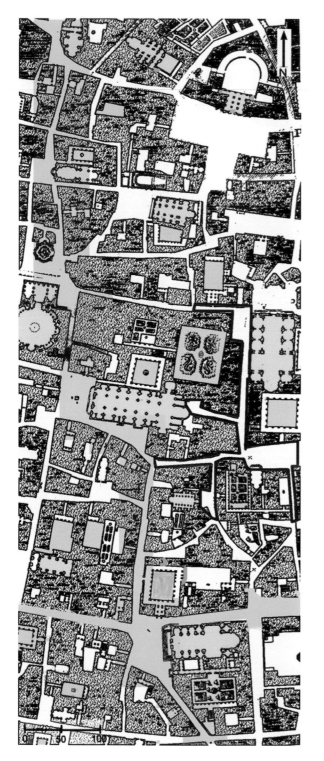

This map will illustrate the connective values and changes in a Roman street, as it serves different city functions, widening or narrowing to include interconnections between squares, other important access into the web, various churches and local public buildings.

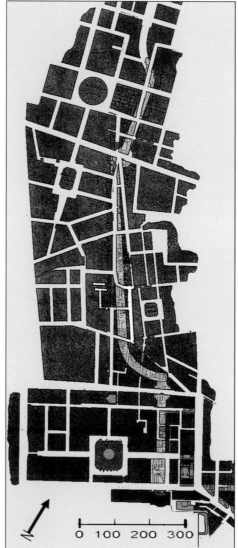

Streets can be the result of a conscious effort to form a certain local passage through a city web, for different reasons. In our case, Regent Street near Soho, formed to serve as a special avenue for monarchial purposes. This sort of formation was not the result of an organic development and is evidence to the way that streets can be formed by the power exerted by a strong government when it imposes its will, at certain periods.

cade. It is reflective of a different type of agreement: a nonrandom meeting place, with a defined objective (such as in new shopping malls). They actually contradict the existence of the traditional street, and to a certain degree, urbanism.

The street, geometrical by nature (street measurements, length, the measurement of surrounding houses by section, general direction in accordance with wind direction, cadence and change), is an urban traffic axis, with defined objectives and purpose in terms of traffic and connections.

The types of streets and their corresponding geometry can be numerous and diverse. They are old, and since they link certain elements (in fact, they are the lifeline of the city), it is fitting that their geometry be analyzed and documented, just as any other issue in conservation. Additionally, they should be classified in similar categories.

Examples of roads abound. There are those that fork and change their definition (changing width and dimensions), with central growth (boulevards), tree-lined, sidewalks, platforms, promenades or simply walkways. They change height, rising above hills, and change direction as well as definition. Extremely long and wide boulevards serve as major axes and create large blocks. Examples of the opposite include extremely narrow streets with many curves, often creating difficulties for traffic. These are the result of early urban structures, based on complex ownership (ancient complicated methods of dividing parcels and lots). Often, the street is disrupted because of public need (Hausman's Paris) and divided within the web. This sectioning is interesting since it reveals things that were previously understood but not seen, thus contributing to the understanding of the principle. The street is the result both of division into parcels and issues of private or public ownership.

The street largely reflects the age of the particular web to which we consistently refer. While buildings may be replaced, the street will preserve itself over years and over even longer periods, mainly due to public owner-

Streets can be the result of a particular city web. In the example above, we can see a few different city webs, including their resulting streets. The middle left, the city of Karlsruhe, experienced radial development, which affected street geometry in its focal point. On the middle right, Moscow's radial structure sustains a focal development.

Discovering a city's character through its different streets or facades, helps understanding. In the case below, we are looking at Rivoli Street in Paris, with its particular design, that is a careful balance of classic elements. Typically Parisian, with balustrades on the main and second stories, provide protection under the colonnade and allow the area to serve as a quieter meeting place, thus constituting the primary function of the street as a place for public meeting, like the forum of ancient times.

Streets can be designed unusually, and still preserve a certain geometrical dignity, when proportions, repetitions and clarity are heeded. These simple qualities can be unique at the same time.

ship. The public's right and duty to preserve the street is in itself a type of conservation, the importance of which is obvious. The relevant codes will not be overly complex since centralized ownership is in the hands of the public. As public property cannot be easily transferred to private individuals, it is clear that the street will have a long life, though its character will be dictated by conservation and planning considerations. While some streets are rivers (Venice or Amsterdam for example), they will still be in public hands.

The complexity of human settlements creates extensive diversity in its quantifiable components, making them worthy of special consideration. In many cases, the streets are accompanied by urban services whose purpose is to introduce essential elements into city life (sewage, water, electricity, rainwater, gas, various energy supply, information supply). Often, these are conducted through ancient aqueducts which may have been linked to the security system and maybe be incorporated in the conservation.

The variety of fronts in a city square is an example of the importance in street design of its principal view, which will serve as a visual link, by using styles, proportions, repetitions and other means to characterize and localize the public meaning of a street.

The happy combination of a street front and its design is brought about when the freedom and scale of a unique public view, the front of a street, with its undulating wave of interconnected facades of buildings, gives a relaxed and acceptable feeling to the visitor, to nature and to the human scale (Bath, England).

2. Intersections

A street has both direction and orientation, and there is a certain cadence in the distance between one street and the next. This cadence creates the street web, which is of importance and can be analyzed. While the web may sometimes be established in a single direction, webs normally intersect at identifiable points. This expresses a central urban characteristic that is emphasized in every urban analysis.

Streets, by definition, create both meeting sites in the form of squares, some of which are more interesting than others. In other cases, street corners meet geometrically at the square, creating an intersection.

The number of streets reaching this type of intersection, their width and angle, are what determine the character of the intersection or square. Historically, corner homes facing the

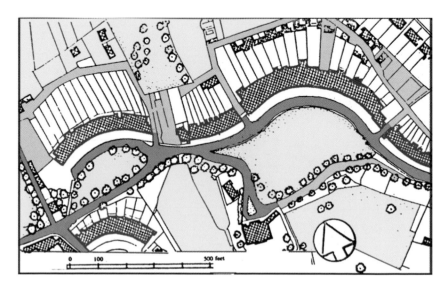

Covered arcades are
a very popular form
of offering the right
of way, on the
actually private
parcel. This occurs as if by a public agreement, making the private plot
a meeting place between neighbors or citizens, in a particular town,
square or residential area, sometimes even through a collection of
neighborhoods.

*The same use of a arcades, and the right of way under houses is, in this
instance, shown as a very natural outcome of the front of the buildings,
owed to their life on the canal. This protection is a chance to use it as
storage and circulating space for all concerned, thus showing another
agreeable method of links to the advantage of the city.*

*Streets are links between different parts of the city. In
this case, Milan's square offers a covered, sizeable
arcade, while at the same time, by sheer scale and
proportion, a forum, or meeting place, which can be
used the year round. It clearly carries a meaning which is
understood by visitors or users alike. These internal
spaces, which offer a protected frontage of buildings look
sometimes similar to a theater set. In this respect, theirs
is a protected, unreal aspect of city life.*

intersection or square are of a unique design. They are frequently designated for conservation in regulations and codes. Streets, however, should only be analyzed when paying close attention to the intersections they create.

3. The Covered Street

Covered streets (often known as passages or arcades) are generally owned either jointly or publicly, though they can be owned by private individuals and used for commercial purposes. Due to their relatively high cost and the fact that they belong to the adjacent buildings, they are generally preserved as is.

This sheltered space is one that is extremely interesting due to its direction and use as a walkway, if it is one.

Protection from weather conditions, relative comfort, use as a marker and gathering place, without any vehicles, often in central location have made the passage conservation-worthy. The passage, essentially a

This sort of street, steps connecting two districts, can be like a symbolic bridge, accommodating differences in heights and alleviates a natural incline; it serves an important role as a connection and as a passage that cannot be envisaged in any other form.

Some variety of styles can be used when the city has a clear cut spatial concept, such as this winding Jaffa street, on the right with its the ancient part, on the left a modern block, typified by its Bauhaus style. The uniqueness is felt by the rounded corners, indicative of a very ancient caravan route that existed in this place, characterized in ancient times by the city walls, replaced on the right during the end of last century.

Bridges can be important streets, due to the opportunity they offer to link a particular town or city. In this respect, they are irreplaceable. Some of them, such as the ones shown as illustrative examples, have trough centuries, offered not only protection but also commerce, as they enjoy this unique place in the city web, and serve as a meeting place to reinforce the existing link.

This further variety of street includes tree-lined boulevards, streets that meet one above the other, one turning into a bridge and streets that are simply steps bridging different topographical levels, helping overcome access difficulties. All three examples are from Jaffa, Israel.

pedestrian walkway, requires relatively large parcels. Often, it takes on the feel of a social meeting place or urban forum.

4. Covered Bridges

Bridges are natural extensions of urban roads. They may be the location of structures, stores, conservation buildings, etc. In such cases, the bridge is a de facto street.

The bridge becomes an axis situated perpendicularly over another one (the river) and represents a break in urban development. In this sense, the bridge is an urban marker, enabling urban links of utmost importance.

5. The Street Front

The front or elevation, which creates street space, can be considered a principal part of conservation, since there is a transfer from general ownership to private ownership, with the city being able to maintain control and encourage investment in this frontage.

There are instances in which only one side of the street is designated or suitable for conservation. In such cases, the tendency is to conserve buildings, and it is important to find elements common to the street front, beginning with geometrical dimensions, various building details, materials, uses of those buildings composing the conservation facade, environmental topography, etc.

Some examples of treatment and variety in streets, starting from Montpelier, then Piacenza, to the Corso in Rome (no. 8) and going on to an avenue in Paris and a Monaco quarter with the straight frontage. Here, the permanence and continuity of the history of the street is apparent, because new functions have been added, such as major city access, interconnection of various squares or reinforcing the city image, from which one can discover something about the nature of a particular city.

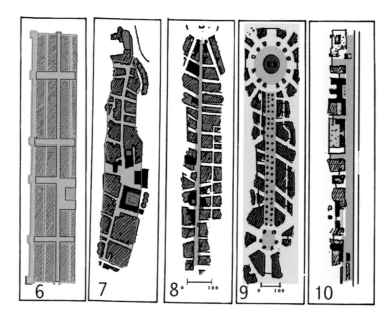

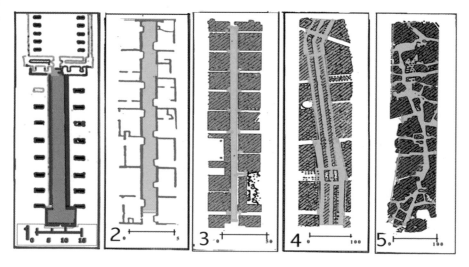

A collection of streets of ancient times, starting from Egypt to (No. 2) Celentium, a Roman encampment, no. 3 - Palmyra and no.4 - Palermo (Italy), shows the different functions that streets have fulfilled since ancient times, such as the colonnade in the tombs avenue in ancient Egypt, through the functionality of the Roman camp, the avenue-type in Palmyra and the scattered old web in Viterbo, no. 5.

Street fronts can be works of art, interrelating different buildings, connecting them visually, so as to make a whole facade, with its own terms of reference and language, creating a particular aesthetic environment which can be analyzed, and may be included in conservation studies.

An example of understanding urban space, as it is viewed from above, showing the marked cuts through the web, including well-designed fronts of buildings, but also a mark in the city body. As a place, it will many opportunities to encounter others experiencing the same urban pursuit, be it by a planned or chance meeting.

Central Brussels, one side of a commercial front, opposed to modern office blocks, serves as a reminder of what our choice is about, when discussing street alternatives.

188

The charm of an ancient technology enhances the urban uniqueness of this street in York. While the fact that it lies in a central portion of town helps its vitality, the commercial zoning is justifiable for contributing to a day to day upkeep of such preservation.

The covered passage in old Jerusalem (the Cardo) is a convenient way of building commercial opportunities in dense areas. From the legalistic point of view, the part of the property concerned cannot be isolated in terms of structural and preservationist requirements, as well as title. Some difficulties in upkeep, will be experienced.

A central street and major traffic vein in Budapest, has managed to keep a decent face of city's history. It is difficult to judge for how long life, aided by centrality, can be sustained here. Clearly, a conservation study is indicated.

A commercial street in Budapest, similar to many typical European urban environments. The clarity of space and its design have an irreplaceable quality to them.

The Street: Essential Documentation

1. Geometry:
· Dimensions: general width, sidewalks, corner radii, topographical characteristics, changes in street length.

2. Urban Objectives and Links:
· Urban hierarchy
· The type of links and quantity of traffic.
· Urban parking, both above- and underground.
· Allocation of urban services.

3. The Nature and Use of Streets:
· Elements included in the street, such as vegetation.

Modern commercial spaces in North America (Chicago and New York) cannot be called streets or familiar "urban space". This sort of planning and design is recognizable by its evocation of a European street, even if it is negative or inhuman. Urban space is maintained on a huge, empty scale.

An urban space (New York) reminiscent of European concepts of streets as a familiar meeting place.

Urban space, though quite standard, is at same time persuasive in its strong and unique clarity. Not many years ago, this sort of space was thought to be unreasonable and its adoption to be inhospitable or backward looking.

Dubrovnik, an example of a clear environment, definable and measurable; this sort of design has long since been abandoned, and lost. We can now appreciate its friendliness.

· Street front (physical and qualitative characteristics).
· The types of division on both sides of the street.
· Objective of the principal floor, as well as of other floors.
· Partial or complete roofing.
· The number of intersections, streets, alleys and gardens.
· General directions.

The tree-lined avenue of the Champs Elysee, is another example of a promenade and an important meeting place, in an important world capital. Its regular proportions, clarity and frontage all handle urban motifs successfully.

Protection from the sun is offered by a natural element, on this tree-lined boulevard in Tel-Aviv, Israel, illustrating yet another role of the street as a promenade in a man-made natural environment. A long garden, which is also a road, serves as a linkage and as a pleasant urban space at the same time.

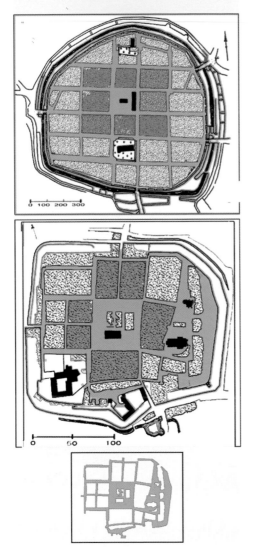

Old German towns have, as a rule, a very central square used as a market place, and as a setting for public buildings on public land. The size of the square is influenced by the modular sizes of the initial blocks and is quite generous compared to narrow streets and approaches (see separate road diagrams).

Chapter Fifteen
Town Squares

Land Uses in the Square
Maps of Town Squares

Dura-Europos - *Development and centrality of the town square in Roman times. As town size progresses and becomes limited by topography and the city wall, some changes are necessitated in the square. The size of a normal block being about 35 X 65 meters, the size of the square starts at some 140 X 190 meters and can bear to be reduced in time, which in fact happened.*

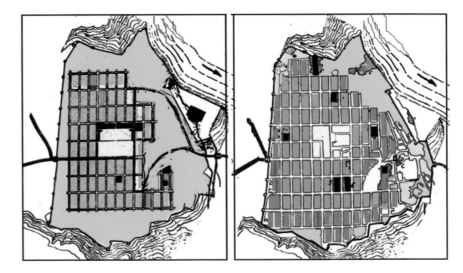

Public squares dispersed through the city help interconnect street patterns and short cuts into the web. They also have a civic spatial attribute. When successful, they can represent the city they helped form.

It is here that the essential differences between urban conservation and building conservation become clear. Urban conservation frequently discusses an issue that is virtually invisible – conservation of spaces.

The urban square, which is not composed of buildings, is an empty, publicly-owned space that is generally surrounded by buildings. These buildings shape urban space – the square.

They can take on various tones and change forms, damaging the square esthetically or culturally. The square, however, will remain. The functional value of the square should be examined in terms (other than geometry) such as the flow of inward and outward vehicle and pedestrian traffic.

1. Land Uses in the Square

Trade, residential dwellings (a combination of the two), existing uses of the square (public or otherwise), the symbolism of the square for residents, its recreational use, social or tourist functions are studied when discussing urban conservation.

The quantitative definition must be strictly adhered to and

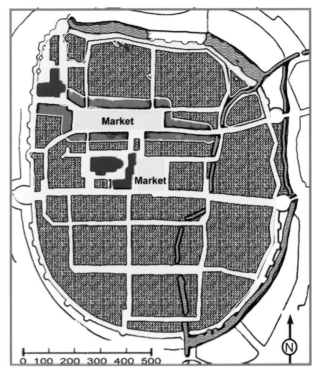

There is no doubt that the essential antiquity of a town square can and has been accommodated, in a variety of situations (Oschatz, Germany). An unusual proximity of two almost separate squares is unified by the presence of some public functions, a church and commercial shops. The orthogonality is the result of Roman influences.

***Paris**, Place Vendome. The antiquity of this monumental square and its location on a major Parisian civic axis promote the standing it has in the Parisian mind. There is no doubt that it is an esthetic and stylistic monument, and is regarded and preserved as such.*

Old Towns
The size of squares in old market towns, having some regional importance can constitute as much as 10% of the town area. On average it will mean about one half hectare, seldom reaching a full hectare. As far as symmetry of design is concerned, it is not a universal quality, especially where old formations are present. Nevertheless, this absence normally adds, rather than detracts from esthetical values.

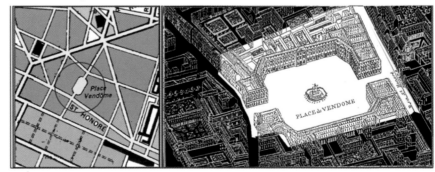

The square of Maubert lies on the important Saint Germain Avenue in Paris. It has undergone some modernization every fifty years, keeping its city role and proportion. Used even today as a clean open market twice weekly, to the full benefit of the area, and introducing life in a conserved district.

Side view of a typical London square (Cleveland Square) in which a central garden part is owned, managed and used by local residents. All dues, benefits and conservation costs are collected in a normal way. Buildings surrounding the square are protected under a few tight preservation acts.

19th century charm is retained in a Brussels square, threatened by the usual sprawl of offices. Proportions and space forming buildings are not replaceable by modern means, as they contain inner courts, established old rights of way, various traditional ownerships and have a life of their own.

exist without any particular difficulty. It defines the environment and the level of intensity of the square's characteristics in terms of regular planning.

2. Maps of Town Squares

In order to summarize the subject as part of the overall urban entity, all squares in a given city should be evaluated. They should be examined in terms of the links between them, their role in the city weave, differences, lookout points and monuments, pedestrian walkways and geographical position. The number and rate of squares should also be noted, as squares serve as important urban markers and meeting points, and are situated along pedestrian axes. Intersections in squares are likewise noteworthy. Their existence must be noted and treated by conservation. A number of examples illustrating this include corner buildings in Brussels, whose rounded corners are emphasized or which have become towers (often, a missing corner creates a square). There are examples in modern Barcelona as well, which although built on an orthogonal grid, had preplanned truncated cor-

Square with old origins and great intimacy, belonging to a specific neighborhood has local significance as it has grown out of an old village, in an old faubourg of Paris (rue Moufetard, Paris).

Contemporary
The presence and impact of a square may be changed over time. This will occur not only by treating the relevant buildings in different ways but also by subtle changes. Buildings can be renewed, but one can find that proportions have to remain constant; that is a quality to be looked for, especially in dimensions of heights related to the plan of the square.

The exact opposite of monumentality, the intimacy of this excellent example of a town square, with friendly, but decisive forming lines, in three dimensions, make it into an exquisite model.(Place de Furstenberg, Paris). Preservation and protection of the totality of such a place call for a complex method in which we involve as much of the components involved in the creation of this cultural asset.

Warsaw (Poland) The rooftops indicate demand and density increase in town centers. Some neglect of buildings is also apparent, probably due to reduced property values because of inability to control the sporadic influx.

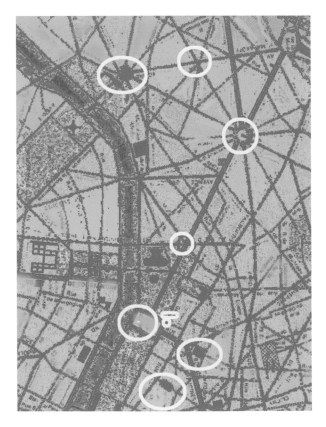

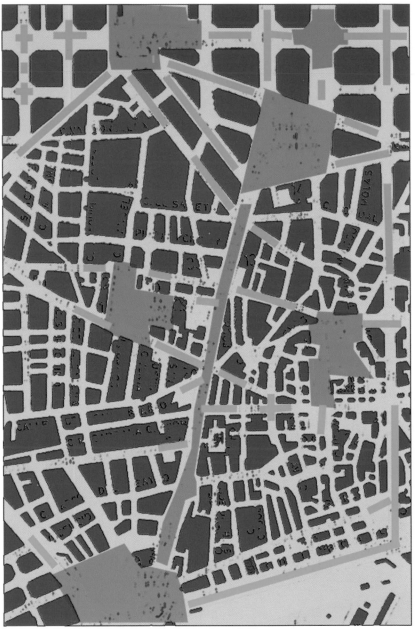

Major squares in Barcelona and Paris have, like in any important city, clear interconnections. These serve well as public squares and are dependent on each other as a system by which a town is understood and its structure remembered.

ners and, within them, smaller squares possessing an octagonal geometry, each one similar to the next. They create a square, an emphasized meeting place and regular crosswalks which then become a meeting place within the district.

Analysis of Town Squares
1. Geometry and principal dimensions
2. Major visual elements
3. Land use and objectives
4. Existing and future transportation
5. Range of the square's borders, including the buildings and axes creating the square
6. Importance to the city, linkage of axes, meaningful urban analysis

Grouping
The grouping of old piazzas has been a noticeable town attribute. In our search for town structure, we look for more than that i.e., links by way of streets and avenues, between different squares. This is a way of achieving not only clarity, but proper functioning of the town when one part enlivens the other, by a good linking artery, allowing proper expansion while maintaining coherence.

Squares in Philadelphia follow the European model of interconnecting the various landmarks. These connections are part of the network that has to be understood in the structure of the city's web.

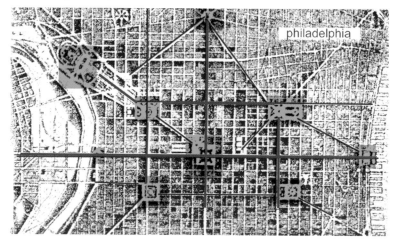

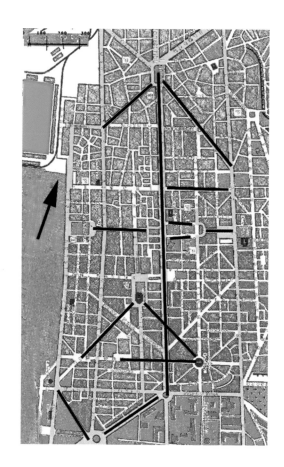

The repetition of the squares created by truncating a corner at each crossroad, means some disorientation in city structure. Conservation being considered, the clarity of the spaces created and the clear ownership makes the task easier, depending on the city will and authority (Barcelona).

Formation

The formation of modern squares has not been particularly successful. New modes of building, especially the full separation between them one encounters, is not beneficial for the creation of urban space, which needs to be protective and clear, if it is too fulfill and function as a cultural open forum, that promotes a sense of urban cohesion.

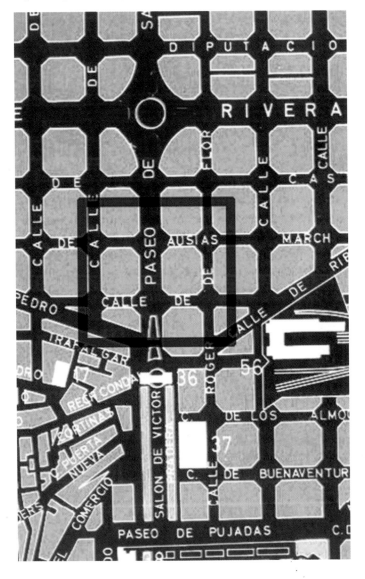

The city pattern in Barcelona is made up of squares, mostly equal in dimensions, and of mixed uses. This regularity creates a mixture of styles, somewhat unrelated, but with a city form which controls plot sizes and building heights, has a proper balance of density and use, and is very conductive to urban culture.

Truncating the angles of buildings at corners to accentuate and help visual lines (Brussels), enriches the visual expression given to the urban space. Conservation will note the design principles involved in creating the urban environment, so as to protect the principle, not the building.

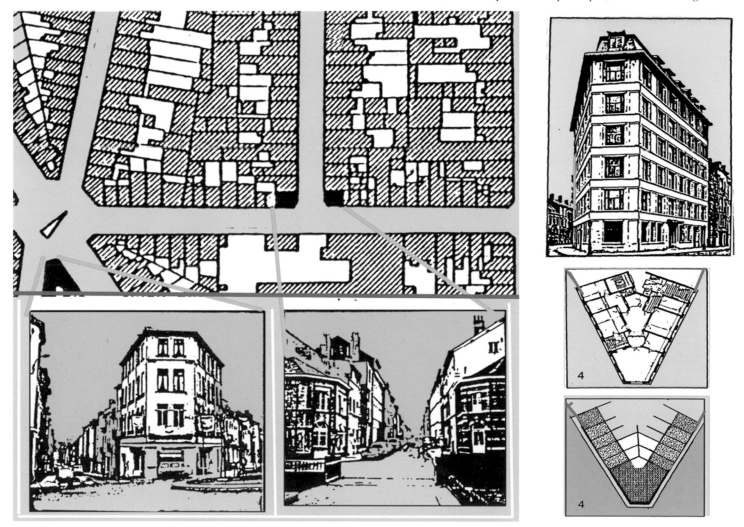

Ceske-Budejovice (Bohemia). Squares in central and eastern Europe have a tendency to a weaker presence, design and proportion. This is sometimes due to provinciality and lack of means. Nonetheless, the unifying elements are easily found in the style and acceptance of a regulatory plan.

The wealth of detail and expression are unique (Brussels) and serve the symbolic value for which they were included. Here, we have to opt for a more complex conservation study in defining preservation. This will deal with workmanship and detail, as well as with proportion and geometry.

Classical

Monumental and classical squares are present in the bigger cities and capitals. They have a role of appealing not only locally; they also carry a symbolic presence of the scale imposed and demanded by a national capital. Up to a certain size, around 150 meters by 200 meters, defined by high buildings, they will be regarded as an efficient town element with a clearly perceived space. Beyond that they lose their meaning as a communal space.

The definite importance as a town thoroughfare (Munich) has to be taken into account here. What can make a square may be the interconnections leading to the whole district.

As the square can be visually pleasing, it can also deliver messages of orientation and relating to major routes, links to other places. The proportion of buildings is such, as they help us to remember their relative position and direct ourselves (Amsterdam).

Town Square in Jicin (Bohemia) has the characteristics of a provincial attempt of a civic design but is left half done. One can feel that the region cannot support buildings on a bigger scale.

One of the oldest squares in Europe, carrying the identity of the whole of Venice in it. It combines religious, official, recreational and maritime standing all in one (not to mention esthetical values) - as the reverse and antithesis to the complexity and lack of clarity in this town. The clarity should be the most valid quality one strives to define and study.

The visual clarity in this somewhat monumental Parisian square, is the result , mainly, of the height of the surrounding buildings, ample in their command and formation of the urban space. The resulting quality, that of a defined and understandable protected function, is a quality pertaining to conservation.

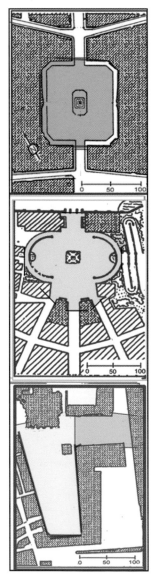

The comparative method, especially concerning elusive qualities such as public space, will be very revealing. Here, we bring together on the same scale, three familiar urban spaces as an illustration. Those are the Place Vendome (Paris), Piazza del Popolo (Rome) and Piazza San Marco (Venice). It may be somewhat surprising that they are all relatively small, when compared to spaces in modern planning. Despite their size they form a very clearly defined visual quality.

The square will often become the excuse and backdrop to urbanity, a lasting symbol of civic unity like a great sculptural presence. Irregularity in the squares presented here can have advantages with proper handling, showing that geometry can often be quite complex.

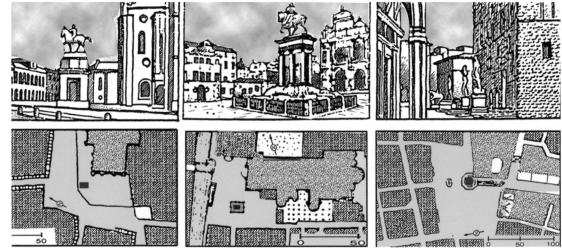

Paris

Parisian squares have a tendency to be formal (i.e. regular) and monumental. The reason may be the self importance of Paris as an immense cultural entity. It is useful to compare monumentality as a quality, to the more organic and naturally shaped squares in Italy. The symbolic message carried by the Parisian civic presence can also be contrasted to the Italian modesty of civic squares as an important comparative habit of study.

The mixed urban uses (one of the buildings is a school) are helped by the covered pedestrian arcade. Introducing city's axes through make this big square have a beneficial effect on circulation. Heights are not very great and allow for the density expected in this central location.

The central part of the square is devoted to a protected city park, very useful for continual life in the square and traffic/ parking eventual solutions. It is situated so that it offers shortcuts and recreation.

A carefully designed city square with beautiful proportions (Place de Vosges, Paris) used to be the seat of aristocrats and monarchs. The regularity of its facade is based not only on geometry (thus facilitating the definitions for any conservation) but on plot sizes as well, which helps in the constant upkeep and preservation of its architecture.

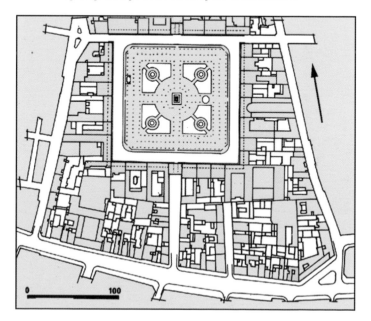

0   100

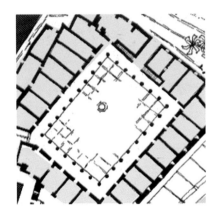

Chapter Sixteen
Markets and Covered Ways

Arcades and Khans

The ease of public interaction in covered spaces and, of course, in markets, has had its influence in the development of a town. Thus, their urban standing is always important and worth preserving.

In conservation, it is important to maintain urban, public and private links, including easy access, permissible usage, maintenance and purchase.

The covered passages of Bologna make up for a lot of the special look of this city, mainly in the historic sector. In this, they constitute a living museum of this particular feature of traditional urban design. The protection they offer is obvious; less obvious is the visual quality of a continuous place fit for human discourse and comfort. The city's hospitality is thus apparent. In terms of preservation, being mainly on private property but used publicly, they point out the agreement on constant and everyday common upkeep and repair.

One of the more attractive city fronts in Genoa (Italy) is made up by the ample proportions of an arcade formed in the main streets. It is an irreplaceable meeting place, protecting shops and restaurants, as well as the permanent outlay of tables on the covered pavement. Because of the important civic use, its upkeep and preservation are assured.

When the public right of way goes through a major building and becomes a shortcut as well - a chance is offered to obtain an internal civic space and turn it into a natural forum. This is the case with our example adjoining the Piazza di Duomo (Milan). The size and dimensions, plus the use of natural light, performs the unique achievement of an internal space shaped and designed as an exterior.

Marketplaces, many of which are located within passages and covered ways, are usually operated by the city, though the land itself may be privately owned. Large interior yards, legally accessible to the public are, by definition, an additional challenge for conservation due to their nature and public interest. We will also mention a Middle Eastern-based element, the urban khan or caravansary (similar to a way station). A large majority of the large urban khans currently act as squares, especially in the Middle East. Khans serve as way stations for tourists and convoys. Their history is sometimes linked to monasteries, assembly centers and prayer halls, as well as to markets. From an architectural compositional perspective, they are different from

The arcade surrounding the public square of the Vosges (Paris) makes it more usable year round and offers a more inviting front to one of the most intimate Paris squares, small in size, very central in location. Liked by all, it serves as a local shortcut and creates an atmosphere of relaxation.

Another example of urban space created by the arcades in Bologna.

One of the rare examples of an ancient court possessing the advantage of a covered passage, acting as a shortcut in a busy street, serving as a market place near the port. This is reminiscent of the same old functions in the Mediterranean tradition which have shaped so much of our architecture. It can almost be called an archetype, its shape and simplicity are evocative and easily adapt to changing and complex uses. (Old Khan in Acre, Israel).

The city of Acre, Israel, contains a few covered market streets that have fallen out of use. As this historic city has lost its regional role since the war of Independence(1948), it has proved impossible to preserve their formations and use, despite a few attempts, because the city has lost its role and function.

the urban squares because they are a planned, homogenous composition of buildings.

The buildings that define the 'khan' are integral to it, and the land on which they are set is privately owned. Property ownership will indicate essential differences – often the fact that the owners are not city residents.

The space is defined a great deal more since the khan is an interior square generally not intersected by streets and traffic.

Conclusion

Study the following:

1. Geometric dimensions
2. Fronts and volume
3. Various urban links
4. Land use

The Rialto (Venice) is a unique example of a covered commercial street, serving as a bridge and shopping place. Title, ownership, and maintenance are unclear, but the usefulness of this example and its location will preserve it well into the future.

The enormous market of Istanbul is a living prototype of the importance of this function in a town. Very spread out, subdivided, correct in function, it does not tamper with everyday life; on the contrary, it contains every activity that in other places would be considered harmful to the environment. Wisely contained and wisely used, it is a major human asset.

Chapter Seventeen
Observation Points

Urban Conservation Aspects

The way we observe our built environment and understand its overall effect and state has been important to city dwellers. This has led to important observation points of various vistas; visitors will always want to understand.

Urban observation points are created in topographical areas that allow or require gardens or open spaces, from where the city can be seen from a distance and from above.

They serve as markers on trails and vista points of city squares or of the general scenic view. By looking down on the city from above, it is much simpler to observe and understand its structure and topography. Just as other urban elements described above, observation points also have specific distinguishing characteristics that are not limited to their geometry. These characteristics are unique, as the vantage points were built to enable long-distance observation.

They will be defined not only in terms of the radius

Historical methods of heavy construction works can be studied from a vantage point. Thus retaining walls, bridges and aqueducts can be fully appreciated as one of the many formations underlying the complexity of a town.

Looking at Toledo from the outskirts, city and hills appear as a view common to many paintings through history; this reinforces the belief that a structured view becomes a symbolic concept. Thus we can perceive the importance of a facility provided as a vantage point.

The old fortress and palace of Topkapi (Istanbul) is a vantage point of importance, controlling by sight the sea approaches, but offering a possibility of understanding city formation. It is both a preserved museum and citadel: its central tie to Istanbul is in the nature of the topography.

Comprehending the town's structure from a vantage point, helps understand the cohesion of life in the city. The occasional openness necessary for civic cohabitation can be obtained by such vistas, quite apart from the pleasure the onlooker can have in grasping the formation of the urban web. (Outskirts of Vienna).

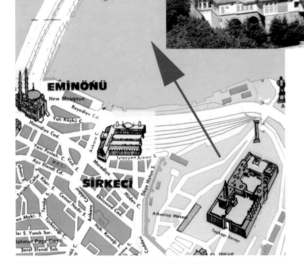

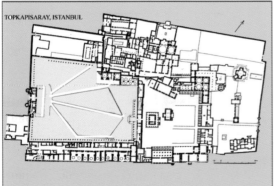

Heidelberg's University and castle are in themselves observation points. Situated in a hilly region , the possibilities of observation in and of Heidelberg being offered by many terraces and vantage formations.

observable from them, but also by what is actually viewed. Access, parking and length of stay are also to be defined. Additional elements in the vicinity of the urban vantage points are inherent to the singularity of the site. These include materials used, age, regional history and unique scenic aspects.

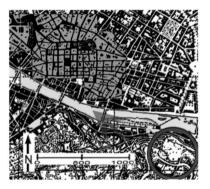

Often, the vantage point itself lends urban significance to an otherwise insignificant area. There are instances when the comprehensive urban picture can only be understood from the well-placed observation point – making it clear in urban terms.

The Urban Conservation Aspect

Conservation, from the ownership and the physical aspect, must incorporate the relation to the element of unobstructed long-distance view.

This can be extremely complicated because of various obstacles, buildings, hills etc. In such instances, scenic or garden planning will be essential, so as to obtain a good view of the city.

Requirements

1. A viewing range of clearly defined urban objects.
2. Planning, sometimes in detail, land use accordingly.

Conclusion

1. Geometrical aspects
2. Land use (zoning)
3. Preservation of the view
4. The natural element, i.e., parks and gardens.

Looking at Florence from the observation terrace, will enhance the sociological aspect of understanding the urban environment and foster the reason for embracing urban culture.

Topography is used in establishing locations of good observation. At a glance, not only town structure is understood, but also construction methods, principal roads, heights, etc. This visual contact can be greatly appreciated in historical sites, which tend to be complex and can be better grasped from above.

PART FOUR

Secondary Urban Elements

I ntricate urban life evolved trough history and calls for a series of secondary elements in its final formation. These have to be evaluated and incorporated into a comprehensive system. Secondary elements are often dealt with, but only on a local basis.

An urban preservation program will introduce a more general meaning to these efforts, by leading to an understanding of their urban role.

Chapter Eighteen
Special Sections

Educational Sites
Religious Sites

As mentioned previously, primary elements are directly related to the urban structure. They are inherent to all cities. The district, block, parcel, street and square are all building blocks of the urban structure and the creative forces behind it. The city is the result of the interaction between the primary components, their physical dimensions and positions. The overall (or local) city web controls the entire entity. The role of urban conservation is to identify the primary components and determine which of them should be preserved, as well as the reasons, conditions and means of doing so. This chapter will identify additional components that are not intrinsic to all cities, meaning that they may be found in some and not in others.

An additional group of elements prominent in urban structure are blocks and districts which appear only sporadically and are not directly linked to the urban structure. These are considered secondary elements. Although a city can exist without them, these elements add a uniqueness and diversity to the city, enriching urban culture.

Secondary elements develop regularly in a receptive city web. They are often involved in cultural presence. Protection is needed so as to retain their central role, an important addition to what cities are about.

Of an exceptional and methodical construction, the Rila Monastery (Bulgaria), is an excellent example of studied preservation. Its size (it covers more than two hectares) makes the building fit for a study of continuous conservation techniques. It is a major tourist attraction of museum quality , making its upkeep possible by its renown, like many similar examples all over Europe.

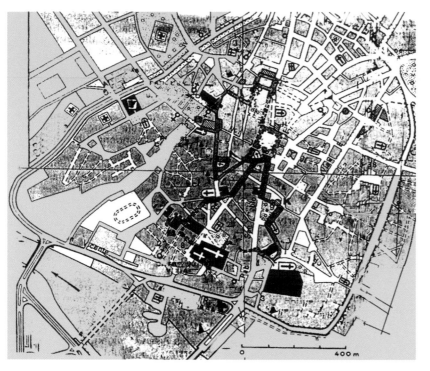

Universities have developed their own patterns, links and internal relations; they are not always related to other city patterns. This may be due to their relatively ancient self sufficiency. (Salamanca, old university town in Spain).

One of the most famous of all religious districts (The Vatican) is noted for its contributing effect to the life in Rome. As far as the city structure is concerned, this fact is striking, because it offers one of the biggest existing squares . Other relations to the town of Rome are not unique and can be somewhat disappointing.

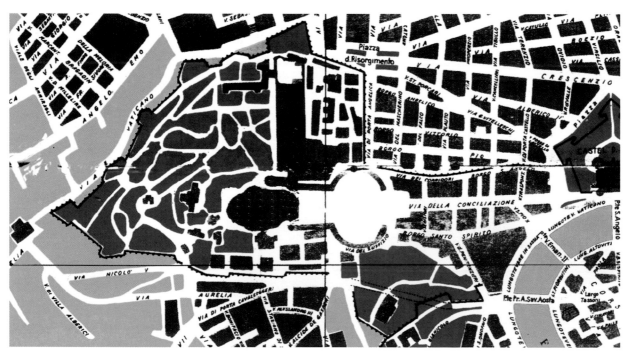

1. Educational Sites.

These districts possess a distinctive character, sometimes resembling a college town and sometimes a monastery (see Cambridge or Oxford, which have old educational districts), and have the feel of an ancient and historical tract, within the existing web.

The internal links are completely different from those found in the surrounding area.

The urban link, generally unique and exclusive, includes a diverse range of solutions and passages, peculiar to these districts.

The university district has its own characteristics pertaining to its areas of construction, the number of users, age of the structures, the nature of public or semi-public passageways, and linkage properties to the surrounding city. By definition, these districts have a

The Monastery of Rila is well documented and measured, as a necessary preamble to its maintenance. Recording almost every stone, this drawing is a good reference as to how preservation studies are conducted .

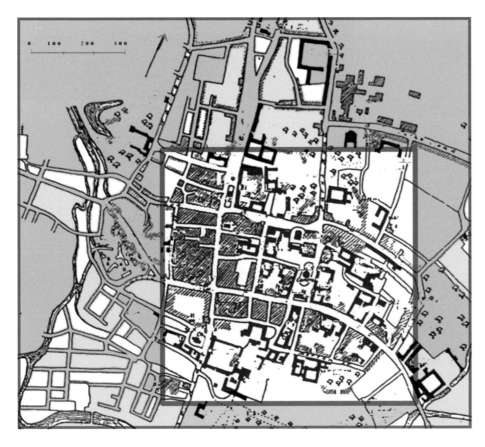

Land ownership in an university town can be disruptive, creating obstacles to development by having an alternative circulation system, parallel to the normal one. It is apparent how this can constitute a barrier in city life, if not organized in a clear, noncompetitive system. These alternative passages with their own rules and a differing urban role, introduce a life of their own into the city. This is the argument for the conservation and the encouragement of such institutions as encouragement to the urban spirit. (Plan of Oxford, England.)

An example of a the well-kept monastery, with an exceptional size and setting (The Rila Monastery, Bulgaria). This is one of a long series of old cloisters, respected and maintained voluntarily.

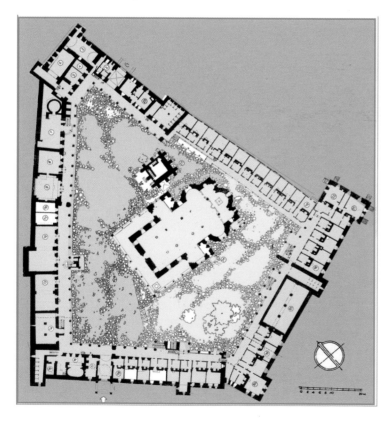

This prominent holy place (the central mosque in Acre, Israel) has an central urban role, and is well preserved and maintained. The unique internal setting is reminiscent of the use of the courtyard in some Mediterranean monasteries.

tighter bond to the city than religious districts do.

Pedestrian traffic through universities should be noted, since it raises the status and nurtures conservation.

Returning to the analysis of urban status and geometry of land parcels, although ownership will be simple, conservation management within the district may be complicated, due to the university's hegemony over its own land.

The university administration's natural desire is to act independently. Nevertheless, a city interested in being known as a 'college town' will want to invest in conservation and ensure that public passageways remain open, thus granting it an advantage in tourism, among other things.

A major part in the city web of Bologna consists of important monasteries and cloisters, which do not always fit the urban network, but have an importance as a regional attraction. The relative repose they bring about, has its own commendable quality, even when this is of a visual nature only.

From a design perspective, there can be no question as to the visual impact of major sites, such as the Vatican's masterly shape. However, the structural effects on street patterns and webs can be seen to create circulation problems, as well as some impairing of visual links.

The Church and Cloister of Dormizion (Old Jerusalem), are not indicative of an urban role; nevertheless they have world renown. A well-kept example of a distinctive section, it has a visual impact on its surroundings, together with the embracing wall and the outstanding visual poise on the turning point of the hill.

The visual impact of the island of Saint Michel has preservation value while being of world renown. It is both distinctive as a monastery, an island, and a fortress of an outstanding profile. This sort of visual impact has its own symbolic values.

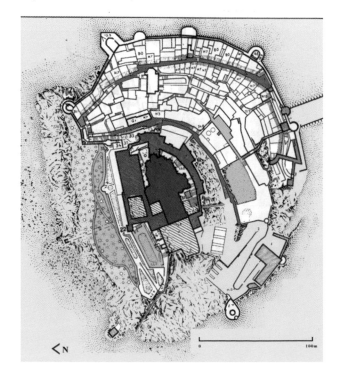

Numerous examples of these types of cities exist, a prime example being Salamanca, Spain. Salamanca's university district is constructed on a Roman web. This district, relatively detached from the city, is difficult to approach since it never established good links with the web. Despite the surrounding difficulties, a link of this type has to be established, to help the status of conservation.

2. Religious Sites

Religious sites are often clusters of buildings with unique histories, objectives and properties. Monasteries, incorporating churches, which have developed gradually, own large areas of land, and serve as a good example.

The monastery, generally made up of a garden, residential quarters, study halls, library, spiritual center, even walls and other security measures, is a special district with a definite religious character.

Monasteries have traditionally been considered worthy of conservation. When the grounds of the monastery contain a number of buildings, the size of the area often justifies referring to it with the term district.

Though the Vatican is a case unto itself, it serves as a superb example of this concept. For the most part, these districts exist in cities that either have rich histories in Christianity, Islam (as is evidenced in cities in Turkey), or the religions of the Far East (monasteries in China, Japan, Tibet).

The crucial factor for conservation is the urban presence of this section and its implications for the environment. Likewise, the geometrical-physical characteristics will factor in to the analysis.

University buildings, especially those of long standing, are functionally distinguished from the surroundings in size, materials, style, etc. The town of Oxford (see map) contains a multitude of such edifices, most of which, even when recently built, contain the element of uniqueness and thus are a subject fit for study.

Distinctive districts and sections have important urban roles. The visual contribution is the introduction of some different organization or pattern in the local web. Thus the quadrangles in Oxford offer visual relief in a densely built urban pattern (see map).

Chapter Nineteen

Cultural Monuments

The Cultural District
Castles and Citadels

The urban monument is created because the city is central. This is where presentation of symbols is most normally welcome.

A cluster of museums can be viewed as a cultural district, e.g., the Victoria and Albert Museum, the National Museum of Science, the Museum of Geology and the Mu-

In this example, the city web is included in the citadel, because the entire city of Toledo, including its major buildings, is considered to be a whole tourist and conservation site. It has all necessary elements to maintain itself, including a seven story underground parking garage (dug into the hill). This conservation attitude to the old urban structure, has been successful and has become one of the major sites to overcome the barrier of cost. It is a living example of urban attitudes and life-styles.

The reason for this success is the link to the town of Madrid, and close parts of Spain. This is accompanied by the understanding of its roads, hills and upkeep, the reliance on a few industries maintaining their place in the town fabric, and the efforts made to functionally operate this major structure, are all contributing factors.

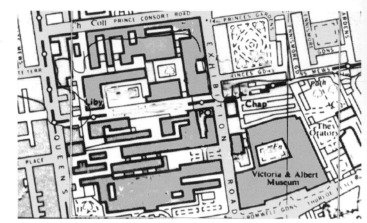

The Natural History Museum (Kensington **London***) one of a variety of important buildings and sites, introduces a unique and special quality to the surroundings. One museum in this complex is the Victoria and Albert museum, with its strong presence added, constituting an important urban element. The presence of important buildings, museums and libraries of various functions in Kensington show that the centrality of a big city is the place where urban culture will develop in a sustained way. Its presence will be felt through centuries, and is naturally pointed out as an important sector of urban conservation.*

The necessity of reinforcing the urban web by all possible cultural additions, and not dispersing them through the entire region, as is very often the case, is presented in the example. This is the way in which the mutual presence helps the creation of unique city sections, better understood and better used. The extent of the cultural complex is quite pronounced, as the map indicates, and it covers approximately 500 meters square (Exhibition Rd., London).

Monuments in public squares have an esthetic and sometimes historic role in enhancing the extent of city structure, showing what the urban system is all about. (Nancy)

Monuments, some with ornamental gates, serve as ornamentation and important focal points and have their own system of gardening and preservation. They constitute another link in urban life with self preserving attitudes. (Nancy).

seum of Nature in Kensington, London. We frequently find large groups of buildings (a district) well integrated within the city, having a cultural role while being publicly owned. Public access and usage makes them unique.

Cultural districts possess an independent life within the city web. Although their appeal and importance can undergo changes in terms of city life, in terms of conservation they are unique. In addition, unique districts that are not targeted for conservation, but have implications, possibly negative ones, on urban structure, cannot be overlooked. Conservation efforts will refer to them with a certain amount of criticism.

There can be centers such as military bases, administrative centers and offices, which though not currently significant, carry historical importance. Their functions, use and definition may have changed.

Conservation, while partial, will assist in treating the different changes over time.

The characteristics required in this district survey include: ranking urban importance (also in comparison to other elements); amount and size; land appraisal; important urban and regional links; existing and potential uses; ownership and maintenance; existing codes; transportation and parking.

Within the above cultural districts, other features such as structural elements, city markets, historical gardens with important ramifications for the city, can be included. In some instances this can go as far as reinforcing walls, ditches, etc.

Portrait of the Cultural District

Function and size:
Property Ownership:
Urban and Regional Link:
Existing and Potential Use:
Maintenance, Parking, etc.:
Existing Building Codes:

Important monumental landmarks are exemplified by the L'Arc de Triomphe (Paris). This has a beneficial influence on its surroundings by forcing a measure of conservation in all that is associated with it, because of its locality and importance.

The old bridge (Prague) serves both as an important link between the two parts of the city and as a monument of the presence and consciousness of the town's spirit, history and style.

The Duke of Norfolk's castle, an English example of conservation of special monuments, contains the symbolic consciousness related to such projects, and plays a role in presenting the attitude necessary in major preservation projects of gardens, parks, old ramparts and castles.

The beneficial influence of the civic presence of palaces, having their own system of design and building. This presence is also maintained by a measure of awareness of what is essential in conservation. In order to maintain important buildings with their relation to the adjoining streets and features, urban conservation maintains a civic function. (Melk Monastery and Castle).

All citadels, palaces and castles that have been created with a protective role are very frustrating in terms of their connection with urban patterns or even civic functions in existing webs. The answer lies in land ownership and possible changes in the principal function of the place, (very difficult to carry out). The necessity of maintenance has to bring about new uses in order to create a new attractive feature of communal life.

Castles and Citadels

Occasionally, in a prominent and important site within an ancient city, a fortress, unlike any intended for military use, can be found. Such a fortress is known as a citadel and has historically fulfilled a different role than a regular fortress. Its function within city limits (either at the city borders or in the center) was not always for defense (in our day, as a tourist attraction) but occasionally was used for trade.

The most unique feature of a citadel is its topographical structure. It is generally situated on top of a round hill with winding access roads, all of which contributing to its uniqueness.

Citadels are generally, but not always, surrounded by walls and contain a variety of structures in close proximity to each other. Sometimes, these structures are from different periods, of various styles and even situated on parcels that are extremely difficult to define. The citadel, with its various structures and links to its surroundings, is situated within a framework of public passageways that were constructed with different purposes in

Some functions of entertainment and sport are included in the city pattern, because they have their own attraction, not always beneficial to their surroundings. Their overall activities necessitate additions of roads and parking, which are not helpful to the environment. They are mentioned because of some uniqueness they may carry.

The old castle of Edinburgh, a citadel and feature of normal city life, has a great deal of activities taking place in it, to the benefit the whole town. However, only the access road is part of the town web. It is the castle's visual presence which is attractive.

Old Jerusalem, including the Dome of the Rock, is considered to be a citadel, and plays an important symbolic and religious role around the world. It looks forbidding in its inclusion in an urban pattern, because it cannot be well interwoven with it, being big and fully enclosed. It is separated from the surrounding area and problematic in the city web; however, it has never ceased to be a major attraction.

The citadel sometimes includes religious buildings. The town may be very closely knit into the citadel, but topographical difficulties will inhibit the challenge of including it into the town fabric.

The Citadel of Segovia with its forbidding structures has not managed to be included in a major conservation undertaking, and it still cannot be cited as an example of urban attitudes.

mind and did not develop as normal urban webs. The physical size of the citadel is important when defining its topographical aspect, in terms of distances, because of the difficulty of access.

Finding a way to make a citadel link to an existing web is almost impossible. The Temple Mount in Jerusalem is a form of citadel. On the Temple Mount are holy sites and observation towers, both connected to the surroundings by some gates. Those can be conserved, even though they vary periodically. When the roads and links to the surroundings are more important than the preservation of buildings, urban planners must look for solutions that can contribute to city life. The district may contain a castle the dimensions of which extend beyond regulation size buildings, extending beyond the area defined as the district, and containing other functions. Just as with other topics discussed, here, too, urban links, beyond ownership and physical geometry, are emphasized.

A special district can also include an amusement park, a zoological park, a garden containing sporting functions, a form of entertainment anyway. All the above can very often contribute to urban life.

The specialized district in Odessa (Ukraine), including the famous "Potyomkin" steps has undergone conservation. The buildings concerned are mostly municipal, containing a local museum and offices

The Alhambra (Granada) is a popular landmark as a citadel, but is not completely included into the city web. Well maintained, it succeeds in overcoming the difficulties by having a good tourist reason for its existence.

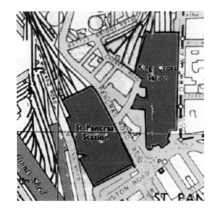

Chapter Twenty
The Unique District

Islands and Ports
Rail Stations

The centrality of cities transforms them into receptacles of specialized function; sectors worthy of study and consideration of preservation are always present.

A district can be considered a unique district, when it contains workshops, industry, transport etc. with a demand of special and controlled environmental quality. It may constitute an important link within the city web, with other parts external to it. Industry or transport, and their influences on the surrounding urban environment (as a train station, platform or port, for example), can be considered dominant, decisive dis-

The port of Odessa contains a conserved, old wall. This will serve us a reminder that conservation can apply to many sections, districts and users. It is the will to conserve that counts.

Ports are sometimes tied to an island and associated with it. This has a close relation with the topography and the seashore treatment, as far as buildings on the shoreline are concerned. The town benefits from the port's presence and has an added reason for continuing the relationship with a major natural element.

Ports can have fishing activities, in which case they exist for the livelihood of the fishermen. These fishing towns have fewer commercial activities; mainly storage and living quarters add a lively presence on the shore.

tricts in terms of a city.

A good example of this occurs in London, which has a series of train stations - Euston, Saint Pancreas, King's Cross (in this order), including the underground as well as the hotels above them and, of course, the railway tracks – that are urban disruption but also a focal point.

This district should be considered in a special way that has a double meaning and requires innovative planning guidelines (partially conservation–oriented.). Conservation cannot ignore districts such as these,

The unique district can be represented by a specialized building like a major hospital (the Hadasah center, Jerusalem)

Many railroad stations at the turn of the century were designed to be a feature of the local urban situation and a reinforcement of urban elements of streets or squares. Train stations are not designed like this any longer, an indication that our century's urban spirit is on the decline. Train stations are becoming less popular and less embedded in the local pattern.

not only because they are mostly located adjacent to webs that should be examined, but also because their presence contributes to daily life, even when it is problematic.

Ports

The natural port: links the city to distant surroundings through sea or fishing expeditions. A key factor in urban formation, rivers and natural ports provide opportunities for trade (necessary for development) and long-term economic growth.

The majority of functional ports have been artificially constructed. They are used intensively and their needs have a tendency of rapid changes, as technicalities of port usage normally do, this in turn making demands on the environment.

The port includes structures, forms of ownership and complex operations which sometimes conflict with the desire to perceive them as natural environments and their existence as an industrial zone. A port can be an urban focal point that adds to the surrounding urban environment. In other cases, ports can be obstacles, delaying and disrupting local development. Examples abound.

Ports have a specialized function in the city web. The function that leads to water communication and buildings facing the water. This is important in a city web, since the external communication enters at this symbolic gate. In terms of conservation, the key points are the promenade along the shore, the port, the commercial activity and what the city shows of its exterior across the water.

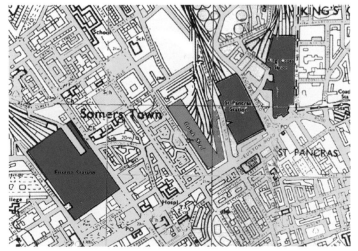

Some great stations of the 19th century in London, including Euston station, St. Pancreas station and King's Cross station, all face a major thoroughfare and were all designed to add their own presence to the center of town. In this respect, they constitute an asset to the city in terms of conservation. The urban features they add offer a great unequalled opportunity and will remain a very useful central attraction.

Chapter Twenty one

Building Methods

Survey of Secondary Elements

Building methods are the external facets of culture. Their development over time, as observed in cities, cite an important human trait - materials and workmanship mark an achievement of coherence and mutual consent.

Building methods, e.g. eclectic (popular construction), specialized technology, coating or processing, can be elements worthy of conservation. Occasionally, the construction materials themselves, the roofs, windows (different from building to building) or methods typical of a period, can establish planning clarity.
This may mean that it is worthwhile for them to be incorporated in conservation plans.

The normal way of approaching building methods is seen in this building of a Bulgarian monastery. Colorful and natural materials have been used with old Roman arches to give a good variety of form, a mixed building technology, without using a particular style, remaining natural and free.

Building methods are normally associated with certain buildings. In towns like Karlsruhe (Germany), building methods can be considered as an organization of an entire city in a radial manner. This is an urban design approach, in a totality that will direct the building methods to be derived from a systematic and centralized formula. Conservation features in such environments will be much easier to formulate, since they closely follow the existing planning approach.

Building methods can be popular and localized systems (Turkey), adopted as a method in many towns and villages, even across Eastern Europe. This particular one comprises the recurring repetition, stories hanging over the stories below. This is clearly a local (no architects) building system. Building methods are normally associated with materials and technology, and should be classified accordingly.

Ancient building methods are also found in archaeological sites and are typical of objects in conservation. This conservation can be termed mosaic, with interest depending a great deal on the type of overall urban link, its potential as a tourist attraction or a site that may be developed in the future, within the limits of conservation guidelines. The land ownership and its subdivision should not be abandoned; as always, sizes of plots or parcels influence the way a building may look. Every study of an edifice must be accompanied by study of the purchase of the land on which the structure is situated, because the buildings are a result of property subdivisions and shapes of the plot of land.

The Survey of Secondary Elements

Urban Geometry
1. Size and layout of buildings, in a geometrical analysis
2. Building methods and parcel directions.
3. Reserve or empty land and future objectives, related geometrical factors.
4. Changes and later additions

Shapes formed by using flat materials, such as copper or lead sheet can be varied. These materials used to be an important way of handling rooftops. (Istanbul).

Thatched roof formation, a familiar building method, seen in the center of the Frankfurt Zoo, is an outstanding example of three-dimensional design formed by old methods and ways of achieving form.

A desert system of domed buildings. The system is illustrative of one form, having the potential of creating a multitude of certain structures. All subsequent filling in, of the urban organization, up to street formations, courtyards and block repetition, stem from this building block.

The well-known method of building towers stems from the Middle Ages and was adopted in San Geminiano (Italy). These towers were used for protection and were an important part of homes. Today, their remains serve as an example of an urban method of developing a protective system on which the building will subsequently be based. A reminder of the early provenience of our modern blocks with their elevator cores.

Urban Importance and Status

1. Urban link: roads and their hierarchy, in the direction of the city and in other directions
2. Types of land ownership and building ownership, special internal division
3. Objectives and existing activities over a period of time

Means of Conservation

1. Development of urban links
2. Encouragement of functions
3. Land arrangement and building regulations
4. Conservation prototypes
5. Renewal of building codes
6. Enforcement of urban and national codes
7. Definition of secondary divisions, land uses and intensive use
8. Definition of responsibility for advancing conservation

A unique building method, the Roman aqueduct in Segovia (Spain) illustrates the preservation qualities inherent in old materials and methods.

A local by-law, introduced by the British Mandate, enforces external building materials in Jerusalem to be of stone. It is an apt conservationist move, which has had good success. The example shows elevations of modern buildings.

PART FIVE

Nature's Role

Nature has always been considered to have a major role in urban life. Cities' well being and function call for the understanding of nature in its underlying effect in preserving town's structure, and participation in its success.

Chapter Twenty Two
Topography

Nature was not generally considered an element requiring conservation protection. However, modern pressures within cities, including new forces (demand for parking, density, air quality, changing demographics) have made it necessary to implement conservation measures for an important urban element: the element of nature, especially when it lies in close proximity to the city web. With the abandonment of historical centers, it is apparent that many elements of nature will be neglected. A study of the urban relationship and inclusion of natural components within directives adapted to the conservation methods, is important not only for gardens or nature but also for the entire city web, as it has implications that may be so major as to transform natural elements into a central component in planning.

Many historical cities draw their uniqueness from natural terraces, hills, winding roads, unique attributes or from their location on lakeshores or mountains. There also must be a link to national plans of the natural environment (such as national legislation regarding national parks, nature and scenic values, shores, etc.)

An excess of nature views is undesirable, especially in relatively densely populated areas as they may hinder man-created space. Urban nature can also delay development or become an obstacle, such as in flooding or land slides. We, therefore, advocate a general measure that forges bond between nature and urbanity.

The way we deal with nature in our urbanity explains our attitudes to life on this planet. Thus, nature has a role in our grasp of cultural development, i.e., the extent of change the human habitat has brought to nature; a contrast full of visual meaning.

Unique topography adds scenic views to the overall urban structure.
The very existence of unique topography or special land, e.g., a mountain, ancient caves or ancient terraces within a city, valleys alongside hills and city parks, must be referred to as a horticultural, and not architectural, element to be preserved, while retaining their urban function.
Naturally evolved cities, built on a hillside or mountain – are a kind of natural, undefined fortress which exploits both natural and artificial terraces which emphasize the topography - and are easily classified in this category.
The daily links to city life - walkways to city districts within it, views, gardens and history are worth emphasizing in

The Jerusalem suburb of Ein-Carem, an old Arab village, is considered a complete conservation region, partly because of its topographical uniqueness. This forms a good example of comprehensive conservation planning.

The old capital town of Bulgaria in 16th century, Turnovo, with its closely built village look, on terraces, perching on cliffs, but systematically facing the same direction as a unique topographical feature. This sort of element in town structure occurs often in towns of the same period.

Topography adds features that normal city buildings cannot have. They are a relief to the eye, adding a system of esthetic approach that has great variability and never ceases to surprise the onlooker. The feature of using nature as a planning quality, can occur in mountains, on the seashore or in the center of existing towns.

When buildings are complemented with natural elements, one can admit that the pleasure it offers is considerable as a planned effect. The force of the basic features added, helps in using technology sympathetically. Technology or building methods are employed in such a way as to sustain good and lasting relations with the surrounding green presence.

A well-known example of topographical features embodied in the structure of a known town (Naples). The visual result of this sort of urban structure is striking. The onlooker has a feeling of understanding the way the town is planned and sees the ties that the town has with the country, mountains or hills. An organization that is pleasing and at peace with nature has its own role as a relief to the urban activities.

planning stages, as they ensure urban continuity and the economics of conservation.

Study of topographical material and its emphasis in city life can be complex, because its jurisdiction is handled by the city parks department and not within the planning department, which is where it should be. Topographical mapping, occasionally lacking and not considered essential, should be completed, while examination of public access links (often neglected), along with future environmental development, etc. should be conducted.

The first feature is the quality and nature of the soil itself. Generally speaking it will influence the size of the buildings with the way they are set out in relation to each other. The fertility of the soil is another feature which might add to the scenic possibilities.

The natural slope, which in some cases may be above 30%, will make an important internal connection potential, especially in terms of access. This can be added to the availability of a view and other exposure of the site, depending on its elevation and height. This qualities are best studied in sections, at the appropriate scale.

Retaining walls and similar structures are a traditional quality of the topography. Those will add major qualities and features to a site, to be considered in proper detail in any conservation.

Further natural elements in proximity with the above, such as sea, rivers, mountains etc. often serve as a natural border with strong visual contribution.

An Italian hill town shows the meaning of the relation with nature, when the town limits itself to an existing hill, leaving the surrounding hills to take their own colorful and natural presence. The town square, the methods of building, the city structure follow the natural dictates of the terrain, offering an interesting and pleasing architecture. This happens even when the result is slightly tainted with a charming poise.

A pleasing aspect, one of choosing a particular building method to overcome the terrain's difficulty (Almira, Spain). Introducing repeatable attitudes and leaving a bare structure, understandable to the human eye. The reasons for this concept are simplicity and acceptable ease, offering a view of the human habitat which can be followed and fully understood.

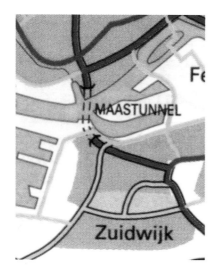

Chapter Twenty Three

Rivers and Seashores

Rivers, Bridges and Promenades
Anchorages and Islands

Elements such as water, shores, river banks, are not to be lost in our present endeavor to maintain cities. A city will always have elements of nature to keep and relate to.

Many cities were established on the banks of large rivers or streams, as they provided a natural defense system, a source of water and easy access route for trade.

Much for the same reasons, cities were often built on seashores adjacent to or in close proximity to river estuaries. These historical growth centers are generally the ancient hearts of the city, containing impor-

It is said that rivers (canals in this instance) are roads on the move. In Amsterdam's web they have the important role of adding unique charm to this city. There is a certain difficulty of interconnecting some parts of the city, with the advantage of quieting down the human environment, offering natural barriers in the blocks of the urban structure.

A river containing all the usual elements, the front of the city towards the river, the basic connections between the two shores, added walkways, the element of nature, all in a natural way. These features meet with the river front and should be specially considered for their urban qualities.

In Positano, Italy, the sea front has added a well-known quality to the urban presence of the buildings surrounding these shores, facing the sea and having the bedrock of the natural mountain side. These undulating shore fronts, roads and retaining constructions, add an additional element to town planning.

tant urban and architectonic values, and representing a unique challenge to conservation.

Rivers

Rivers function as a traffic conduit, facilitating the development of markets or regional commercial zones, as well as serving as a focal point of regional development. Rivers are often internal borders between various sections of a city, to an extent that they may limit development. This phenomenon is true for ports as well.

River and shore conservation actively promotes urban quality and should be encouraged, for they are one of the primary factors leading to the establishment of the city. Focal points such as boardwalks, bridges and walls, are generally established on river banks. River banks, a natural attraction and an urban creation, should be preserved. The river or seashore can contain boardwalks or bridges. Their preservation will not only be determined in accordance to planning and conservation issues, but also by their links to the nearest urban environment streets as well as its link to traffic and pedestrian movement, trade zones and other urban centers. Excessive establishment of parks and other similar elements can often interfere with a city's productive web; it tends to cut parts of the web. Conservation measures will take this into account.

Natural Promenade

A promenade on the shores of a beach, lake or river, or near a park, can be viewed as a natural element designated for conservation, even when it is an **artificial promenade** (e.g., the Brighton pier - a promenade that extends into the sea), and on which commerce or entertainment are conducted; a special construction with large dimensions that grant it the status of important urban asset. Ownership would be joint, or sometimes public. The promenade may include recreational elements, such as swimming in the ocean, sailing, which are welcome, but require planning arrangements and different codes.

Canals and large rivers are an added feature to existing towns and urban culture. We seldom stop to ask ourselves why fronts like this are basic to many towns, but it is when we lack this natural element or it suffers some neglect, we remember instances (such as below), where great care has been taken to maintain and preserve the qualities inherent in this relationship between the natural element and the city core.

The town of Portofino offers the seashore as an instance of city preservation. This place is extremely popular and admired for obvious reasons, one of them being the front line of the buildings which have a systematic repetition and easy flowing contours related to the natural shape of the street and promenade, acting like a port.

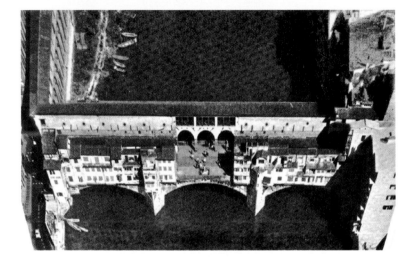

Urban culture and an example of cohabitation with the river, are presented by the Ponto Vechio (Florence) where a mixture of urban qualities are part of the bridge formation itself, a very unique construction and use of natural features, plus an outstanding piece of design.

Old towns built on a reinforced peninsula often have a close, intimate relationship with the seashore, full of design ideas and preservation fit qualities, in materials, shapes, volumes, systematic arrangements and architectural ensembles which are worth following in detail. (Dubrovnik)

Bridges

When bridges serve as passageways between various parts of the city, they are continuations of roads with characteristic designs. A large majority of bridges have been assigned historical significance due to their function as a defensive point in signaling wars. They are frequently independent and defined elements, not necessarily connected to the street designated for conservation. Other bridges located within the urban nature district function solely as access routes.

Natural and Artificial Anchorages

Anchorages are introduced in this chapter when they function mainly as gardens, and not as trade points or human passageways. Their main role is to meet tourism and recreational needs. In doing so, they complement the park, boardwalk and other such elements.

A river is bridged by an old Roman arch (Yugoslavia), showing the opportunity and importance of the visual quality of such a structure in nature, simple and austere in character.

The sea town of Molfetta (Italy) is well related to the sea. The beauty of this relation is achieved through an experience with local shapes, building habits, materials and treatments. Thus a natural quality seldom accomplished in conscious design, is full of invention and elements that can only be admired, suggesting the importance and the necessity of conservation attitudes very often based on local natural development.

Old seaside reinforcing wall can be considered as a good asset for preservation. These walls often take the natural shape of the hill, especially when local materials are used. The above promenade is on the sea front of old Jaffa.

City promenade on the sea shore of Tel Aviv offers an advantage of adding nature, sand and sea shore, to the urban environment. Some natural elements, like the clean sand and natural reefs, are preserved by a man-made reef in the fore of the shore.

One of the many islands surrounding Venice, with an incredible esthetic quality seldom seen elsewhere. The treatment of shapes and the feeling of esthetic proportions, reaches its full scope and extent in dense urban relations.

The Lake within the City Web

A lake, or rivers that create a lake, within a city web is also a scenic element. The lake may be natural or artificial. The city absorbs and creates this element which belongs to the category of natural elements, with banks, vegetation, various water sources and which serves as a recreational facility for the residents while relating to the urban environment. Relevant conservation issues should be taken into account in special circumstances. They should take into account that the lake belongs to the wider natural environment, such as a park or wildlife area.

Natural and Artificial Islands

Within the aforementioned lake, city, river or ocean are islands (either natural or artificial). Although there may not be any buildings on these islands, they still represent an essential element in the scenery, belonging to the same venue of nature incorporated into the web. We can measure their proximity, treatment, use, and cultural or other importance within the city (i.e., the island may be reached by bridge or boat). When the island is populated, it can be viewed as a residential area.

River side promenades are abundant in central Europe, and are a fit subject for preservation. The example above treats the entire environment as a tourist ensemble, responsible for the overabundant color in Carlovi Vari (Chech Republic).

The strong presence of an island connected to the shore, is where preservation and study of the human habitat can take place. This is an admirable opportunity to analyze the esthetics of compositional ability, which has a maximal in a given urban situation, in a unique natural formation. (Sveti Stephan, Montenegro).

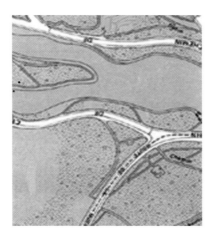

Chapter Twenty Four

City Parks

**Documentation of Natural Elements
Means of Conservation**

The urban park is a necessity understood all over. Conservation is related to life around it and will retain its role in the city's web.

Large public parks on urban scale (beyond an individual square or neighborhood garden) are a subject for research, conservation and treatment. These gardens are categorized as belonging to the urban web (such as Central Park in New York), because they create a relationship with the streets and surrounding city, or belong to nature (like in Washington) and create a large recreational park.

The presence of a large park on a big scale, such as Regents' Park in London, has a recorded history and has been preserved through hundreds of years. It has a major role in the midst of an urban development of considerable density. It is maintained and appreciated throughout. The influence on neighboring estates and buildings is beneficial. The local ideology of upkeep and the natural elements it offers are the reasons behind this extraordinary relation with the park.

The presence of a large park in the vicinity of a neighborhood, is not an excuse not to keep a smaller town square nearby. This small garden will be included in the city pattern and will serve as an intimate meeting place and offer some orientation in town. (London, near Regents' Park)

The large park (Bois de Boulogne), an integral part of Paris, has always been an important presence in the townscape. In a town such as Paris, where building density is one of the highest in the Western world, the vicinity of a park is regarded by many as an essential compensation. It is preserved accordingly.

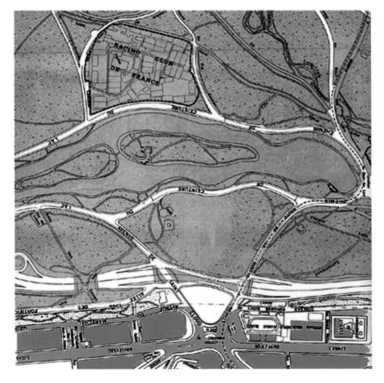

The plan of the Bois de Boulogne (Paris) shows the abrupt way in which the town ends on its circular roads. The park begins and starts with a completely different design, one of free natural forms and handling. The map shows the care with which this is achieved, when the web and the park come into contact. Nothing is left to chance in this careful and appropriate design of conserving both the park and the city web one next to the other.

These types of gardens or parks will be larger elements in terms of conservation, because they contain more elements, both in terms of historical record and biology.

They display enormous vitality (e.g., Hyde Park and Regent Park in London). Vegetation is ancient and complex, while topography is intricate, involving the creation of lakes and streams, paths and roads (see Bologne Forest, Paris).

Their decisive importance for the neighboring city is their size, which transforms them into a significant topic of distinctive value. This requires special attention. In these cases, conservation and legislation are the general rule, but that cannot be overemphasized since the park is dissociated from the neighborhoods located nearby. Therefore, at present, normal conservation which does not refer to the urban web is barely reflected in outline plans. This is one of the reasons why overall

A park can become a visual focal point, where some of the city can be observed. It can include several important monuments and have a symbolic meaning. At the same time, it can be a place which is included in the daily life of its users.

In Galloway County, Ireland, it is clear that parks can be very useful in the web of an existing town and become a large garden, giving the impression that the city lives in nature. The care undertaken by the city to maintain such a large public space clean and functional, is a large task, including many studies of the natural elements involved. It will mean reinforcing walls to keep floods at bay, maintaining bridges and vegetation, topographical studies, etc. which go on continuously behind the scene and help to create this unique element of conservation.

A central and well preserved urban park of large dimensions, containing the old monastery of the Mazleva Valley (of crusaders origin). Situated in central Jerusalem, it combines visually some of the city westerly districts.

The city park in Haifa, on the eastern slopes of the Carmel, built by the Bahai, plays an important role in the city structure offering a focal element of orientation.

Garden design has developed a special and separate taste in Europe. The memory it evokes is often of Italian Renaissance influences. One of the results is that conservation of the above elements is a natural endeavor. (Henley, England)

attention to urban characteristics is important. These parks are occasionally grouped within national conservation plans that cover cities possessing different needs; local aspects should be examined.

Summary of Documentation of Natural Elements

1. Definition of the size of the element, complete mapping of borders, hills, etc.
2. Identification of the extent of and solution for ecological problems.
3. Identification of vitality and microclimates, determining their extent and solutions
4. Inclusion of ownership or primary responsibility, within the city's statutory scope.
5. Examination of urban links to important city points, traffic and pedestrian axes.
6. Definition of responsibilities, operations and maintenance.

Means of Conservation:

1. General inclusion within the urban planning system and type of responsibility.
2. Planning and development by experts in the field.
3. Urban links and responsibility factors of maintenance.
4. Relation to the national infrastructure of nature conservation.

The esthetic element of design involved in garden conservation, is not difficult to envisage in terms of the historical public garden and its appearance. Style, dimensions, vistas and nature are well coordinated and have always been well documented. (Versailles)

An historical Paris park (the 1900 exhibition's site), whose pavilions and buildings have since changed, was included in the system of parks and avenues of Paris, as a part of the Seine Valley system. It is clear that a major focal point has thus been created in the city.

Ma. Romes

Monte Donzella

Monte

oncezione

Arenella

l'Architiello

Soccavo

Antignano

il Vomero

bello

Villa Floridiana

Villa Belvedere

Cast.º de Santa Maria in Portico

Infrascata

Bottone

Logerot

Bottone

Castel S. Elmo

Monte

V. Ereme

PART SIX

Methodology

Planning, as a system, will be more concerned with preserving components of the urban web. Urban preservation's role is a part of this tendency.

By incorporating conservation on the urban scale, we will be reinforcing good planning and promoting a sound basis of general planning considerations.

Urban components will be better understood by preservation criteria, evaluated and introduced into the planning system.

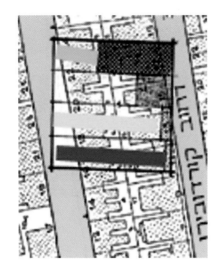

Chapter Twenty Five

Background Data

Selecting a Region
Study of the Past
Urban Structure
Urban Background

After identifying the urban elements that dictate urban conservation, and clarifying the critical influence of the past on conservation, the hierarchy of urban structure was outlined. Conservation on an urban and regional scale is not independent of urban planning, for they are symbiotic.

In order to establish a methodology, we incorporate urban conservation within the context of planning, when urban outline plans are under conception. In order to illustrate the approach, the aspects of conservation will be emphasized, with planning serving as a backdrop. In reality, the importance of planning will certainly differ in each case.

Background data is collected in normal fashion. It will be used first in a condensed form, when the selection process of a region is complete. Other preliminary data acquaints us with the site and its region.

1. Selecting a Region

For the purposes of this discussion, it is assumed that the area selected is an urban region, that is, having a population of some 50,000 persons. When discussing changes in planning within the historical centers of cities, the majority of the area within those cities will be marked for examination for conservation. The area will be divided by its underlying webs and quarters. As we have summarized, conservation considerations may have a minimal, though critical, effect on the results of urban planning. Since this is the case, conservation is a positive force in extensive planning, not just in preserving places, but also in the study of webs and districts.

2. Study of the Past

Experts in the field of archaeology are often called in to provide a thorough analysis of the significance of ancient findings and their importance to the conservation process.

The archaeological analysis will shed light on the uses and size arrangements in the past, thereby enabling a comparison between findings from the present and the distant past. An analysis of the historical material will be conducted by studying the following central questions. Answers, taking the form of maps or graphs, are an additional step towards making effective decisions based on background material.

A. The ancient division between roads and private parcels.

B. Intensity of land use in the past, at its peak, including roads.

C. Size of parcels and secondary divisions, with promi-

The study of the chosen region will include studies of proportions between heights and plans, (such as the one shown below) overall dimensions, with the principal elements of urban structure included. Geometrical dimensions, especially when used as comparative information, are always revealing.

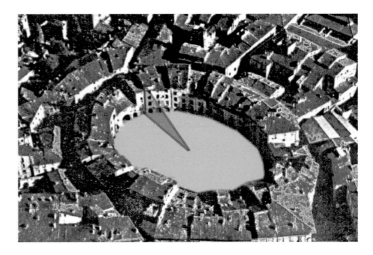

Studies of an urban web will include elements such as the roads, different blocks, the size of the parcels, sections and elevations, small perspectives, roof plans, general dimensions of the area. Elements of nature such as trees, plants, vegetation, etc. are to be pointed out(see example below).

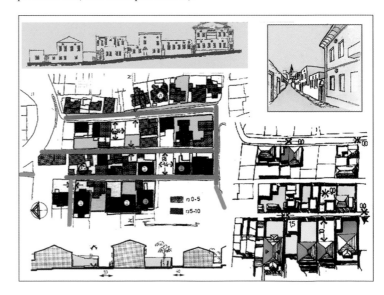

The study of the region chosen for possible conservation purposes will include maps, aerial photographs and some preliminary analysis. The example illustrates the nature of the study, with some emphasis on the borders of the site, and some important links.

Further studies to be conducted involve relative densities, detailed land use in the blocks included and some general diagrams of the preservation intended. The present example is one of many, and it gives an idea of the nature of the information to be collected.

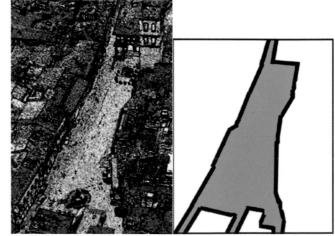

nent changes that occurred over time.

D. Natural barriers that existed during several eras, such as rivers, walls and topography, some of which still exist and others which are solely historical.

3. Urban Structure: Identification of Elements

It is impossible to discuss district conservation without identifying urban structure. Urban structure consists of the web, constructed by districts, which result from land division for public property (mainly streets and roads) and private property (adjacent parcels for construction). The principal elements which make up the city are individually identified within an area that has been designated for conservation or study. The primary and other elements will be marked as such on maps, with a registry of their main characteristics and without getting into explanations (those are to be categorized at a later stage).

The classification will be start with the general city web, after which districts and blocks, including squares and streets will be located and marked on the maps. Elements classified in the "nature" category will be discussed in the relevant chapters dealing with those elements. They will be linked to the geographical environment in order to emphasize the importance of the scenic background.

Urban Structure, a suggested summary:

	Identity	Size	Basic Dimensions
1. Basic Web			
2. Districts			
3. Blocks			
4. Land Division			
5. Primary			
6. Secondary			
7. Nature			

The regions and districts have to be well pointed out, with delineation of their extents and limits, as well as any important relations to surrounding regions.

Marked buildings will include present uses (harmful or useful to the urban web) according to zoning or present status.

General plans to be included in the conservation study can take the form of intended planning attitudes, such as major access and future alternatives for the district. These can be noted in terms such of changing roads, zoning, new avenues, treatment of existing street patterns, small parks and squares, relations with existing industry, etc.

The urban character of the analyzed section (south Tel Aviv) will be made clear by some photography.

4. Urban Background

The background material for an urban conservation area, which generally accompanies outline planning in order to assist in the planning process, will be conducted in accordance with the following generalized check list. At the present level of analysis, background material is used principally as an aid to the decisions as to the suitability of the region for conservation purposes.

Ownership maps – showing private and public ownership on the general background map of the region and environment, by the individual parcel.

Principal maps - of 1) primary land use, 2) age and condition of buildings, 3) identification of major urban links.

Demographics – on a rough scale: population according to income levels, family size and age, and main changes in the population over time.

Residential Density – the number of individuals or rooms per net hectare and the number of individuals per room

Major Public Services

Extraordinary Uses - including obstructions (documented and based on surveys)

Level of Services - in terms of roads, electricity, communication, etc.

Elements of Traffic - major access routes (city and local) for pedestrians, motor vehicles, mass transportation, stations, and existing and predicted traffic volume.

Mapping the conservation areas will equip researchers with a general evaluation, as well as with some detailed appraisal of the dimensions of the conservation project. The above material provides some general background necessary, as conservation cannot be carried out on its own. It also ensures that the basic urban structure is well documented up to a certain degree, and the planner is well equipped to become familiar with the planning effort one is going to invest. This effort will reflect on the level of future conservation. The study is to be finalized later, when the practicality of conservation is considered in the methodology section.

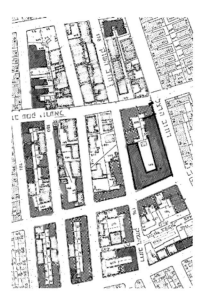

The further study of the blocks will include heights and elements of style and design. This may mean a more detailed look into the block origins and the need for maintenance and upkeep, as well as present state of repair.(Examples shown of similar studies in Tel Aviv.)

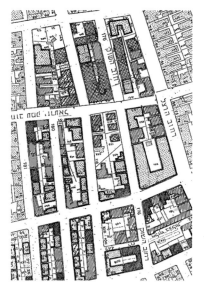

Another example (age of buildings) included in the study will be helpful as a source of evaluation for the process of the urban conservation study. These maps are the normal procedure undertaken in planning, and some can be used in conservation.

Chapter Twenty Six

Reasons for Conservation

Estimating the conservation potential :
1. Character of the Urban setting
2. Locality and Sense of Place
3. Internal Proportions and Relations
4. Style and Design
5. Construction Methods and Materials

It is important to know the reasons for conservation. A necessary method has to be adhered to. Intimate knowledge of what is to be conserved is essential. It is also important to be able to compare qualities to other sites.

The selection of urban regions designated for conservation, even if that conservation is to be partial, can be examined with the assistance of positive criteria.

An urban district marked for conservation should possess certain properties that can be classified in an organized manner. Such urban areas should be examined in this light, in any normal planning stage.

The following properties are the main reasons behind an ordered determination of conservation. We are not

The following illustrations start with those containing a low conservation potential (around 50%). Urban conservation potential cannot be precisely calculated. However, in the present chapter, we will try to make it the result of an analytic endeavor, to estimate quantitatively what is to be conserved and the reasons for it.

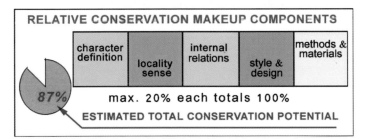

RELATIVE CONSERVATION MAKEUP COMPONENTS

character definition	locality sense	internal relations	style & design	methods & materials

87%   **max. 20% each totals 100%**

ESTIMATED TOTAL CONSERVATION POTENTIAL

Legend : The necessary analysis for estimating the conservation potential of a site consists of :
1. Character - clear definition of local character and size.
2. Clearly formulated sense of locality and place.
3. Internal proportions of spaces and volumes.
4. Well defined design of the volumes.
5. Building methods and materials employed are of clear and exceptional nature.

All the five components have unique features, as compared to similar components in other places. What is calculated is the sum total of every component, each max. 20%. This serve only as an indication and is not a precise rule.

The low conservation potential in this example stems mainly from the fact that it has only a high character definition mark, around 20%, which is maximal. The other attributes have quite low marks. The total sum is not much above 50% (see % in pie diagrams). In that respect it can be compared to the example above it, with the strong locality sense (approx. 17%).

attempting to assign various purports to each one of the planner's personal opinions (despite the fact that it can be done). The attempt is to clarify the different elements and qualities which can undergo the process.

The following demands will receive validation only when they are unique, clear, and formatted within a precise table, with the certitude that in terms of conservation, requirements are clear before the planning phase begins.

True, in certain historical cities, conservation is considered so important that it becomes a central consideration in urban planning trends. In these instances, however, it should not be viewed as being completely detached from overall planning, as conservation cannot be divorced from the necessary planning procedures.

Good overall qualities make for high character marks. Conservation potential does not achieve a high mark due to the fact that some of the qualities are not deemed unique. We determine that by comparing to similar sites. This is to be judged, in spite of a clear and interesting situation . This does not mean that other opinions cannot be relevant and that a final judgement has been made. Opinions or different emphasis of the relative makeup of a site can completely change the outlook when the decision of conservation is being made; the method used can lead to a possible debate. Style and design, in the square below (Place Vendome), as well as the methods and materials used, are not very special (comparatively) for a town like Paris.

In this slightly higher estimate of conservation potential, the marks are the result of some inherently rare internal relations (quality no.3 in our table, in green) and a high degree of design and style (4, in blue). This raises the potential. On the other hand, it is lowered back by the lack of definition in the site area (1) and mild locality sense (2).

The only stipulation is that each one of the conservation features has to be unique to some degree, either in terms of esthetics, or historically significant values.

Estimating the conservation potential and its components

The qualities we will look for will undergo a process of value judgement in a two directions, namely: A. Comparison to other, similar sites, and B. Esthetics and historical value judgement. Admittedly, it is not the most accurate of all procedures, but it is easily understood and possibly amended in due time. An elaboration of this method is obtainable by assigning different values to each component, thus performing a basic sensitivity check. We have already noted the five physical qualities necessary to grade and judge some proposed conservation. These are briefly put as follows: **A**. The clear border of the site; **B**. The sense of locality. **C**. Internal relations in their variety; **D**. Style and design; **E**. Materials and workmanship. If each is examined on esthetic and historic grounds, using some comparisons, they can be valued as a percentage of a whole. This done, a scale will be created to constitute an average judgement of the values attached to the site.

It will be necessary to elaborate on these qualities, as they become the prerequisites to the necessity of preserving a region.

1. Definite physical character of the urban setting and its borders

The region is given to definition by clear, physical borders that are traditionally accepted and well marked.

The strong definition in the outlines of this quarter has good potential in terms of character (light blue in our charts). The remaining characteristics, however, score rather low marks. The total potential is not greater than 50%.

Very low conservation potential because the site limits are not entirely clear, and contains low makeup components, except for some building methods in their repetition and uniqueness (5, in yellow).

By its very nature, the region serves as focal point. Comprehension is guaranteed, be it urban or regional, and that is the primary force behind conservation.

The physical definition has lent uniqueness to the site, which can then be well identified and qualified to become the subject of a subsequent and more detailed analysis.

It is somewhat imperative that this requirement is fulfilled for the sake of the clarity it implies.

2. Locality and sense of place

The self-evidence of a locality as one in which one experiences a unique sense of place is important. Historical associations, scenic views, fusion with some defined issue, shade, comfort, feeling of local importance, vegetation and relation to the topography, are all contributing factors. The reference is to the extensive position

The emphasis given by different components of conservation is not always very material. The important measure is that every quality is weighed, discussed and annotated as carefully as possible. The lists prepared for the estimation of these qualities help a great deal in defining what we want to preserve and the means we will need in order to implement our decisions.

The two strong characteristics of this place, with its clear border, are good character definition in light blue (1) and a very good sense of locality, in orange, 2) to be preserved . The internal links, design and style do not raise the potential in this site, neither do the building methods.

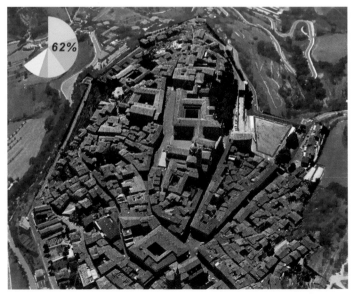

of a site's uniqueness as a human asset. These properties have to be formulated and clearly defined.

3. Internal proportions and relations

Sites examined will have to prove recognized and accepted relations between structures and spaces, guaranteeing the understanding of the environment, at a public and urban advantage. The understanding may only be partial or require some emphasis and clarification. The internal relations imply special proportions between the various built volumes and the spaces thus created. In this section the urban space will be fully appraised, as a basic abstract quality of the urban elements.

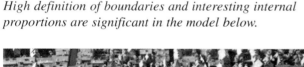

Some components, varying in their importance, carry different implications. The conservation potential may not be high, we may strive to preserve some definite characteristics, and not necessarily the total site. In the uniqueness of the design and style, in blue (left), one can spend a great deal of funds to maintain the particular design one admires, perhaps neglecting other necessary measures of conservation, not being able to apply them because of a temporary lack of means. Perhaps some care should be taken not to overlook the totality of a given situation.

In preserving a totality of parks, squares, streets, building blocks and street fronts, each item must be evaluated. An overall opinion will help the decision about every separate component. It is not an easy task, and one has to control as much as possible one's esthetic judgement, giving chance to a variety of opinions. This variety will manifest itself in the quantification we are trying to pursue.

High definition of boundaries and interesting internal proportions are significant in the model below.

4. Style and design

The site will have to reflect a good level of mutual comple-mentation as related to architectural style and design of structures. Here, due to overall considerations of design, the immediate esthetic rationale will come into play. Design involves proportions and silhouettes, not only de-tails or artistry. It must be said that we are looking for a common design factor, which applies to the whole site and area.

5. Construction methods and materials

A high degree of processing and a traditional use of mate-rials according to architectural specifications is apparent, with the ability to implement a certain defined building

It is interesting to note how conservation potential rises when the overall quality of the sample is seen at a glance to be superior, even intuitively. Our decisions are influenced unconsciously by the totality of the situation. The case is clearer when qualities that lower the potential will have to be repaired in order to enhance some of them. For example, the character definition of the space involved in our example may be stressed by dealing differently with the way the square has been treated in detail, and resort to some planning or finishing measures. These measures may necessitate some corrective design by environmentalists, architects, etc.

Components such as design and style (blue) and building methods (yellow), comprise the singular building attributes and not just the abstract qualities we are trying to quantify. In this respect, it may be easier to find reasons for conservation when the clarity of the building involved is more pronounced. This does not mean that the abstract qualities related to history and to the sense of local feeling should be neglected.

technology.

All workmanship is authentic and has undergone a valid process. It also has an overall quality, which is related to all the site.

The Conservation Potential

If each of the preceding qualities is given 20% in an evaluating scale, a measure of the comparative degree of the conservation potential can be arrived at. A total of more than 50-60% will confirm our choice of the site or region as a viable one.

A sum of less than 50% is to be reconsidered. A measure of changes may be all that is needed to raise the potential. This may be achieved by some planning, providing the upgrading is not substantial.

The total influence of the above components will tend to make the site more universally accepted because of the objective restraints involved.

This will be important especially in public debate, and can be presented methodically.

The total is called "relative", so as to imply that conservation is a matter of social agreement and conscious choice. It is not to be based on political or mythical conjectures only, but should enjoy a consensus based on an open public

We are fortunate in that conservation principles are multifaceted. In this respect, we are helped in our decisions, about a site like the one below, by a sense of locality that is not altogether abstract. In adding to our reckoning the building methods involved, as is strongly indicated in this case, we reach a more balanced opinion. The precision necessary in our conservation methods is thus not impaired.

*This **Tel Aviv** square is an example of modern design. It is not often that modern designs, in this case from the 30's, are preserved in an urban manner. Very few urban spaces have been successfully designed in a modern (Bauhaus) international style. We are raising our total marks in the explanatory process of the principles involved. This being a good example (and not an old one as is normally the case), we may add that its preservation failed, the roundabout altered and raised, because of local traffic problems.*

The weak parts of this example are the internal relations (in orange) of the zone, because of neglected shapes of the volumes involved, when judged by considerations of uniqueness. Other weak elements are the definition and clarity of the boundaries of the region.

This example is lacking in terms of its uniqueness in design and style and a badly defined region, esp. in heights. However, it is considered to be outstanding in the other aspects, reaching a high conservation potential.

We have an example of clear architectural merit, but it is a single building. It suffers from an undefined sense of locality, lost in the similarity of its neighbors, and is therefore not perfect. The workmanship is exquisite, the style is clear and the building method is uniform, thus illuminating the principles involved, and this is where the example is duly appreciated.

It is the full extent of Venice that is brought to one's attention. It indicates the conservation potential in all its variety. The design and style are somewhat unclear in terms of repetitiveness and so are some internal relations.

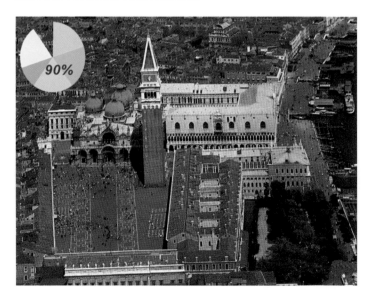

debate.

The numerous examples given in the present chapter are meant to serve as guidelines. It is clear that the sum and the percentages involved illustrate the method and the principle. It is also certain that different appraisals are possible: the method cannot be scientific, its range of precision is about 10%. The method presented only proves that estimates are possible and should be employed as a base for possible future debate.

As one can sense, the above estimates can vary considerably. The sensitive planner, aided by comparative knowledge, will make sensible adjustments.

Venice is one of the prime examples of urban conservation and can be analyzed to show that the principles we are proposing here make some sense, leading us to reach a very high conservation potential.

Chapter Twenty Seven

The Town Planning Approach

Structure: The Physical Dimension
The Urban Mix:
1. Land   2. Buildings   3. Usage

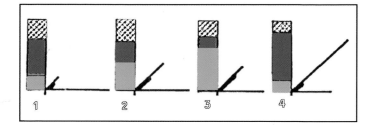

All cities and towns are made up of a certain mix of qualities. These are primarily contained in land, buildings and their use. The planning approach is summed up in the above urban mix of qualities.

Data

This is where data collection should become more intensive and available, as the clarity and the necessity of a conservation study become apparent. The following background material has planning overtones. It is to be used in a more conservation-oriented manner later on.

Planning standards and requirements progress, both in subject matter and in presentation. The example provides some diagrams of urban analysis, comparing different quarters, as a simplified way of showing quantified research. Strong blue is the actual built surface (residential), light blue the proportion of the open space, and(dotted) the total road surface. Some waste is apparent, and so is the excessive density, in "3". The diagonals indicate amount of floor space and open space, per inhabitant.

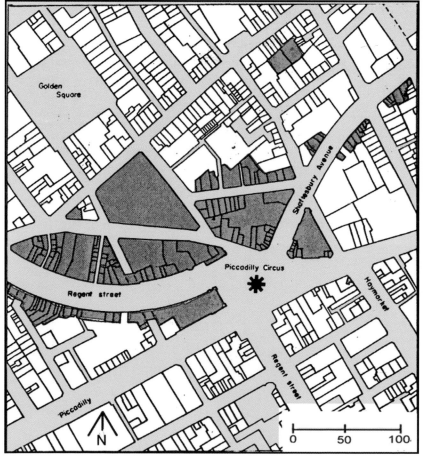

Background material of regional and general importance, as well as some historical features are brought in the form of maps. Changes in planning recommendations can take various forms. In the map considered we can judge previous structure and formation of plots. Some of the plots were cut and changed when land acquisitions were made in the formation of Regent Street. Form of present buildings stems partly from that fact.

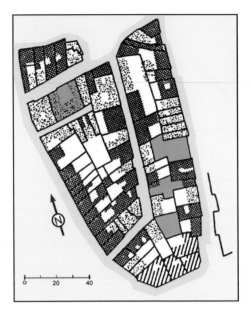

Building types, their maintenance, age and standards for their preservation are noted. In historical places we will encounter many of these old building types, and as their value is difficult to estimate, we have to collect as much data as possible, showing the future scope of our planning intentions.

Assembling data about parks, is best left to expert landscape designers, equipped for such tasks. The scope is enormous and consists not only of horticultural aspects, but of topographical measurements, better left to a later stage. The illustration of a park in Washington can illustrate the size of the undertaking, which will include links to city as well.

The need for surveys and records

The region or the site to be dealt with has been selected and its urban structure as well as close environment have been identified. Likewise, the major reasons for their conservation have been formulated. All of the data must now be arranged in an analytical order, creating a final summary of classifications and screenings before an operative planning decision is made. The planning approach to the region is helped by maps and a detailed background. Only the major planning considerations will be outlined here, without the immediate connection to urban conservation. These will be discussed in the next chapter. The purpose of the presentation of the material in this manner is to make clear that conservation is not promoted outside the context of overall urban planning, but is included from the very onset to have an influence on this plan.

Planning has the objective of instituting and renewing the urban operational function of a region. It may be useful to quote some planning directives, especially those which have a bearing on conservation procedures. These directives, plainly quoted as the informative background used by planners, are added to the primary investigation ones, mentioned in chapter 25.

1. General Background of Selected District

A. General objectives and functions of the district,

with their regional link

B. Planning Standards – (existing, model and future oriented) health, education, energy, industry, safety and environmental quality

C. Social Background – demographics, social and educational needs, work force, domestic tourism, population transport (both internal and external)

D. Culture – history, tradition, archaeology, museums, local flavor, preservation of the site's cultural tradition

E. Nature - local ecology and geology, topography and land, suitability for development, vegetation and climate, life forms, microclimates, hydrology, natural disasters, energy sources, parks, preserving values of nature

F. Economic Background – urban expense, realization of land values, zoning, trade, tourism, agriculture and industry, different forms of taxation

G. Residential Response – local unions, neighborhoods, media, public relations on various issues (including conservation). Comparison between planning goals and residential desires

2. Structure: The Physical Dimension

A. Principal past forms in urban history, general urban framework, densities, permitted heights, building lines, building coverage, and building types

B. Public Services and Buildings: culture, welfare, education, sports and gardening

C. Roads and Traffic, in all their aspects: regional links, transport, parking, bicycles and pedestrians

3. Construction

A. Visual Background – color, textures, proportions, visual and scenic singularity

B. Town services - sewage, waterworks, electricity, etc.

C. Buildings – types of buildings, forms of management and existing building laws. Treatment of

Age or antiquity of construction has planning, conservation and social implications. In the Parisian quarter illustrated, sanitary conditions of low standards and dilapidated dwellings made preservation almost impossible. From a cultural point of view, Paris lost a considerable amount of its charm, due a century of neglect, compounded indifference of the central government. Complex and intelligent diagrams can be used for illustrating long developments.

	1800
	1860
	1900

0 10 20 30m

285

Maps of urban structure are commonly used, when they contain helpful, condensed data. The subdivision of the block into plots being essential, we add building contours, parcel size and form, private open space, all marked in our illustration.

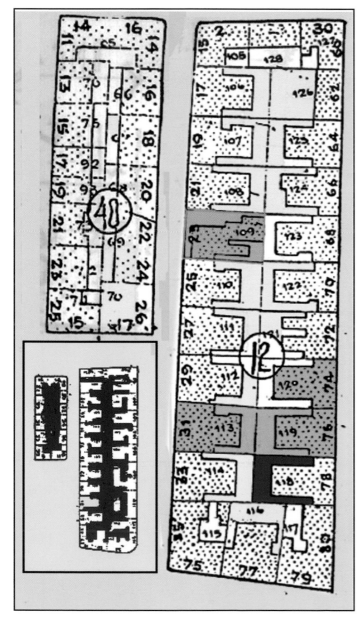

new and existing buildings and comparison of the levels of maintenance

4. Living Standards

Detailed determination for living standards within the selected region:

A. Residential Dwellings - in terms of known standards

B. Public Services and Public Welfare – parks, health care – in accordance to their comparative levels

C. Entertainment and Culture – urban and local

D. Urban Continuity – or detachment

5. Suggested Changes

These will come to our attention as local malfunctioning of some nature, necessitating planning intervention.

Major steps for the formulation of a plan to initiate local changes, in accordance with accepted planning clauses:

A. Residential Dwellings – changes in standards

B. Land Exploitation and use (zoning)

C. Various Requisitions – roads, public property, and buildings

D. Social Recommendations and Improvement

E. Changes in Urban Links with surrounding areas

The preparation of the above planning data will take place alongside with conservation data recording.

The Urban Mix

It is not practical to enter into detailed planning considerations pertaining to conservation on the urban scale. This is one of the reasons we have to find terms of reference that will permit us to briefly outline planning. The following remarks are written with that intention.

We will make planning considerations much clearer by dividing them into three major categories. These three entities will set our planning priorities to a considerable degree.

Planning deals with three principal quantities that make up the so-called urban mix. Urban mix is a multifaceted concept that can have a significant effect on our understanding of urban planning.

The **urban mix** contains the following items to one degree or another:
1. Land
2. Buildings
3. Usage by people

Any change to urban plans will have a direct impact on the aforementioned entities, thereby altering the urban reality. Furthermore, the mix of any human settlement (especially in the dense urban environment) with its fragile interrelations demands a high degree of control (i.e. by planning). The above components are of course interrelated and interdependent. Planning can, therefore, be called **the balancing power of the urban mix.**

It is illuminating to elaborate on the above and to try re-

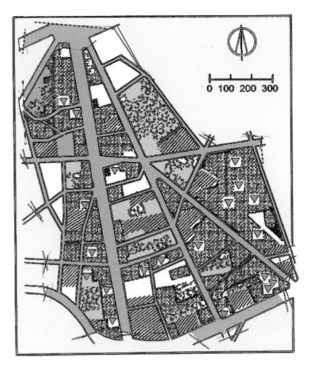

Economical aspects have to do with the expected investment, in different categories, needed for the planned conservation. Land values and their expected increase, for the properties concerned, have to be registered and estimated. Public revenue from taxes can be calculated. All this is to be done in the preliminary stage, with the help of maps, areas and intensity of use calculations. An example shows the spread of different land uses, mainly in the nature of open spaces, empty plots, and the quantity of the usable floor space, all in a present state of affairs.

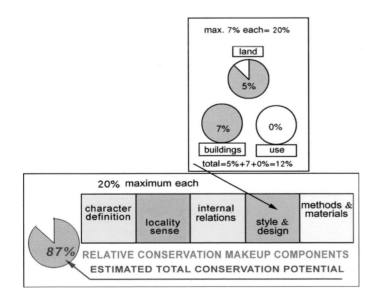

Urban mix considerations are introduced and the weight of different conservation components is further refined. By the division of the 20% separate category weight into three headings, (each of 7 %), we can adjust the contribution, (style & design, in our example) by considering the contribution of every part of the mix. Thus, land is responsible for 5% of the uniqueness of the category (its subdivision is of interest), buildings add a further 7% (containing the style considered), while use is nil (0%), as nothing comes from it. A total of 5% + 7% =12% is calculated (fictitiously of course).

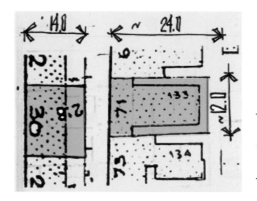

The formation, sizes and front lines of the various plots cannot be overemphasized. The type of information needed will be used for considerations such as the reshaping or remodeling the plots . This will influence not only living conditions, but any future preservation, or even rehabilitation.

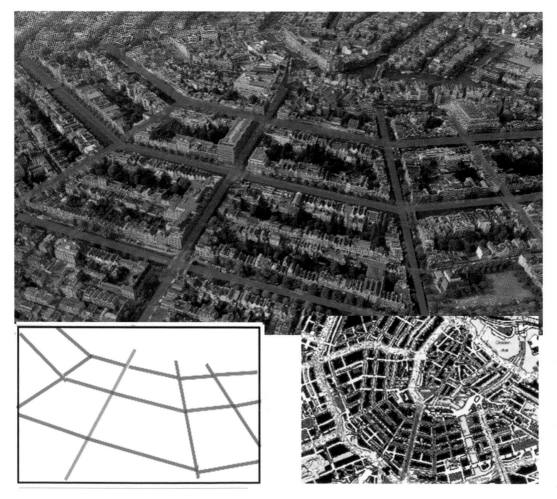

The extent of the web, marked here by roads (and canals, in our example) has to be studied. If public buildings are added, we will be familiarized with the structure in terms of public ownership and presence. These particular maps are also used to mark public services, such as canalization, electricity and gas, and other technical matters. The planner has to be familiar with web characteristics (see insert of road axes), as their structural influence is the major urban feature and forming force.

solving the complexities that seem to be implied.

1. Land

All land is divided to a certain degree, with the help of surveying, in order to conceive the parcelation needed to ensure continuity and ownership. Land division is essential and preordains any building or usage of the land. It is essentially the raw material of planning. Other than parcelation into plots, 30%-40% of urban land is owned by the public. The necessary public involvement relieves frictions (especially as densities increase), and serves as a regulating formation, enforceable by law. This public involvement includes: a) roads and squares, approx. 20%; b) public buildings (e.g., schools) or public grounds (approx. 10%); c) parks, gardens, etc. (approx. 10%). While the publicly-owned land has an simple system of subdivision, all privately-owned land undergoes the much more complex process described below:

a. Division to ensure access from a public space (roads in modern times). In most cases, this is decreed by law, as a basic premise.

b. A degree of simplicity (i.e., geometry) to ensure simple identification and measurement as well as possible further subdivision.

c. A degree of street frontage beneficial for access to air and light as well as for commercial value.

d. A clear relationship with neighbors of similar private standing, with party wall, common boundary, etc.

Due to the resiliency of this land division, which results from an inherent arrangement of a substantial social contract, it can remain in service for hundreds of years. Land division is the strongest proponent of abstract and historical values. Much of urban culture has developed through this division and will continue to develop. All oddities and irregularities in the plots have been and will be handled by planning, but this imprint (i.e., the

A survey of building types will introduce an element of architecture with it. This will be done with the help of photographs and drawings. In the case illustrated (European typology in Tel Aviv), style is somewhat stressed for clarity's sake. This may also indicate the intricacy of the conservation envisaged.

A semblance of a catalog of existing building types is needed. This is also a guide to the difficulties to be encountered in a preservation project (Tel Aviv).

Another compilation of building types, Bauhaus design of 1930, interesting in its variations. Mixtures of building types, some times incongruous, adds complexity and visual interest (left).

shape of the subdivision) will be the last to change. Thus, form arrangements have resulted in the formation of the city block (a conglomeration of plots) as well as the street frontage. Other typical qualifications are the creation of repetitive patterns (the recurring width), shortcuts, right of way, common line of buildings, subsequent colonnades and other design qualities that are found in cities (regularities in skyline being not the least important). Design is then clearly the result of the creation of parcels and plots, thus highlighting its standing as the most important element in city formation and planning.

2. Buildings

Parcel formation and plans, creation of plots under different management and ownership, have the purpose of erecting buildings, and their majority is constructed to serve residential purposes. The following is a brief summary of established principles.

The first characteristic of edifices is their relative bulk. That is best qualified by a few objective relations.

a. Coverage ratio is the "shadow" of the building (its imprint), relative to a percentage of the plot. Normally, in dense cities, it starts at 40% and can even rise to approximately 70%. (This is rare, as ventilation of rooms may become virtually impossible).

b. Coverage multiplied by the number of stories is the total area built. In normal conditions, it will stop at approximately 100% (of the parcel) and very seldom reaches 180%, where the land usable as the private open space on the plot will be minimal, regardless of heights.

c. The former quantity, i.e., the total area built to a certain height, creates the visual qualities of cities by forming the

The visual background needed for the study we contemplate, is made of drawings, diagrams, compilations of building types, photographs etc. (mixed elements, south Tel Aviv).

public spaces (streets and squares mainly) and allowing built environment to be habitable (using different bylaws and regulations).

d. The bulk of edifices thus created is responsible for the creation of usable public space, immediately influencing the visual formation and quality.

e. Buildings can and will change every 50-75 years, and so will their ownership, possibly at a greater rate. This can also happen independently of land ownership in some cases.

3. Usage by Residents

The last quantifiable and planned element of the city mix is the least resilient one. This can be attributed to the reason behind the association between land and buildings, namely their use. This association's primary purpose was to form the habitable human organization into a certain controllable system. However, the secondary attributes of such an endeavor change somewhat with time, sometimes rapidly, as the developing economies progress dynamically. Land use can be applied to land only (i.e., open markets of different descriptions) or buildings only (technical use, such as water pumps).

Land use can also denote use of floor space, assigning different uses to differing floors or heights, up to a certain height (such as in parking structures). It can be restrictive in heights (ground floor commerce limits) and applicable as a mix (i.e., no more than 40% office use on upper floors). Tenants can be restricted by occupation or trade, as well as by disturbance or harm to the environment.

Zoning depends on planners and users alike and can be regulated to a certain degree. This form of use in the built environment changes over time, some of the uses refined by conservation or public will. Change of use can be the result of betterment and rise of living standards, as well as change of tastes. It has been established that as technology develops and habits change, areas will be rezoned, sometimes every twenty years.

On the other hand, deterioration and drop in intensity are the marks of blight or degradation of a district. Hence the

Living conditions in an historical and central place will be problematic to record. As conditions change rapidly, esp. in the last 50 years, questionable living conditions have influenced the desertion of central districts. However, it is a collection of a multitude of facts that has contributed to this deterioration, living standards being just one of these factors. Present day zoning in central districts has quickly set in commercial and office use, to form this nondescript reality.

Public appropriations of property, as well as public ownership, give a good chance to central districts. This central part of London will illustrate that as the density of nonresidential use is lowered, standards rise and deterioration can be halted.

It will always be necessary to look into the actual plans, sizes, etc. of residential accommodation. It can be collected at the preliminary stages in a perfunctory manner. Plans of flats and other types of dwellings, are illuminating. This is where some necessary changes will occur, so as to increase living standards. Small flats, like the ones illustrated, may need to be renovated, enlarged or refurbished. This has happened in many London boroughs, as a part of some urban renewal programs.

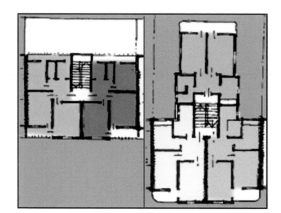

Changes in planning are undertaken as a part of renovation or preservation. Paris municipal plans are allowing changes in a controlled way, up to the local skyline, modernizing the section of the upper rooftop floors. Giving geometrical and precise guidelines, has every chance of a positive effect in restoring urban life. The example also shows changes which have occurred in the last 100 years, as a guide.

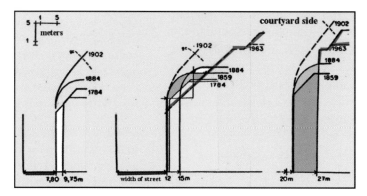

Future urban design plans and intentions are collected and studied. Some major effects will take place from pressures other than conservation principles, such as additions of urban links, to ease the traffic, in the eve of new design approaches. (Virtual design study in conjunction with urban renewal in Tel Aviv).

note about the low resiliency of the third factor in the urban mix.

An important measure of use will be its intensity. In the same way that quantity of traffic is a suitable indication of intensity, local elements such as measures of occupancy, family size, use of educational facilities, in percentages or comparative terms, will be a suitable indicator.

The factor of the urban mix

We can now adopt the above terms to create concise and systematic urban profiles for sections, boroughs and districts.

A model of a fictional profile can read as follows:

1. **Land** : plots of 500-1000 sq. m.
Narrow 8 m. street fronts.
Party wall construction.
Low public ownership (30%)

Two major applications of land division. To the right, the roads have been established , and alongside them, the city blocks. The size of the block, an important component of the way the city will look and behave, is calculated. This is done as the land division's contribution to the urban mix. Such is (left) the more delicate subdivision, showing the plots left for public use.

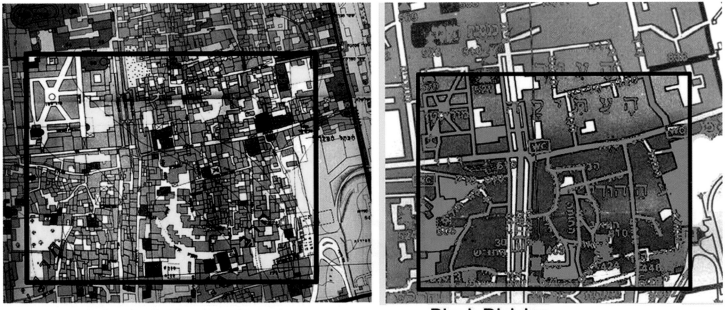

Private & Public Plots   Block Division

JERUSALEM - Old City

Shapes of buildings emerge after land has been divided (two east European squares). A recurrent repetitive pattern in both shows the above fact clearly. Heights, once decided upon, will perpetuate the ensemble. Architecture will clarify the public importance of the site. The second element of the urban mix, building, has played its part.

2. **Buildings** : 120 % utilization factor in 4 stories
Regular front lines.

3. **Use** : restricted to residential, at the
intensity of 1.2 persons per room.

This very simplified form of identity, based of course
on the proper surveys, will help in comparison and
study, as well as form a basis for conservation studies.

*A city will be a reflection of its land division. That, in its turn,
reflects the history and the current cultural practice. The web
and plots in the present example show two approaches. The
lower one is a land division for agricultural use. It was turned
over, 50 years ago, to residential use. The unsuitable land
division as it was, is completely inadequate, and will not fulfill
its purpose. Land division (at top) has the overtones of the
"garden city" practice, and was indeed created under auspices
of British planners of the same period. It has its drawbacks,
but is not deteriorating. It certainly reflects modern planning,
and shows the influence of land division.*

Chapter
Twenty Eight

Methodology
of Conservation

The Urban Mix
Appraising Conservation Potential
Quidelines for Conservation Planning

The methodology of conservation will use background data, structural identity and preservation potential. This will affect the urban mix, which has planning injunctions concerning present and future clauses.

The Urban Mix

This somewhat innovative planning tool was suggested and elaborated upon in chapter 27. It is used primarily as a planning tool, but its terms of reference will help in all other aspects concerning cities.

By adding additional criteria, the components of the urban mix will become clearer and increase the practicality of our procedure. We have stipulated that all cities are made up of the following:

1. Land – that is, the plots, local topography and ownership information (especially public).
The land division creates the subsequent public space in streets and squares, and other urban elements.

2. Buildings are never entirely separated from architecture. Thus, some measure of the design and appearance can be introduced here, alongside with the measure of the general bulk of the existing buildings. Buildings are articulated by architecture, by symbols and elements of design, to make them understandable and self-explanatory. This is achieved by forming exterior elevations fit to perform some measure of urban order with the help of some natural light. Interiors will have a secondary role, lacking that natural light and becoming less important in the urban context.

3. Use and zoning are better quantified by a measure of intensity and the urban role they play and not just by their local aspect. The local aspect can then be weighed by some measure of comparative intensity.

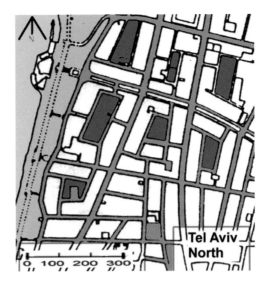

The Geddes plan (Tel Aviv) has the advantages of a modern plan that "works". Conceived as a mixture of commercial streets, with a backdrop of residential quarters, it results in some north-south arteries (mixed uses), and small protected gardens, for residential purposes, and relatively stable in time. This land division and plan can be read as the happy combination of an urban mix with a strong character all provided by a good land arrangement.

CONSERVATION POTENTIAL					URBAN MIX
CHARACTER DEFINITION	LOCALITY SENSE	INTERNAL RELATIONS	STYLE & DESIGN	METHODS & MATERIALS	
					LAND
					BUILDING
					USE

Formation of a city or a borough as the result of land allocation and division (Jaffa, Israel). Choosing a particular direction will in itself be a major factor of normal use. This direction need not be very precise or outstanding. From the point of view of urban mix , this is where we read the "land" influence, as a quality in existing and future planning.

Jaffa | 0 100 200 300

The intensity is manifold as it is manifested in many kinds of uses and possible activities, where every category will be judged on its own.

Estimating degrees of intensity will help in the understanding of the urban hierarchy.

Appraising Conservation Potential

One of the central questions in the matter of conserving parts of the urban entity is the worthiness of a district for conservation. If the potential of the given area is analyzed thoroughly, an answer can be found.

City sections and districts under our consideration are qualified in two ways. The first deals with physical dimensions and appearance, the second is the qualitative one, handling esthetic and historical appreciation. They are both aided by a comparative appraisal of those qualities.

1. Structural Basis

Introducing the land / buildings / use mix into the structure analysis.

The following is a brief summary of the physical aspects of urban structure, 1. The urban webs which are spread through the city; 2. The pertinent local pattern. 3. The particular site, section or district, made up by a collection of similar or different blocks and composed by: 4. Buildings on plot divisions. The locality will also contain some (5.) primary, secondary or natural features. All or some of the above may have been discovered as the existing structural components of the site.

We now use the urban mix summary in conjunction with the urban structure in a table form. This table will enable some systematic arrangement of the source and nature of each element, to point out whether it stems from or is tied up with the nature of the land, the buildings or the local uses.

Some squares in the table are filled in to illustrate the concept.

This table will provide some clarity as to our intentions as

URBAN PROFILE RELATED TO THE URBAN MIX						
SITE:						
URBAN MIX	**STRUCTURAL ELEMENTS**					
	WEB	DISTRICT	BLOCKS DIVISIONS	PRIMARY ELEMENTS	SECONDARY ELEMENTS	NATURE
LAND	regular					
BUILDING	3 stories					
USE	housing					

planners. We have to note that not all the squares are relevant or can be filled. The structure is obviously created solely by a particular kind of mix. Only then can one go into the planning process (conservation oriented), because the urban structure will have been understood in its mix, as well as in its geometry. As we become aware of how diverse conservation activities can be, this methodology will enable us to control conservation, the care taken to prevent us from damaging the contents and prevent planning errors at the level in which detailed decisions are made.

2. The indicator of the conservation potential

The second and more subjective measurement was helped by the use of a diagram in the form of a pie chart (see chapter 26). This diagram constitutes (in percentage values) a measure of the potential conservation quality present in the given site. The five qualities we have defined are a) a clear definition of the site b) the unique feeling of the locality c) internal relations of bulk d) the prevalent style and design e) local materials and workmanship. Each of these prerequisites is allocated a measure of 20% in the total estimate of the potential, and a total is reached (clearly a rough estimate). When this is judged to be below 50%, the case for conservation is rather weak. The examples provided in chapter 26 allow some

The urban mix, i.e., the definable and somewhat dynamic components that make a city, starts with land division. A borough in south Tel Aviv, built about 60 years ago, is clearly based on block arrangements frequent in Europe. Plot sizes being around 250 sq.m. , and division allowing a party wall, density was set at a high figure, with building coverage at around 230%. This had a difficult effect from the start, with a strong deterioration potential, which did happen in the next 20 years.

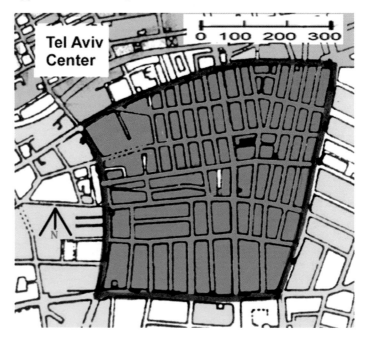

The old city of Jerusalem, in this aerial photo, shows the effect of the built environment on the urban mix. It is clear that urban density of this nature is achieved by a peculiarity of building arrangements (admittedly on a special land subdivision). This peculiarity is limited in height (usually three stories), as air and light have difficulty reaching ground floors.

Actual Buildings

The urban mix component we call "use", is meant to be an indicator of the way people use their cities, and at what comparative intensity. An extreme example will be an open-air market, shown here. In this case it is not influenced by buildings or land divisions; it is pure "use". Uses have a tendency of a comparative high rate of change. They are the easiest to be influenced by municipal by-laws and regulations. It is clear, however, that the use by people is the life quality of a place, and its asset in many respects. Nonetheless, it is also tied to land and to buildings.

clarification of these calculations. We note that our estimate is always based on either esthetical or historical considerations.

It will serve as a reminder to repeat the conservation makeup components in detail:

The five criteria , used in estimating the conservation potential:

A. Clarity of borders

These can be recognizable urban elements, such as city squares, parks, side streets and elements of nature.

B. Feeling of locality

The site's atmosphere and urban spaces, with links to the city and to nature as well as a sense of protected urbanity.

C. Internal relations

Mainly proportions of the urban space as created by the volumes of the built environment.

D. Style and design

This concerns mainly the overall design approach and the principal style prevalent at the site.

E. Workmanship and Materials

A high level of performance in building technology. To that can be added considerations of the special materials employed in an authentic manner.

The aforementioned qualities, summarizing the appreciation of esthetic and/or historical resources, (sometimes by comparison to other and similar sites) concerns cultural and civic meaning. It is normally the result of an identification and understanding of an urban hierarchy and symbol, helped by the prevalent architectural ambience. This appreciation is necessary in order to create some common agreement as to the necessity of a planned formation of urban conservation. This is, in fact, preservation of an urban context of identity, not clearly definable and made more complex because of that. However, an attempt is worth the effort of trying a measure of further analysis.

To show the prospects of a deeper investigation, we estimate that our judgements, whether esthetic or historical

The webs are made of stronger or weaker strands, as this photograph of Paris indicates. The bigger arteries are the main structural ties. Considered as the outcome of an urban mix, we have a special land division, with many triangular corners, the result of cutting across old quarters, frequent in Paris. Other divisions may be more regular, in a mix where the buildings themselves are the major contributors.

Block creation in the city of Rome. The seemingly haphazard size and nature of these old blocks is quite unique, and widespread in Rome. The result of the city's long history, it results in an urban mix not easy to analyze. However, the mixed uses present in every block are a major factor; the changes and adaptations the use goes through, shape the block much the same as land division and building changes may do. One can find a similarity in the shapes of the blocks, esp. in their respective size, but it is the mixture of a church, a government office plus some apartments that is the striking quality here.

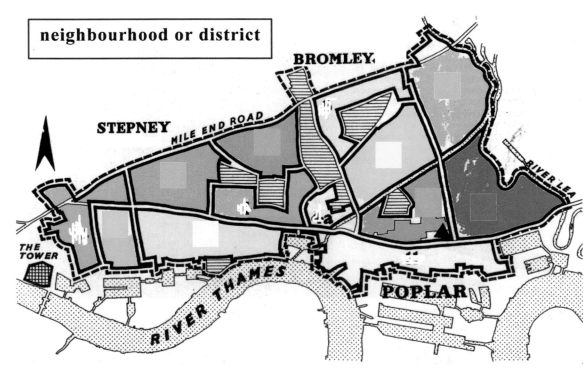

neighbourhood or district

BROMLEY

STEPNEY   MILE END ROAD

RIVER LEA

THE TOWER

RIVER THAMES   POPLAR

The creation of various districts in time, containing differing neighborhoods, is a mixture of old land division, with dense, but boring and suburban typology, in intensively dense, overcrowded residential use (East London). These neighborhoods or districts had a life of their own, tied with the former docks, or with industrial establishments, which have since all disappeared. What is indicative are their poor connections to the central city, as well as their inner links.

(of the conservation potential), are established on the basis of some urban facts. Those are not always self-evident, but nevertheless, they make up the urban environment. We will try to be more precise by using the adopted term "urban mix".

Further precision of the conservation potential

Each of the three primary elements of the urban mix influence one another. In fact, each component is based either on land qualities or on buildings, and in some cases on the peculiarities of use by residents. It can therefore be illuminating to create three pie charts, each for every component of the mix. The roughly 20% allocated to each makeup component, is the sum of 7% contributed by each of the three separate elements of the urban mix. Thus, for example, the category of style and design quality may stem up from land division (say 5%), buildings with special features (say 7%) and the use, (which may be non existent) - (0%). This makes for the 12% addition to the total potential. Our table will be clear and easy to follow, when conducted in the above manner, with a section for every separate urban component, rather than the more visual pie charts in chapter 26.

Further analysis of the conservation potential can now be achieved by weighing each of the five conservation potential elements on the scale of the urban mix that makes them. Thus, apart from esthetic and historic comparison of fitness on a percentage basis, we use the module of the urban mix (land/ buildings/ use); this will refine our search and present it in a way close to planning procedures. Each of those three quantities contributes to what was basically a value judgement.

Summing up and clarification

Urbanity is initiated by the necessary division of the land, so as to place buildings in a certain way, mostly predeter-

We have found a variety of urban webs (Tel Aviv), each outstanding in its own right. Each has to be well connected, as efficient as possible, some creating better ties with close districts than others. From the structural point of view, separate land divisions, originating in different periods, have to be examined for the links they create. The building component can bridge those gaps, with regular use. In the case below(see insert) natural land barriers (a local river) have not been bridged, and constitute an unhealthy barrier.

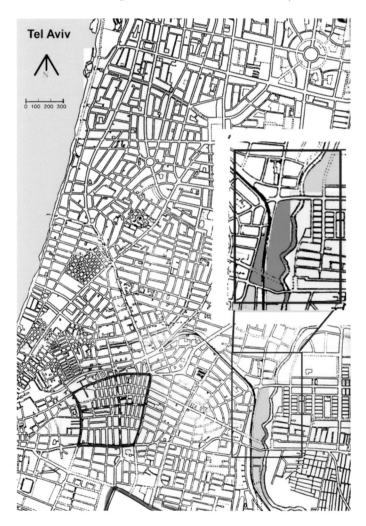

The conservation principles involved in the preservation of the Bahai parks (Haifa) is self-evident, as it plays a vivid urban role, helped by local topography.

mined. In order to enable this urban conglomeration to function in a permissible and coordinated fashion, the process is facilitated by introducing a hierarchy of urban functions (zones and use), controlled and implemented by the urban mix.

Conservation Procedures

Decisions regarding what is to be conserved are to be made before the selected tools are used. The tools will be those that can in some way change the peculiarities in the urban mix. That is why the difficulty lies in planning, and the importance of not freezing a given situation should be remembered. The site is to be allowed to develop as freely as possible in all respects, the only directives being the terms of the mix, controlled and amended. It is futile to plan and establish lifeless cities, containing some half-preserved sites.

Conservation can be done with the help of the comprehensive nature of the urban mix, with the view of raising the level of the economy and the standard of living.

A greater opportunity to create a strong base for conser-

Primary elements in the city structure are mostly streets and squares. Those are the principal visual urban features. They are again recognized as such during the past decades, as exemplified by renewal in adjoining photographs. A central renewed square in Frankfurt (Germany), and a subdued, widened street in Prague, are therefore quoted.

vation will transform it into a beneficial tool for the environment. The city will not become incapacitated by an undesirable frozen situation.

In many instances, it has been proven that if conservation is properly conducted, it can improve the regional economy by an increased activity. This is one of conservation's desired results: the increase of the standard of living and the transformation of the whole region into an active, vibrant one. The site can be used as a mixed residential area within the city web. This can be attempted by observing and studying various approaches to conservation and comparing examples from other locations, some more successful than others. Comparison of similar aspects will be carried out in an orderly fashion, with factors of equal value, so as not to stray in value judgements.

The study will culminate (but not end) in the determination of the percentage of the conservation potential. This has been explored to provide a familiarity with the subject matter, in a measurable and objective manner. When one feels confident that all ingredients have been understood and ready for some public accord, by a methodical system, one can proceed into recommendations.

The existing mix of land/ buildings/ use is going to be affected when we finalize our findings and recommendations, and we must organize the expected future planning changes.

General guidelines for conservation planning

As experience is gained, it becomes apparent that urban conservation is a planned process that accompanies all other urban planning. Furthermore, a plan that incorporates means of conservation will be preserved longer in this respect. Every region undergoing new planning can include conservation clauses so that they ensure continuity, allowing for permanent tools in maintaining and conserving the web. Experience has shown that this concept has proven valid on an operational level. If we do not ensure the use of such tools, the region may soon degenerate.

The secondary urban element, containing a park, in which a cultural landmark is set, serves as an illustration of one of the structural urban elements (Carlovi Vari).

The primary urban elements, mainly streets and squares, are abundant in Rome. Their principal and very prominent quality is the constant presence of the interconnections in this system. This has helped the promotion of the present urban mix.

Urban structure, with its background of an urban mix, is illustrated in the example bellow. The Place d' Italy, Paris, is one of the big squares of Europe. When we analyze its structure, we will find a few anomalies. The table used for that, serves as a kind of check list.

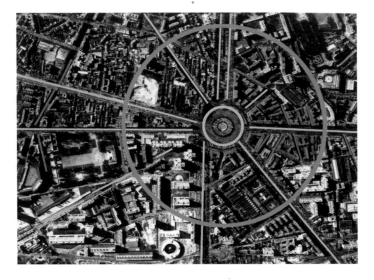

URBAN PROFILE RELATED TO THE URBAN MIX

PLACE D'ITALY, PARIS RADIUS OF 90m.

URBAN MIX	STRUCTURAL ELEMENTS					
	WEB	DISTRICT	BLOCKS DIVISIONS	PRIMARY ELEMENTS SQUARES STREETS		SECONDARY ELEMENTS	NATURE
LAND	radial	shape of squares	old	round	1	—	
BUILDING	—	few left	changing	!	changing	municipal	—
USE	—	mixed	mixed	!	!!		boulevard

Additional planning factors of a discussed site and its internal and external relationships must be included. In order to determine a final framework for a site worthy of conservation, outline plans should be drawn up and analyzed for flexibility in future use. Eventually, this determination will be linked to urban planning codes and buildings, with the conservation clauses to be recommended.

Realistically, we cannot predetermine at which stage of urban planning actual conservation will become a factor, as it depends on economic and, occasionally, on political issues. We also cannot predict what the conservation guidelines in national or metropolitan outline plans will be. It is extremely difficult to make any such predictions. We can be equipped with the conservation material and analysis and attempt the formulation of building regulations and codes, until they become necessary.

We can also anticipate the preparation of long-term conservation plans in addition to overall national or county intentions. In specific instances, urban or metropolitan conservation plans will be such as to require addition of conservation clauses in every outline plan for the future, such as infill, demolition, restoration, etc. Implementation of these recommendations is more complex. The majority of the implementation will be conducted with the assistance of conservation codes in various designated boroughs, analysis of possible progress and guidelines regarding detailed planning, as development dictates.

The urban planner's intentions are, by definition, inclusive. It is not too difficult to incorporate the suggested changes and procedures as issues of planning measures. In terms of methodology, we should choose the suitable codes, and rewrite some of them, within urban plans that are either being prepared or are in effect. At any rate, conservation codes will be required to reflect the changes in the various forms of hierarchy, some of which already may exist, but may be disoriented or misapplied.

Summary of the conservation procedure

The concepts of our investigation steps were:
1. The structure
2. The urban mix (a planning concept)
3. The conservation identity and makeup

Those can now be summed up. The element linking the whole is the urban mix. It is the only one to contain quantities and precise regulations.

All urban changes of plan will be achieved through a measure of change in the mix.

The table we have to form contains the full analysis of the existing situation, in the form of an urban profile (see table at the end of the chapter). The right side contains the structural elements, reflected in the urban mix , and recognizable as factors in existing planning statures, codes and zoning. The left side contains the relevant sum of the conservation components. This is where planning will decide which are the necessary elements which have to be reinforced or preserved, helped by the structural features on the right.

The above deliberations will result in some recommendations for the future. On the right, decisions as to what urban components we want to keep, in an hierarchical order and in detailed urban mix. On the left, we can mark the qualities that need reinforcing, changing or elaborating upon.

The result of these deliberations will be marked by "change" (from present to future), which calls for a change in planning notions. The change may occur either in the structure of the site, which is a planning recommendation, or in the conservation makeup or upgrading, which has a more complex role. It is precisely these changes that become the input of conservation into the statutory planning procedures.

Methodology serves only as a guide to the approach to conservation. Solutions will come with actual work, which may require separate alternatives. The restored web, renewed in its potency, will come as the result of the inclusion of new economic uses. This being the

A clear definition and structure of a quarter can be the result of a major artery in the city. The dark colored urban section, near the Opera, in Paris, is clearly the outcome of the location of such arteries. As far as the urban mix is concerned, the buildings help in forming the above definition.

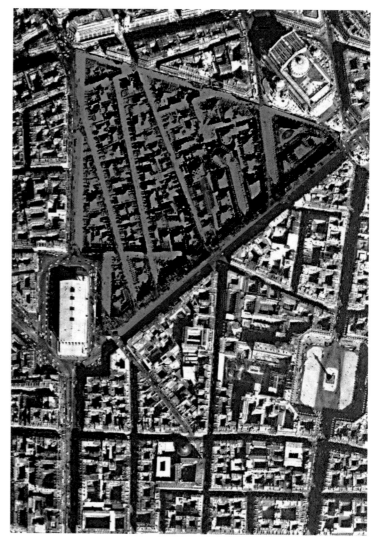

case, planning has an indirect influence on the results. As this is not the purpose of the present volume, it is best not to enter into planning suggestions. Instead, we will add a chapter entirely devoted to examples. We have selected several examples of conservation on an urban scale. The overall approach begins to become apparent in each example, even if there still is no final formulation or system.

Close attention should be paid to the entire entity the planner has established. If the problem is not properly defined in physical terms, the planner will unintentionally preserve items that are not influential and often reduce the quality of conservation.

URBAN PROFILE RELATED TO THE URBAN MIX
SITE: ST. PAUL'S, LONDON

CONSERVATION POTENTIAL					URBAN MIX
CHARACTER DEFINITION 20% max	LOCALITY SENSE	INTERNAL RELATIONS	STYLE & DESIGN	METHODS & MATERIALS	
3%	2%	3%	1%	1%	LAND
3%	6%	4%	5%	2%	BUILDING
7%	3%	2%	2%	0%	USE

LEGEND	Total Potential 44%	Present state ☐ %		Sub total 7% max

As a subject for conservation, this part of the City in London is analyzed by the urban mix method, in the table on the left. One has to bear in mind that as a each makeup component, (each one out of five), carries a weight of 20%, we will devote a third of that, i.e. 7%, to each of the three urban mix qualifiers. We analyze a slightly noncoherent site just to illustrate our method. The total arrived at, 44%, indicates a rather low preservation potential. The table also points out the simple fact that the "building" total (i.e. the horizontal sum of nearly 20%), has the largest contribution to the mix. As we are looking for a comparative uniqueness, we may note that the reconstruction of the area after the war, which obliterated the peculiarities of the historical land division, retained only one kind of use, not very significant or special, and this is reflected in the table.

The city of Basel offers an admirable example of a well-defined region. Its clear borders stem from a mix of the land division, which has its source in the middle ages, and of the regularity of its buildings. This is a way of saying, when weighting the potential for conservation, that the use of the region does not contribute to its defined borders.

The easiest definition of a region comes when the clarity of its borders is achieved by an existing city wall. In such an instance it is recommended to look for connections and links with the vicinity, to check for their efficiency, needed to reinforce the site. (The old town of Avila, Spain, above). It is the building of the old walls that contributes here, rather than the land division or the actual use.

The sense of place offered by the eastern Europe square (above in black and white), is the result of a mix, in equal measures, of all the components of the historical urban mix. This characteristic is normally sensitive to the possible change of its components.

The relation of the unique methods employed to build these protection towers (in the early middle ages) is mainly to the old plots. Their present use being minimal, alongside with the crudity of their appearance, may became an incentive to discover the old land divisions, and perhaps retain them in a prominent manner, so as to reinforce it, thus helping the mix.

photo

JERUSALEM - Yamin-Moshe quarter   N →

plan

URBAN PROFILE Related to the urban mix
YEMIN MOSHE QUARTER

CONSERVATION POTENTIAL					URBAN MIX	STRUCTURAL ELEMENTS					
CHARACTER DEFINITION	LOCALITY SENSE	INTERNAL RELATIONS	STYLES & DESIGN	METHODS & MATERIALS		WEB	DISTRICT	BLOCKS DIVISIONS	PRIMARY ELEMENTS	SECONDARY ELEMENTS	NATURE
7%	6%	5%	3%	4%	LAND	-	!!!	0	!!!	!! / 0	!!! / 0
6%	7%	5% +2%	6%	4% +3%	BUILDING	-	-	!!!	0 / !!	0 / 0	!! / 0
2% +5%	4% +3%	2% +4%	4%	3%	USE	!!	-	0	-	!! / 0	!! / 0

Total potential		Present state	%
Present	Future	Upgrade	+%
68%	82%	Sub total 7% max	

Degree of influence on conservation: 0 !

Present state ☐
State in future plan ☐

(Table above, plans and photos to the left.)

Forming one table, in which we clarify simultaneously the relation of the urban structure and of conservation, as they both relate to the urban mix, helps create an urban profile. This is done in order to amend any future conservation plan, upgrading the situation. Using this tool, we can sum up a present, given situation, in terms of the urban mix, (it serves as the common denominator here), quoted in planning terms. The next step is to note in the table the future planning moves needed for conservation purposes. These will be reflected as the future urban mix, either as a change in structure related planning clauses (right side), or as changes related to conservation needs (left side). A comparison between the future needs and the present conditions will be summed up as "changes", i.e., necessary planning directives and new clauses, to function as amendments in the prospective conservation plan. The advantage in this procedure is the clarity of future changes in the three components of the mix which are to be affected.

311

PART SEVEN

Examples of Conservation

Comparison is a very good way to proceed along the preservation axis. This will show the growing concern for urban preservation on a global and comprehensive scale.
Establishing a method for the inclusion of such concerns will clarify many issues, saving time and energy for all concerned.

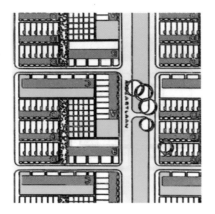

Chapter
Twenty Nine
Modern Planning

Misguided Modernism

The culmination of modern building abilities and town planning has brought about an environment nobody can admire or use culturally. It can only be perceived as some kind of necessary evil.

This view of post-war urban renewal in Brussels illustrates very well the loss that occurs with attempts to be modern. Facing long and maybe "obsolete" forms on the left, there is no inspiration or motivation to offer design on a similar level of intricate feeling.

Even the mixed use, on the planning level, which is allowed on the left only, is more appropriate to the locality, a center of town, urban street.

The popularity of scaled models can be understood to be an indication that the general public likes to observe the intricacy of urban architecture, when it is presented in a clear way. It is not the sympathy and respect for the workmanship involved, or the momentary pleasure of the Swiftian proportions that are at play. Identification with spatial observation, the realization of the clarity involved in good design and the need to identify with the built environment are what we observe in the above instance. Similar cases of public participation and sympathy are hard to find in modern exhibitions of projects. In the very rare occasions that those are presented.

Why are some places, even in the form of a model, grasped and liked at a glance? Can it be that the eye and brain feel relief when reality, in our case urban reality, is resolved in a formulated and "grammatical" way, i.e., according to the rules? Are not these rules manageable structurally?
A lesson can be learned from the need the public has to understand the environment. Is it not the role of the planner to explain and formulate the urban space? The proportions and the spaces we admire in models of old cities are found in the historical centers we can preserve. We can also admit that the rules are there to be formulated.

Since the 1950's, modern plans which do not have urban dimensions and do not create viable public space have become widespread. Planning has completely disregarded the concept of the urban web and of cultural continuity. Lax treatment aided by this attitude has left us with buildings that astound us with their inability to replace historical cities. The true alternative to the failure of urban conservation in many places is to live in suburbia.

The new towns, neighborhoods and quarters appear to resemble an organized and temporary camp. Although they are suitable replacements for poorer neighborhoods (relative comfort, cleanliness and low prices), they cannot atone for faulty, superficial and cheap urban planning. It is difficult to believe that architects and planners created these suburban "camps".

In the 1990's, things begin to look better, when planners attempt to retry traditional city webs and not shape them to fit the will of the governments or entrepreneurs. We are currently discussing a policy of infill, web conservation, creation of convenient, eye-pleasing spaces. In other words, there is an attempt to preserve the city and learn from it.

One has to make do with an haphazard shape of reality, ("dynamic", or is it " imposing"), whose effect is the disruption of eye level-urbanity. One cannot fight the giants. The only possibility left is to understand what went wrong. Urban culture has lost to the skyscraper, and there cannot be any way of undoing this reality. Planners can contribute only on the basis of viable and structured alternatives, based on cultural premises. The proposed debate will start at the conservation level.

What can be the urban contribution of diagonally placed blocks thus presented to the eye? It creates a composition on the lines of a different orthogonal direction, perhaps more dynamic. Is it what the environment requires? (Chicago). The sensible plan would have been an effort of resolving a visual conflict, and offering the public some usable outdoor space.

Many instances of modern planning, such as shown in the examples, are rudimentary and very regimental. They still manage to induce a slight feeling of hysteria. The urgency to house people, especially after the war, was the main excuse, along with "freedom" offered by modern principles. One is very much reminded of ancient Roman army camps; they happened 2000 years ago. Is it then true that people can survive in any condition, and will embrace anything they are offered ?

At the end of the present century, architects and planners alike begin to feel that the mistakes of planning were great. Some of them are inexcusable. Thus, one of the reasons of looking back is the search for the possible solution to a wrong approach. This is where the research into urban coherence will help.

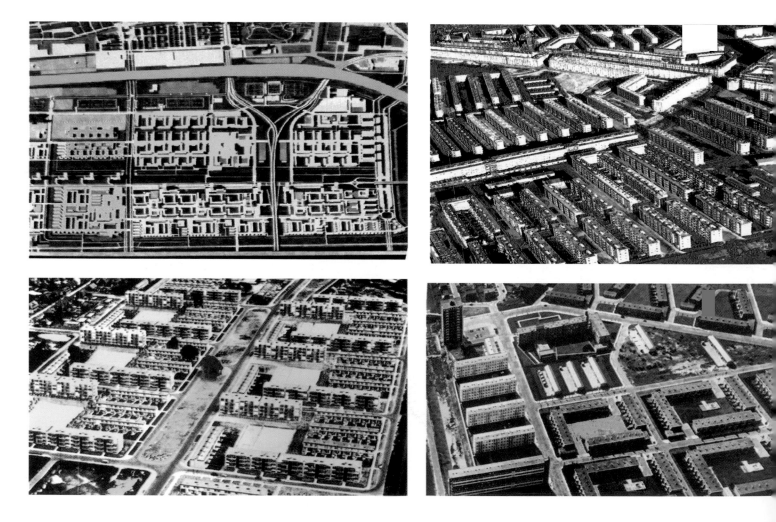

The examples cited are brought here as a reminder. Are we going to turn our urban environment into an alien one, with no alternatives to speak of, while at the same time advocating tourist attractions of classical and 'premodern' architecture? It seems that this double-talk attitude towards design has been the order of the day for too long, and is not strongly criticized.

The naive habit of showing tourists scaled models of famous buildings, illustrates the above even further. People are normally attracted to objects and environments they can understand and use easily.

The architecture of city space they are admiring in

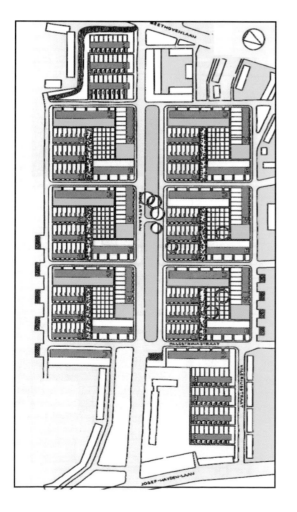

Old town centers are cleaned up and modernized, with the inclusion of indifferent buildings. It is to be suspected that architecture is indifferent, because it has lost the function of explaining and giving clarity to urban elements and situations. When the urban structure is changed irreversibly, without any degree of conservation of past assets, one suddenly loses the urban "raison d'etre", and with it the public, civic and urban presence of the single building, which can become an isolated, well-designed edifice.

A central, partially renovated square in Frankfurt (Germany). This isolated and admirable attempt looks futile relative to the disregard by surrounding plans and reality.

Many cities carry this imprint of modernity, which becomes another way of saying that nothing is even attempted coherently way. The disruption of urbanity becomes established, meaning a break with a cultural achievement. Discarding past achievements in the name of expediency results in other losses we incur, one of them being the social cohesion inherent in urban principles.

The unified street front containing different architectural principles will serve as a reminder of the history of the present century (Chicago). Old planning principles have helped to contain the eruption of modernity here, and some beneficial physical order is observed. However, architects designing along this street have differed in the way they have interpreted the role of their building in the spatial order of the urban space, and no real contribution is created, except for the demonstration of some personal ability.

models is the one we are trying to preserve.

The urban planning perspective that we have suggested can only distinguish implementation to a certain extent. This is why we attempt to provide several actual examples.

A minimal amount of examples prove that there is still a great deal of work in this new and developing field. The first example discusses San Francisco and includes unique old neighborhoods. We see that the lack of well-planned conservation has caused a number of distortions in judgement and fundamental planning guidelines. An additional example will illustrate the attempt to judge urban conservation in an ancient city.

Preservation measures have resulted in an environment which was not subjected to a disruption of its history and cohesion. Some buildings were kept, others respectfully renovated. Block shapes were positively adopted and a local sense still persists. The proportions were found sensible, land utilization high, a sensible continuity maintained, proving that urban conservation is a matter of decision and choice, which can be extremely beneficial. It is possible that individual speculative gains were reduced, but so was the cost and burden to the immediate environment.

A possible emblem of the achievement of the present century. As we turn into a new century, an alternative is not presented . We are burdened with an incredible technological ability of building, advanced in creating tall structures composed of similar compartments, possessing a repeatable and doubtful identity. We manage to use these achievements at the cost of a divorce from a stable and viable community.

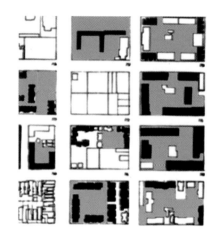

Chapter Thirty

San Francisco, U.S.A.

The Existing Situation
Conservation Attempts

A beautiful section of San Francisco is undergoing transformation. The clarity of conservation aims was not challenged and the results raise some questions.

The example illustrated below was excerpted from Anne Vernez Moudon's excellent and highly recommended book, *Built for Change* (MIT Press). The book is a result of well-conducted research, acquiring immediate relevancy.

The region researched is San Francisco, U.S.A., and includes the Alamo Quarter, established in the mid-1800's with a rigid geometrical land division. Topography, as well as codes that enable division into smaller parcels, were not taken into account.

The condensed summary of the approximately one hundred years of the neighborhood's existence leads

Seeing changes such as these, one feels that they need not have happened. The simplification of the building methods have not been beneficial. They are the complete negation of the prevailing old methods. More should be done in this respect if preservation is wanted. The effort needed is to classify the technology and regard it as valuable.

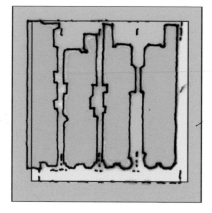

The repetitions of the dwellings, in height, frontage, details, and their individuality, are all a valuable asset to the city. Present day technology is very seldom individually developed. One does not find examples in the same vein any longer. When appreciated methodically, the existing qualities can be preserved. In all events, local codes can emulate some principal qualities, but those should be first typified and analyzed.

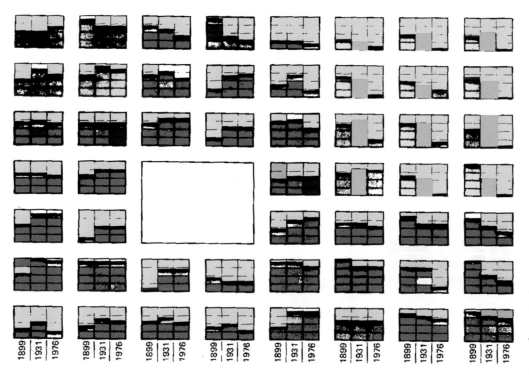

This table shows the fall (between 1931 and 1976) of the number of dwelling units per block. One can see clearly the vacancy created in that area (blue in 1931), until a complete emptiness results. This points to the long presence of a problem, as is usually the case. The other data will reinforce this fact. Allowing an uncontrolled mixed use is, at the very least, partly responsible.

one to realize that the city eventually failed in its attempt to preserve the nature of the neighborhood. We witness the gradual well-documented destruction of the web, which need not have happened, had planners been sufficiently aware of the necessary conservation hierarchy that determines what is to be preserved and by what measures.

The local style developed with significant Victorian overtones. Its scale is a very friendly, and because the entire neighborhood was developed in the same period, it looks as a typical site for conservation on an urban scale. It also has a recognizable system of detail, carried throughout. The changes the site is undergoing are typical of our period, and have been dealt with in some similar places.

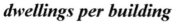

dwellings per building

These excellent maps show the result of the urban renewal meant to correct the declining use in the northeast corner of the neighborhood. It becomes clear again, that the renewal was not conducted in conjunction with some conservation purpose in mind. The result is a successful upgrading of the blocks concerned, but a failure in terms of the visual environment.

One of the clues provided by maps such the one below is the probable reason for the deterioration observed, as non-residential uses, in big portions, overcrowd the vicinity. The blocks thus occupied are getting numerous as time goes on, resulting , apart from the negative effect on neighboring dwellings, in the obliteration of the traditional land division. Thus, when the opportunity of easy development and renewal presents itself, it does so neglecting   lost values.

The result of the former table. The clearing of small plots means losing contact with at least part of history, the sort of "memory" persisting after buildings are gone. When small private owners are involved, this will not easily happen and the locality will preserve itself, at least partially. In the case above, bigger owners on the blocks concerned, have gone into the unification process, creating shapes that will cause a new set of rules.

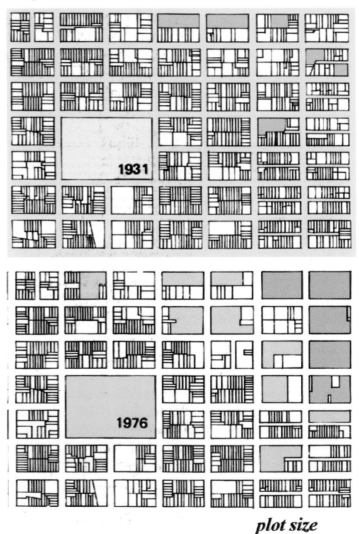

non residential use in black

plot size

Analysis of the Existing Situation

The neighborhood, a residential area with an allocation of mixed use and a great deal of flexibility in the selection of the subdivision, is the product of European influences in the United States at the beginning of its independence.

The flexibility, however, is not necessarily European. On the contrary, it has a definite free-for-all touch. As the book's title indicates, we begin with an open situation subject in advance to changes, since it is defined by flexible land use and characterized by secondary divisions too unruly for control. These changes become unhealthy over time.

In this respect, we have a prime example that constitutes a realization of how an over-divided grid influences conservation motives (sooner or later). Under such conditions, future preservation is doubtful. It is only natural that the prominent example is situated in the United States, bound for failure, due to the excess of laissez-faire. The three factors influencing urban planning: land division, manner of construction and population – the urban mix – were not taken into full account. No wonder regions that undergo serious changes eventually move towards their own destruction if the process is not well understood. The region fulfills all of the criteria for conservation and its urban role is not especially vulnerable.

This is a warning sign for modern planning, which tends to scorn rational land division.

Conservation Attempts

In the example provided, the study of the conservation components (what is to be preserved and how) appears to be a study in wrong directives. Planning authorities did not select changes in codes, evaluation of prototypes and new outlines. Hence, the lack of clarity in plans that stemmed from a lack of clearly defined goals and of no definition of means to achieve them. Preliminary conservation studies on spatial components, parcel sizes, construction methods and geometrical expanse were, however, conducted. Changes that had far-reaching

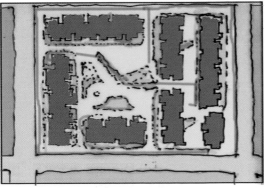

Complete disregard for the typical block, which has some very definable attributes, points to the simple fact, that conscious conservation was not even attempted. It is relatively simple to notice that many qualities in the local street stem mainly from land subdivision, which has some typical sizes and depth measurements. Those have been utterly discarded. The result loses the sense of uniqueness prevalent all over the site. It can be noted that it is not only a matter of style. It is the urban structure that should have been respected.

When the subdivision, with its strong local presence, is emulated in an half-heartedly way, and everyday technology is used, we are faced with an unacceptable cultural fact - modernity thus used lacks visual quality, and cannot compete with traditional methods. This of course is not the only reason, it is motivation that was lacking; once conservation is adopted, and agreed upon, ways and means are always available.

implications, such as the nature of ownership or the size of the subdivisions, were not prohibited so as to become the much needed conservation factors.

It becomes clear that at the middle of the present century, when it was understood that the district was going through a difficult period and would deteriorate, nobody took conservation steps or even a study of the factors involved. It also becomes clear that the main concerns should have been the existing land division regulations (where no law governs conservation), the size of the plot and its shape and orientation. These factors were not even considered. Eventually, the disregard of the design factor helped to arrive at urban shapes completely unfit for the environment concerned. Had this factor been considered, one imagines that some design restrictions might have been adopted in this direction.

As things stood, the restrictions imposed were of the wrong implications and character, thus not contributing to any real conservation principles at all.

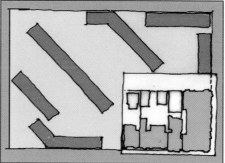

A diagonal direction of the new design, in a strongly orthogonal space, is a doubtful approach. The clarity is gone, and the original intention is now questioned. The appreciation of the space presented is marred in a very substantial manner. Or was that done so as to include more dwellings? In terms of design, those buildings could be anywhere in the world, all the local touch has been lost.

URBAN PROFILE RELATED TO THE URBAN MIX
SITE: Alamo, San Francisco

CONSERVATION POTENTIAL					URBAN MIX	STRUCTURAL ELEMENTS					
CHARACTER DEFINITION	LOCALITY SENSE	INTERNAL RELATIONS	STYLE & DESIGN	METHODS & MATERIALS		WEB	DISTRICT	BLOCKS DIVISIONS	PRIMARY ELEMENTS	SECONDARY ELEMENTS	NATURE
7%	6%	3% +4%	5%	5%	LAND	!!	! [!!]	0 [!!]			!!
6%	4%	0 +4%	4%	3%	BUILDING				! [!!]		
4%	1%	0 +3%	2%	–	USE					0	

LEGEND

Total Potential	
Present	Future
50%	59%

Present state — %
Upgrading — +%
Sub total 7% max

LEGEND — Structural Elements

0	!	!!	!!!

Degree of influence on conservation

☐ STATE AT PRESENT
☐ STATE IN FUTURE PLAN

Urban profile and planning directives for conservation, Alamo quarter, San Francisco, in conjunction with the present chapter.

A. Good preservation potential (50%), though not a high one, indicates that conservation measures need not be dramatic or expensive. Land division has a strong effect, so do the existing buildings, in defining a local and unique character.

B. Upgrading will be beneficial in emphasizing some focal points and a better hierarchy. At present, lack of hierarchy is causing some uniformity.

C. Local structure, in right side of table, stems from the strong effect that the local web and surrounding topography have.

D. It seems that stronger borders to the site and a better block emphasis (by building higher buildings around the limits of the site) can have a good effect on the definition needed.

Chapter Thirty One

Capua, Italy

**The Current Situation
Conservation Attempts**

S tudies of urban preservation are in many instances a process initiated in Italy. The following attempt is an illuminating one, as it creates some basic principles of urban understanding.

The next example illustrates the attempt to conserve on a large scale, though not on a comprehensive urban one, resulting in architectural conservation of individual buildings. It is taken from *Il Centro di Capua* by Brock, Giuliani, Moisesco, (Marsilio Ed. 1972). The extensive professional analysis conducted in the city of

The flat street front and similarity in heights appear constantly in the town. Stone treatments are elaborate and deserve attention. Their stylistic content is special and identifiable. Neglect is almost constant and runs trough most of the used materials. Buildings are related trough a party wall, always problematic in terms of ownership and sharing of preservation costs.

An entry to a common yard in Capua. Sharing the internal court (used for ventilation of upper floors), are many tenants, using differing stairs. Those internal spaces have their own uniqueness, but have to be maintained by a common agreement and good neighbor relations. The fact that mixed uses are introduced and not only on ground floor level complicates relations even further.

A normally prevailing section through front and courtyards of a building. The section shows the circulation trough the internal courts, turning them into "public right of way" on private property, and occurring in a substantial number of cases, making this usage a typifying one. This local peculiarity (not uncommon in medieval towns) does not help or simplify matters. It may be worthwhile to note that the density in the local web achieved through the land division, ancient party walls, topography, etc.

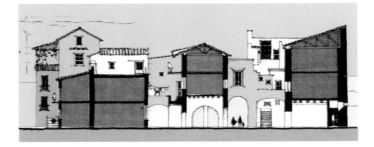

A typical street in the township of Capua, Italy. The following structural peculiarities are encountered: buildings follow the same line, forming a street with no step-back, entrances are receded into a courtyard, balconies project as overhangs. Many uses of buildings are intermixed. Ornamentation is of stone and plaster. Roofs slope sideways and meet in valley gutters.

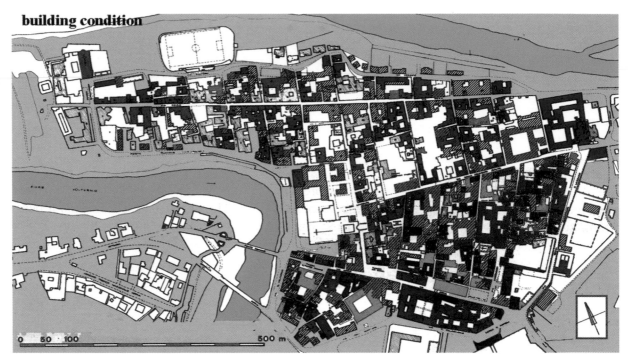

building condition

Building conditions show a deteriorating state of affairs. Many of the buildings are in serious need of repair. However, this does not mean that they have to be razed. The terms of conservation will involve systematic repairs with the assistance of a methodical technology, as has been done elsewhere.

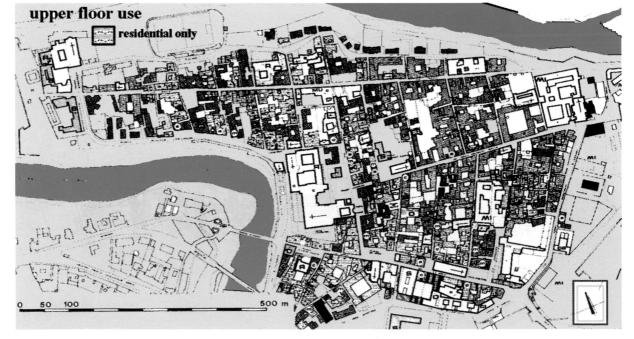

upper floor use

☐ residential only

Upper floors are less harmed by negative users. However, it is normally thought that upper floors can contain residents only. Any different state of affairs will soon deteriorate under normal conditions. Public buildings are of course of a different category.

332

Capua focused mainly on conservation of buildings. While most attention was directed towards technical conservation, other important overall aspects such as urban analysis were slightly neglected. No long-term conservation codes were formulated, or even attempted.

The Current Situation

Apparently, although extensive and orderly documentary effort was made, it focused on only one aspect: identification of the typology, so as to restore and conserve buildings. The authors of the research established a number of formulations systematically defining buildings, volumes, physical conditions, internal spaces, etc. – an innovative and valuable concept in our time. The research, however, lacks any reference to the region or overall urban area. The important factors of land division and ownership remain unclear. Only the center of the ancient city was documented (the documentation aspect being for restoration and rehabilitation purposes).

On the other hand, there are a number of references to demographics, to dwindling population as well as to economic values influencing urban blight. The authors acknowledge that it is not enough to deal solely with the center and with building restoration. In this respect, they are pioneers. The book also calls responsible politicians to draft a more comprehensive policy that includes a mutual relationship between planning and urban conservation.

Conservation Attempts

The analysis itself reveals a pessimistic trend, since modern pressures on historical city centers create frustrating situations, which regular means of conservation are incapable of solving. In contrast, the web approach, which attempts to create a planning order in every district – in the example before us, in every block – may be possible since it enables more relevant principles of land use. The problem here is on a higher plane: many of these cities are built on the "0" line and have a party wall on all sides. Definition of ownership and registration are thus

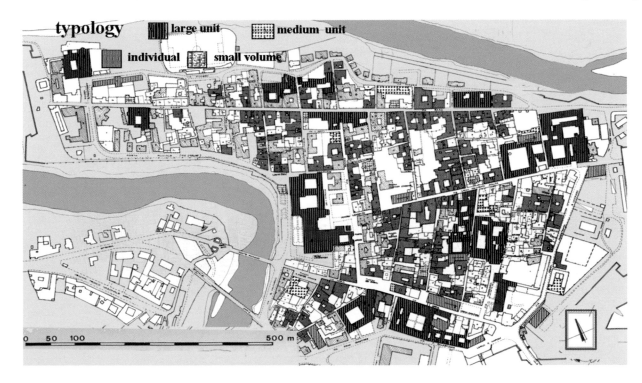

Typology of the existing buildings shows a series of particular units, but also a quantity of large complexes like churches and monasteries, having a considerable volume. All are similar in their inclusion of internal courts, pointing to the unifying identity of the local appearance.

As far as
architectural
merit is
concerned, one
finds a good
number of
buildings
responding to that
qualification. In
urban terms,
however, it is
clear that we are
faced with a
coherent
historical fabric.
The systematic
arrangement of
the structures is
one of the main
contributors to the
situation.

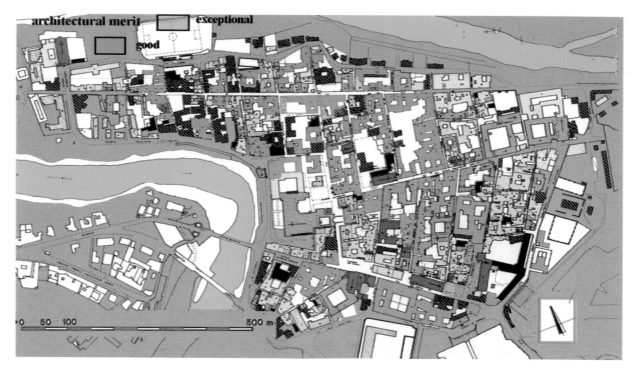

The range of the
age of different
buildings is
considerable,
especially up to
the nineteenth
century. This
serves as an
indication of the
suitability of the
present city web to
maintain a
continuous life for
a sustained
period. Reason for
deterioration is to
be searched for
elsewhere,
perhaps in the
details of land
division and
ownership.

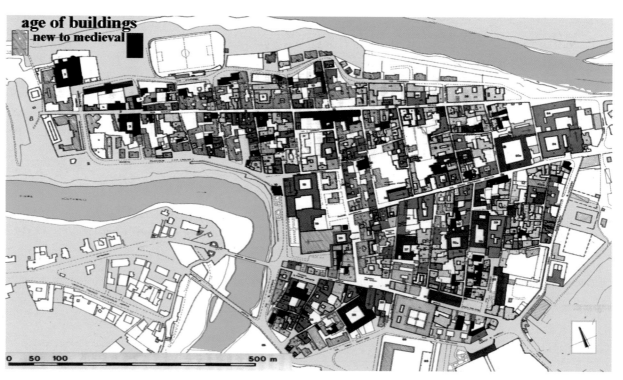

extremely problematic.

Conservation in such places of mixed ownerships and un-clear divisions calls for an even more complex approach, where cooperation of owners has to be imposed in some degree.

URBAN PROFILE RELATED TO THE URBAN MIX
SITE: The town of Capua

CONSERVATION POTENTIAL					URBAN MIX	STRUCTURAL ELEMENTS					
CHARACTER DEFINITION	LOCALITY SENSE	INTERNAL RELATIONS	STYLE & DESIGN	METHODS & MATERIALS		WEB	DISTRICT	BLOCKS DIVISIONS	PRIMARY ELEMENTS	SECONDARY ELEMENTS	NATURE
3% +3%	5%	5%	1%	0%	LAND	geometrical !!		courts !!	streets		river
7%	6%	4%	4%	4%	BUILDING		similar method			churches	
4%	3% +3%	0% +5%	0%	2%	USE				0 mixed !!		ancient road

LEGEND						LEGEND				
	Total Potential		Present state	%				0 ! !! !!!		STATE AT PRESENT
	Present	Future	Upgrading	+%				Degree of influence on conservation		STATE IN FUTURE PLAN
	48%	59%		Sub total 7% max						

Urban profile and planning directives for conservation, for the city of Capua, Italy, in conjunction with the present chapter.

A. Good preservation potential, not a high one, indicates that conservation measures will be relatively restrained. Buildings, as the marks indicate, strongly influence the potential. Good internal relations and volumes, aided by genuine locality sense are primarily the result of traditional land division.

B. Upgrading is important and will affect the potential by clearing some uses and helping the definition of land ownership.

C. Local structure is created by geometry and unique internal courts, aided by secondary structures and elements with clearly definable blocks.

D. Future plan will have to reconsider the mixed use and restrain it.

Chapter Thirty Two

Tel Aviv, Israel

The Renewal of South Tel Aviv
Renewal in Central Tel Aviv

Tel Aviv as the central town in Israel is changing rapidly. Conservation is attempted on a reduced scale, but has its success.

Tel Aviv is a new city (approximately 100 years old) and includes a number of webs, some of which are leftovers of the 19th century, the beginnings of modern planning, Bauhaus influenced districts, new Garden City approaches, working class neighborhoods and some high density, high rise areas. For this reason, and because of the city's close proximity to Jaffa and its ancient city, it is a living museum of planning styles. Since the 1980's, Tel Aviv has been subject to planning approaches that include a diverse range of conservation. This was promoted by city patrons, city engineers, and planning departments encouraging young architects. One of the interesting examples of this work is the renewal and conservation of Bauhaus buildings. (See *Batim min HaHol,* a special publication written by architect Niza Smok. Although not translated yet, the book provides many superb examples and graphics).

The majority of the approximately 600 Bauhaus type of edifices built in Tel Aviv since the 1920's have been documented and designated for conservation. Conservation is mainly architectural, which, though relatively easy to formulate, encounters legal problems, requiring a special code of urban planning, renewed occasionally by the county's preservation committees.

The difficulty in the codes stems from the fact that the buildings are privately owned. The conservation problem arising from such a situation is obvious. Although the

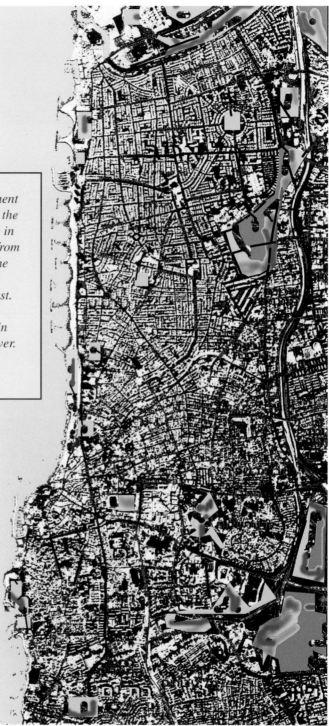

The final result of the development of Tel Aviv, shown with Jaffa at the bottom. A very strong influence in this rapid development comes from the direction (north-south) of the sea, and the narrow formation, limited by a river bed on the east. The clarity of the orthogonal direction is finally established in the north, again limited by a river. Jaffa shows a radial scheme, typical to historic centers.

*As Tel Aviv reaches its limit , the old central
section , related to Jaffa and the sea front,
deteriorates further. This region was always
problematic. Historic relations to Jaffa were
never too good, and planned changes have
not materialized. Land situated on the
borderline with historic cities is bound to have
late development, as ownership, grids and old
roads, all hamper building. The area shown
has the unclear tendency to develop office
blocks and hotels, undistinguished from each
other. When developments are delayed in
central areas, diverse, sometimes opposed,
undertakings are encouraged.*

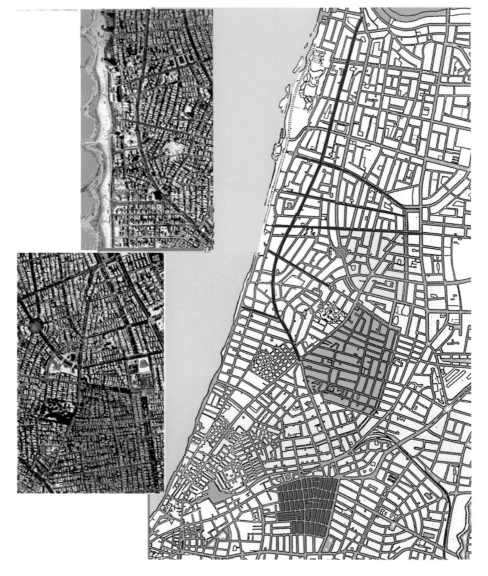

*The developing grids are shown alongside
their air photos, and colored respectively.
Their initial formation is not always the result
of clear planning, and can stem from odd
shaped ownership with oddities of
topography. It is also indicative that the main
thoroughfare (in red), changes its direction,
from one perpendicular to the radials of
Jaffa, to the one sensibly parallel to the sea.
The purple marked grid denotes the south Tel
Aviv grid.*

buildings are now being successfully preserved, the immediate environment undergoes normal changes or neglect. 50-60 year old buildings are being renewed while their immediate environment, of the same age, disintegrates, and we are left with preservation in a deteriorating environment.

The scope of urban renewal and conservation in Tel Aviv is considerable, despite its age. Of the first order is the difficulty that it was built not long ago around the ancient (5000 years) historic port town of Jaffa. The two city webs, the old one completely radial in nature and the new one, predominantly orthogonal and parallel to the sea front, cannot be easily reconciled. The approach to the city of Jaffa will be closely examined in the next chapter. It can only be added that as the full name of this city shows (Tel Aviv -Jaffa), it contains two centers, not resolved into one as yet. The meeting place between the two major webs

The main value of this south Tel Aviv quarter is clear in the example. Unique building design and style, like the one shown, has a strong presence in the neighborhood. The encouraged preservation has succeeded to some degree, even though a more radical approach, one of alleviating the local residential density is not easily manageable. Other efforts, such as weeding out harmful uses, and establishing public and community services to some degree, are beneficial. It is an open question for how long such sustained efforts in similar places can be maintained.

The clarity of the structure establishes itself in a northerly direction, with sizes of blocks and similarities of planning principles. A rather smooth transition has occurred between a strong radial direction (Jaffa) to a characteristic and somewhat complex grid, parallel to the sea, which contains a marked difference in width of roads (East-West and North-South), helping directly the orientation. Dizengoff square is marked in orange.

Influence of renovation is felt on buildings not strictly of Bauhaus origin. The effect of attention paid to the whole built environment, causes some return to the center of Tel Aviv and to the urban way of life. Conservation may be catching on, and is now in vogue.

The plan of the south Tel Aviv grid , shows primary direction in 1918 (marked in blue). The blocks' size and their direction have their origin in a forceful plan. The building of this borough took place in the short period of 30 years, some of them at war time. Streets are formed by the blocks edges, and a minimal elongated ventilation shaft is left in their center. However , the clarity of the street formation helps the establishment of a viable and vibrant public space, enhanced by its mixed uses. This often happens in slum areas, unfortunately not for very long. To become really usable, a lot of effort and control have yet to be spent.

1984

1918

The general development of Tel Aviv. The view taken in 1918 shows the system of the rudimentary beginnings. In blue, the major street, starting to develop, seen again at 1984 (left photo). In red, the existing connections to and from the old city of Jaffa (bottom of photo). It is clear that a town develops according to set rules and geometric principles, beginning with land division. On the right, the somewhat European grid of the south of Tel Aviv fills out. Marked in light orange, two early grids are established by 1984. The major grid (upper left) which started (in blue) at a westerly direction, receives its final form.

is undergoing a critical change with an undecided future and nature.

The renewal of south Tel Aviv

As a part of the attempt to introduce restoration into Tel Aviv, a major section possessing a very strong and unique urban character of a very dense, mixed residential area, will be examined.

This unique pattern, imported by planners from Western Europe, consists of a very dense, unventilated urban grid.

Influence of the Bauhaus approach on present day design, showing the beneficial continuity that current renovation has caused in cities.

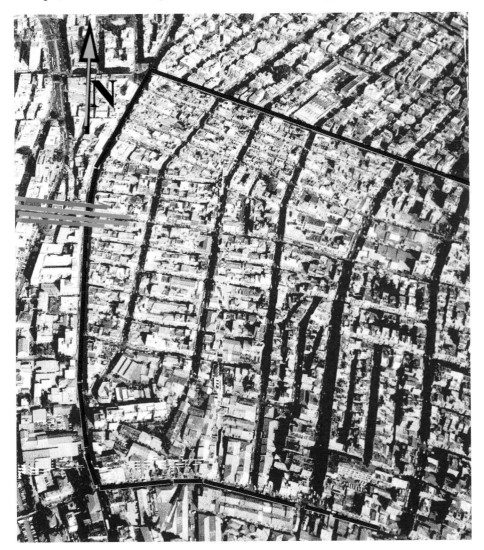

The grid at the south of Tel Aviv , as it finalized its development at around 1950. A very dense neighborhood (up to 70 persons per 0.1 hectare of parcel net), with a quantity of mixed uses, it was destined to grow as a slum area. Its uniqueness in terms of preservation had some influence on decisions of renewal based on minimal conservation principles, all undertaken in 1986. The district is certainly unique in Israel, and deserves the above preliminary effort. The primary direction shown, at 1918, is marked in blue, for orientation purposes.

It is by details such as these, than one recognizes the uniqueness of some sites. When it becomes clear that they have a continuous presence , as well as a convincing and authentic identity, they will become a relevant issue. Such is the case in the quarter we are looking into.

URBAN PROFILE RELATED TO THE URBAN MIX
SITE: SOUTH TEL AVIV

CONSERVATION POTENTIAL					URBAN MIX	STRUCTURAL ELEMENTS					
CHARACTER DEFINITION	LOCALITY SENSE	INTERNAL RELATIONS	STYLE & DESIGN	METHODS & MATERIALS		WEB	DISTRICT	BLOCKS DIVISIONS	PRIMARY ELEMENTS	SECONDARY ELEMENTS	NATURE
5%	2%	4%	4%		LAND	!	!	!!		0	0
6%	5%	2% +1%	4% +1%	2%	BUILDING	–		!!		–	–
5%	4%	0 +2%	1%		USE			!! !		–	–

LEGEND	Total Potential		Present state	%		LEGEND				STATE AT PRESENT
	Present	Future	Upgrading	+%			0 ! !! !!!			STATE IN FUTURE PLAN
	44%	48%	Sub total 7% max				Degree of influence on conservation			

A. Estimating the conservation potential (see pages 340-341 and chapter 25). Land division is the main characteristic as it creates a unique pattern. Buildings are placed in a repetitive and clear way. The total of 44% is low indicating that preservation will be of a mild nature.

B. Upgrading is possible by enforcing a better quality of use, i.e.; getting rid of light manufacturing.
C. Urban structure has a definitive influence in the special blocks, unique and containing mixed, high intensity use.
D. No clear possibility of changing the local structure is possible except by enforcing a less intensive use.

Built over a period of twenty years, it is consistent in design to a remarkable extent, and shows a good instance of urban clarity. A study prepared the way for an overall urban renewal concept, where changes were minimal and the character of the region cleared up. Some of the blight attacking the area was stopped; urban renewal, thus encouraged on a major scale was successful. This was due without a doubt to the clarity and adoption of the recurrent urban pattern. However, the task is not an easy one. The internal nature of this borough has many drawbacks, the principal one being the fact that it contains mainly small, two-room apartments, which are difficult to upgrade. Another difficulty is that neglect has swept prices down, and it is not economical as yet to use much "infill".

Renewal in central Tel Aviv.

A major part of the Tel Aviv grids are the result of the adoption of the Geddes Plan, a unique masterful approach to modern planning advocating a comprehensive and co-

New attempts at preservation and renovation of the Bauhaus buildings in Tel Aviv, usually by agreement with owners, is the late result of a realization that the city has unique qualities. Some introduction of lively color was not exactly on strict Bauhaus formulas. At a rough estimate, around 50 -60 buildings are thus rehabilitated at present (1998). It is a local restorative measure that is at work here. In some instances, owners were encouraged by the offer of a license to build an additional floor, as an economical incentive.

The special and unique nature of the Tel Aviv "Geddes" plan, makes it a worthwhile element of study. One can note clearly in the vicinity of the marked square (Dizzengoff), the formation of squares of residential portions, with the small garden in its center, well protected of noisy, wider roads. The repetition of the plot size (around 0.350 hectare) adds to the local identity. It is in this sort of regulative plan that one of the unique examples of modern urban planning has flourished, as Bauhaus graduates emigrated to Tel Aviv, to start the first "Jewish" city. These facts contain their own strong conservation argument.

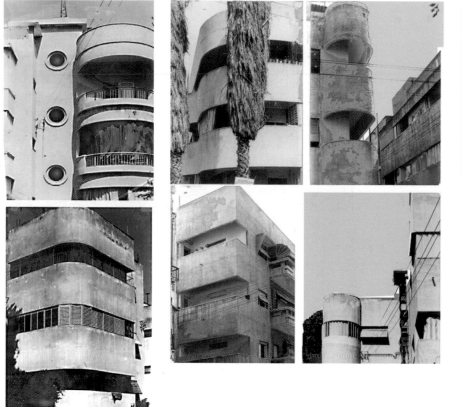

Some early examples of the Bauhaus architecture encountered in Tel Aviv. There are around 500 examples of varying quality, spread out in the city, some as far as Jaffa (author's collection). Balconies add a charm to these designs, built well to withstand the weather damage. Protecting these unique examples has proven to be more difficult, as no conservation plan was envisaged, and they are still regarded as an architectural, and not urban, contribution.

The changing Tel Aviv skyline, as office use, along with commercial and some hotel building, is rapidly changing the nature of the city. As conservation plans have a minor effect on the city's center, and development has been delayed for long, a dispersed collection of tall buildings is going to win the day. At present, the residential potential of the center not augmented in a serious manner, it is felt that the city may lose its present attraction, and become just a big Central Business District.

herent city structure.

This is a complex grid mixing major streets, basically orthogonal, with inner neighborhood type of alleys, small blocks, uninviting to traffic.

The clearly delineated plan is now studied and conserved to a great extent. It also remains uninfluenced by a modern sweep of high rises in Tel Aviv.

As yet, this aforementioned web is not connected to the conservation of the hundreds of Bauhaus buildings in Tel Aviv.

The hope is that it will be incorporated and thus keep its two major modern contributions – Bauhaus design in the highly successful and rare modern contribution by the Geddes plan.

The presence of the renovated Bauhaus buildings has a striking effect. It is rare to find many examples of this particular period in Europe, despite the fact that it has had its impact on post war designs, even then on a minor scale. The rediscovery of these buildings in the web of Tel Aviv, with plots of a conveniently small size, has drawn some international interest. However, it is also clear that the drawback of not having a comprehensive plan, may leave its mark. In the example offered, the neighboring buildings, long neglected, reduce the clean effect of a considerable restoration effort, because of the lack of such an urban conservation plan.

Chapter Thirty Three

Jaffa, Israel

Urban conservation is being carried out and reaffirmed in the old city and port of Jaffa, after many years of neglect.

The ancient city of **Jaffa**, which expanded at the end of the 19th century and gave birth to Tel Aviv at the turn of the 20th century, was neglected in terms of planning for the entire fifty years of Israel's statehood. During this period, Jaffa has survived several crises related to demographic and ownership changes (from private to government ownership). It is rare to find an ex-

Air photograph shows a disrupted and degenerating urban web. This meant that research was to be conducted into the origin and nature of the site, so as to establish some resemblance of structure, some of it conjectured. Effects of neglect are clear, starting by total disregard for repair, up to haphazard filling in of a length of the original shore. Nothing was done to maintain roads or services, allowing the environment to disintegrate.

Structure of the ancient town of Jaffa is shown to have a strong radial and one-sided web. Major roads include the old coastal Egypt - Syria road, the eastern connection to Jerusalem, and other interior links. The importance and persisting use of these roads are the reasons they still exist. This radial structure is difficult to connect to an orthogonal one, as we have seen in other parts of the world (old towns in Spain). The insert contains the prevailing internal web of Jaffa, vaguely orthogonal.

Results of complete restoration and repair show the extent of preservation, in terms of architectural examples. As these are outstanding samples, their location is immaterial, and their contribution is purely local. Materials and colors are close to the original buildings, in many cases of a superior , modern quality, which can be a drawback in restoration work.

This old aerial photo furnishes the origins of the radial grids, in the ancient port town, situated on the hill, and slopping to the east.

Old parts of Jaffa , pointed out in yellow, and some results of the radial web, as triangular shapes of blocks develop.

The old web in the southern part of Jaffa is obliterated, but shown beside an old air photo, it is clear that its qualities can be studied and identified. As a result of studies like this, and with the help of old maps, a revival of the webs can be attempted.

ample on this scale, of an ancient city undergoing such a crisis. At the same time, regional services, not sufficient to begin with, were somewhat neglected. In addition, many buildings were destroyed (in some districts up to 60%). Other houses simply collapsed. In the original ancient city of Jaffa, situated above the port, the British Mandate government destroyed approximately 30% of the buildings during the 1930's. The Israeli government, choosing to avoid the severe problem and exacerbating the situation, destroyed an additional 40%, this in one of the world's oldest cities. Since then, it had been designated a protected area – mainly a tourist attraction. The valuable land of the rest of Jaffa – with its enormous urban potential became unusable due to similar neglect in the mid-1980's. The trend changed, at least partially, when urban upkeep became intolerable. A decision was made to return to innovative urban planning, although this was limited to areas outside the ancient city. This planning had certain conservation goals in mind, mainly regarding buildings. The plans ignored to a certain degree the historical situation.

The history of the regions adjacent to ancient Jaffa in the south is recent, and is not obviously opted for conservation. Certain delays in planning authorization were also caused by modern traffic problems, which often attempted to carry a great load into the existing districts, damaging the web. In addition, numerous other local entanglements, such as the presence of a fishing port (with a great deal of unnecessary structures) as well as spillage of building wreckage into the Mediterranean, which, although it created 80 hectares for construction, turned to be unusable.

There was a need to rethink and reevaluate the conservation approach. The author of this book was requested to conduct a new survey of the southern area of the ancient city. Web-oriented thinking in relation to conservation had not yet been established. In fact, the aforementioned treatment was to be some **urban renewal**, lacking cultural connotations. Study of this region revealed nu-

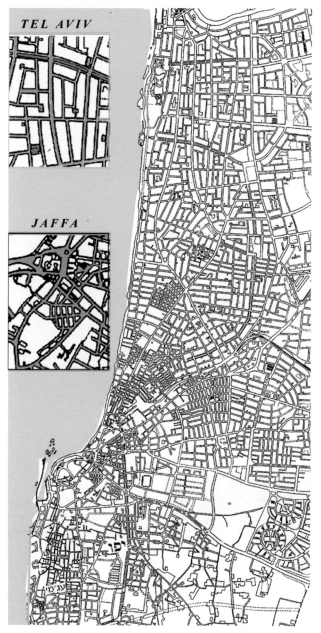

The structure map of the Tel Aviv - Jaffa township with the considerable differences in their basic structure. For a close-up reference, the detailed insert can be consulted, with the Tel Aviv structured regularity, and the seemingly haphazard Jaffa irregularities. The planning has had to reconcile between these two basic qualities, with no real success.

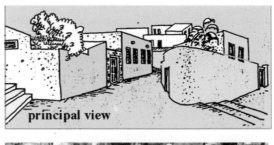

The final result of analyses conducted in Jaffa. The extents of an old local village are presented, with qualities fit for preservation attempts in the future plan. An essential vertical photo, with the relevant drawings, elevations and sections, and a perspective view. The plots and the buildings' heights (0-5 m. in blue, taller in black) are inseparable in studies of this nature.

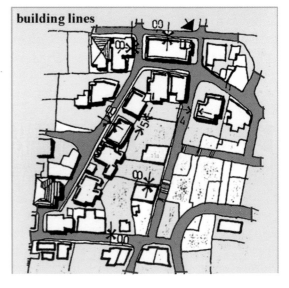

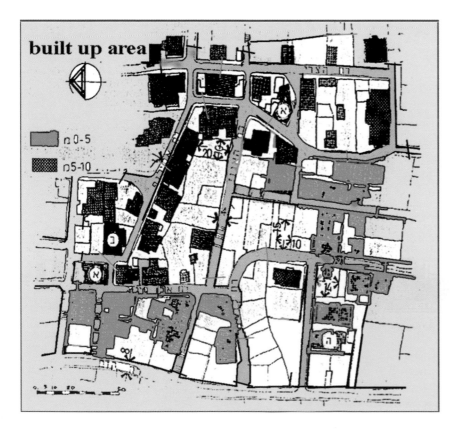

principal view

elevations

The former systematic classification methods are used in relation to the area undergoing a detailed plan preparation. The study prepares the background for future decisions, some related to planning procedures, and others to conservation clauses or recommendations. The most valuable in this instance is the aerial photo, as it alone indicates the past intensity of the site.

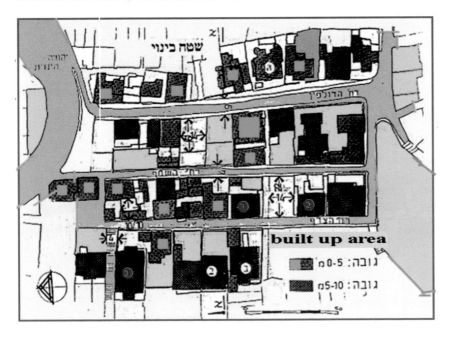

שטח בינוי

built up area

גובה: 0-5מ

גובה: 5-10מ

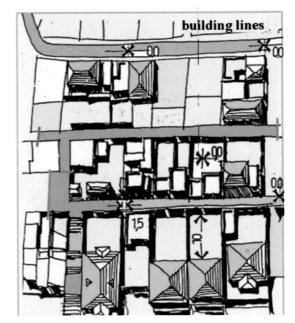

building lines

The effort of restoration work has been considerable in some instances. Some old buildings, quaint and peculiar, while authentic and unique, can be of an inferior quality in the original, and almost impossible to restore. This sort of work can be described as reconstruction, and has an element of guesswork in it.

When the radial web meets some more modern developments, it tends to create and form some odd shapes, interesting in themselves and worthy of preservation attempts. These local grids are not very old, as they were created at the end of last century, and are mostly based on land ownership, rather than any ancient structures (roads in red, land division in light blue, and buildings in blue). An old village compound is shown in green , and indeed its land division is uniquely irregular.

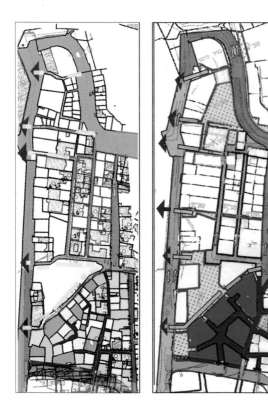

Ajami, Jaffa, existing situation, (first on the left) , is the result of old plans, not very comprehensive in nature, and having no recourse to any elements of conservation. The "S" shape is a cut into an old Arab village, performed by the British Mandate, as a cut to serve the newly erected port. The new plan (second to the left) follows some peculiarities of the site, allowing as much of the old land divisions to retain their effect. The only major difference is the allowance of an higher land utilization factor to come into effect.

New plan, in its final statutory form, with color denoting different intensities of use, to the right (Nahoum Cohen, 1992). Green marks the new public open spaces, demanded by Israeli planning law, and not exactly in total harmony with existing regional web characteristics. Perpendicular passages down the hill become statutory, and some roads are closed. The bottom green space contains an observation point, with visual contact to the south and the north, the whole of the sea front of Jaffa.

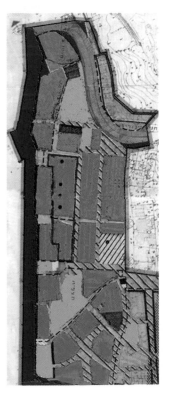

merous possible approaches to planning in an urban area of approximately 200 hectares. Some sections of the area were relatively ancient (result of Arab fishing villages), other sections were modern (from the British Mandate). The Ottoman Empire influenced the majority of the area. Obvious differences in the urban structure were discovered. Districts, with potential for independence and having properties that should be studied in detail, were revealed. The fundamental properties of these districts were marked, separated and formulated. The study indirectly gave birth to the present formulation. Following this research, a special staff of planners, set up in city hall, conducted a number of urban evaluations. Thus began a planning procedure in accordance with a new perspective. Economic evaluations were also conducted by the landowner (the government). In addition, city transportation advisors contributed. Formation of a formulated conservation plan put an end to demolition while initiating individual outline plans, in accordance with recommendations and division into sections with independent characteristics. Separate staffs studied the individual implications of single buildings as well as the architectural elements stemming from the decision to conserve.

Currently, a decade after the decision, buildings are being restored and even rebuilt based on an overall urban perception. Innovation in conservation on an urban scale is difficult to implement in its entirety within planning, though the possibility exists for a planning approach parallel to con-

One of the most revealing efforts will be the conservation of a totality of the local urban mix. In the presented case, the proposed roads are shown, with the formation of navigable streets, answering modern requirements, but influenced by local and land division attributes. This information is supplemented with a map of the former village, with its divisions. This answers the "mix" demand for unique land division.

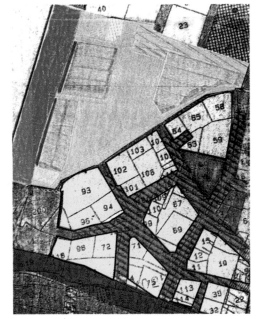

Some of the existing and surviving buildings have the authentic quality of local mixed improvisation, basically eclectic, of old village dwellings. Their arrangement and masses can evoke our sympathy, but they are almost not given to restoration. Some of the attempts may therefore come out not convincing in the end. In the photograph, only local ruins can indicate the direction of our guesses.

servation principles. These principles were incorporated into the plan, referring to the entire web rather than to individual buildings. This great professional contribution, though not very ordered, is general and successful.

We should again mention the planner Geddes, who created the urban plan for modern Tel Aviv without involving Jaffa. Like his attempts to renew historical, problematic cities, Geddes approach to Jaffa reveals his methods

An oblique view of the concept behind the new plan. As the site is on the sea front, behind the old port, it will be looked upon as the entry to this part of Jaffa, and necessitates an appearance of a somewhat walled city. The old approaches to the sea front have been kept and accentuated, and this was done as a result of the study into the old grids and archaeological peculiarities.

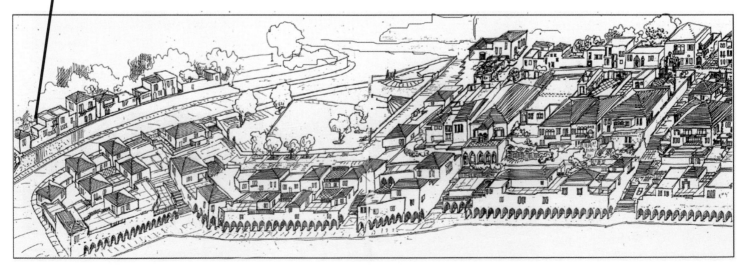

in India: a very partial cleansing, in order to revive the web; this attitude may continue to be relevant here.

On its own, conservation cannot solve a city's economic hardships. The rarity and historical importance of ancient building values can serve as a lever for economic success. This requires a great deal of public investment, including expropriation, in order to renew the web, establishing comprehensive urban projects. Political apathy, lack of private interest, complex ownership, all hinder efforts to establish a new system of ownership that includes conservation codes. This is an extremely difficult process, due to legal precedence, legislative delays, etc. Significant government involvement is necessary and this is not easily obtained.

Successful conservation, such as seen in central Prague and certain sections of Paris, London, many towns in Italy and isolated places in Germany, prove that urban conservation can be formulated, and successfully conducted.

Some precision is needed when plots and old ownership are to be observed. Some old maps have to be obtained, and the proposed changes in roads (red in both maps) have to be annotated against a background of measured parcels. Every effort was made to preserve as much as possible the nature and the sense of the local, even though all buildings have disappeared. As far as new building and use are concerned, a suggested approach is attached to the statutory plan. These suggestions, by nature, are not compulsory, and have an illustrative status.

This vertical architectural conception is an interpretation of the local conservation plan, and its detailed future manifestations. Thus a large degree of future work is conceived as reconstruction based on some local design principles, and is not strictly a conservation effort. However, by necessity the long neglect has to be overcome by various means, restoration mixed with new and some what related structures. (Illustrated by the author.)

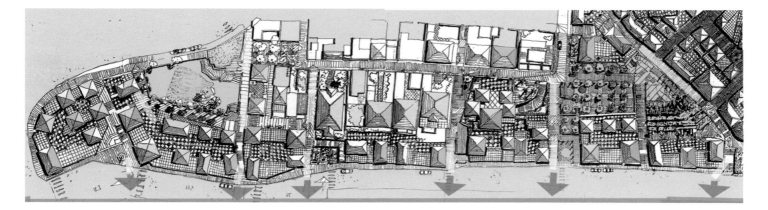

One of the unique qualities of the region is illustrated by examples of authentic design and workmanship, like the doors which combine an oriental entry. These designs originate in Lebanon and are part of the Mediterranean culture.

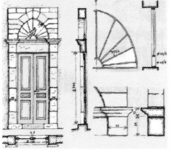

Cataloguing the authentic local details was necessary, for the execution of their repair, and sometimes for their restoration. The drawings concern stone work, wood and metal.

URBAN PROFILE RELATED TO THE URBAN MIX

SITE: ajami, jaffa

CONSERVATION POTENTIAL					URBAN MIX	STRUCTURAL ELEMENTS					
CHARACTER DEFINITION	LOCALITY SENSE	INTERNAL RELATIONS	STYLE & DESIGN	METHODS & MATERIALS		WEB	DISTRICT	BLOCKS DIVISIONS	PRIMARY ELEMENTS	SECONDARY ELEMENTS	NATURE
3% +4%	3% +4%	+4%	3% +4%	—	LAND	!!	!	!	!! !!!		!
4%	6%	5%	3% +4%	3%	BUILDING			!	!		
4%	4%	4%	—	3%	USE	0		! !!			— !!

LEGEND

Total Potential	
Present	Future
45%	68%

Present state %
Upgrading +%
Sub total 7% max

LEGEND

0	!	!!	!!!

Degree of influence on conservation

☐ STATE AT PRESENT
☐ STATE IN FUTURE PLAN

A. Estimating the conservation potential, (see pages 352-355). The main contribution seems to come from existing buildings along the streets in the north part of the plan (second row in the table). The present use is very clear in forming a unique residential quarter, creating a good definition, a sense of the local and relative proportions of volumes. The total of 45% potential indicates a border case.

B. Upgrading is possible in the new plan, by stressing the unique land divisions pattern in the former villages (see illustrations of land division).

C. Urban structure is special in its land division, a pronounced web and clear streets, thus influential in preserving the site (right side of table, first row).

D. The future plan will emphasize the streets and observation points, as well as some elements of nature (parks). Existing topography is to be used in a more pronounced way.

BIBLIOGRAPHY

Architectural Design 11/12-1980, Publisher and Executive Editor dr. A. C. Papadakis: Urbanity. Paris Bienale. London.

Architecture in continuity. Buildings in the Islamic World today. Edited by Sherban Cantacusino 1985. New York: Islamic Publications Ltd.

Bacon Edmund N. 1992: **Design of cities** (Revised edition). London: Thames and Hudson.

Benevolo, Leonardo 1988: **The history of the city**. Cambridge, Massachusetts: The MIT Press.

Bertrand, Michel Jean 1980: **Architecture de l'habitat urbain;** (La maison, le quartier, la ville). Paris: Dunod.

Brauman, Annick; ... 1982: **L'immeuble et la parcelle**. Bruxelles, Editions des archives d'architecture moderne.

Brock; Giuliani; Moisescu 1973: **Il centro antico di Capua**. Metodi di analisi per la planificazione architettonico-urbanistica. Italy: Marsilio Editory.

Chermayeff, Serge; Alexander Tzonis 1971: **Shape of community**. Realization of human potential. Penguin Books.

Crosby, Theo 1973: **How to play the environment game**. Arts Council of Great Britain and Penguin Books Ltd.

D'Ollfus, Jean. **Les aspects de l'architecture populaire**. Paris: Editions Albert Morance.

Deilmann; Kirschenmann; Pfeiffer: **The Dwelling.** Use-Types; Plan-Types; Dwelling-Types; Building-Types. Stuttgart: IGMA.

Dell, Bruno 1994: **Histoire de Paris**. Paris: Hatier.

Die neue BauNVO '90. Kurzkommentar: **Alte und neue Fassung**. Germany, Augsburg: Herm.-Deiml-Verlag.

Dodi, Luigi 1972. Citta' e territorio. **Urbanistica tecnica**. Milano: Tamburini Editore.

Donnison, D. V. 1967. **The Government of Housing**. Penguin books.

Egli, Ernst 1959: **Geschichte des stadtebaues**. Erlenbach - Zurich and Stuttgart: Eugen Rentsch Verlag.

Ferguson, Francis 1975: **Architecture, cities and the systems approach**. New York: George Braziller.

George, Pierre 1952: La Ville. **Le fait urbain a travers le monde**. Paris: Presses universitaires de France.

Goodman, Robert 1972: **After the planners**. Penguin books.

Goodwin, Godfrey 1987: **A History of Ottoman Architecture**. London: Thames and Hudson.

Hall, Peter 1989: **Urban and Regional planning**. London: Unwin Hyman.

Hall, Peter G. 1990: **Cities of Tomorrow**: an intellectual history of urban planning and design in the twentieth century. Cambridge, Massachusetts: Basil Blackwell.

Hristov, Hristo, Stojkov Georgi, Mijatev Krastju 1959: **The Rila Monastery**: History, Architecture, Frescoes, Wood-Carvings. Sofia: The Bulgarian Academy of Science.

Human identity in the urban environment. Edited by Gwen Bell and Jaqueline Tyrwhitt. Penguin books.

ISOCAP 1992: **International manual of planning practice**. Second edition.

Johnson-Marshall, Percy 1966. **Rebuilding Cities**. Edinburgh: University Press.

Jones, Edward & Woodward, Cristopher 1983: **A guide to the architecture of London**. London: Weidenfeld & Nicolson.

Kato, Akinori, 1990: **Plazas of Southern Europe**. Tokio: Toppan Printing PTE(S) CO, LTD.

Koolhaas, Rem 1994: **Delirious New York**. A retroactive manifesto for Manhattan. New York: The Monacelli Press.

Kostof, Spiro 1991: **The city shaped**. Urban patterns and meanings through history. Boston-Toronto-London: A Bulfinch press book. Little, Brown and Co.

Lewis, Harold MacLean 1949. **Planning the modern city**. Volume one. New York - London: John Wiley & sons - Chapman & Hall.

Lichfield, Nathaniel 1996: **Community impact evaluation**. London: UCL Press.

Mazger-Smok, Niza 1994: **Batim min ahol**, 1931 - 1948. Tel-Aviv: MSTB.

Mann, Roy 1973: **Rivers in the city**. Great Britain, Newton Abbot Devon: David & Charles.

Manuale del recupero del comune di Roma, 1989. Rome: Edizioni dei Roma.

Morris, A. J. F. 1995: **History of urban form before the Industrial Revolutions**. England: Longman Scientific & Technical.

Mumford, Lewis 1991. **The city in history**. Penguin books.

People and Plans. **Essays on Urban Problems and Solutions**. (Abridged edition) Herbert J. Gans 1972. Penguin books.

Perenyi, Imre: **Town Centres**. Planning and renewal. Budapest.

Planning London, Edited by James Simmie 1994. London: UCL Press.

Radiografia di Milano. **A cura della Unione Repubblicana Milanese**.

Sitte, Camillo 1986: **The birth of modern city planning**. New York: Rizzoly International Publications.

Teritorialno I selishno ustroistvo. Sofia: Askoni - Izdat, 1994.

The City: problems of planning; edited by Murray Stewart 1972. Penguin Education.

Tonev, Luben; . . . 1974: **Gradoustroistvo**. Sofia: Technica.

Virolleaud, Francois; Laurent Maurice 1990: **Le Ravalement**. Guide technique, reglementaire et juridique. Paris: Editions du Montiteur.

Yaffa. Jerusalem: Kardom, April 1981.